Checkpoints

Checkpoints

Developing College English Skills

Fifth Edition

Jack Page
Merritt College, Emeritus

Leslie Taggart

PEARSON
Longman

New York   San Francisco   Boston
London   Toronto   Sydney   Tokyo   Singapore   Madrid
Mexico City   Munich   Paris   Cape Town   Hong Kong   Montreal

Vice President and Editor-in-Chief:	**Joseph Terry**
Senior Acquisitions Editor:	**Steven Rigolosi**
Development Editor:	**Meegan Thompson**
Senior Marketing Manager:	**Melanie Craig**
Senior Print Supplements Editor:	**Donna Campion**
Media Supplements Editor:	**Nancy Garcia**
Production Manager:	**Douglas Bell**
Project Coordination, Text Design, and Electronic Page Makeup:	**Elm Street Publishing Services, Inc.**
Cover Design Manager:	**John Callahan**
Cover Designer:	**Keithley and Associates, Inc.**
Manufacturing Buyer:	**Alfred C. Dorsey**
Printer and Binder:	**Courier Corporation—Kendallville**
Cover Printer:	**Phoenix Color Corporation**

For permission to use copyrighted material, grateful acknowledgment is made to the copyright holders on p. 301 which are hereby made part of this copyright page.

Library of Congress Cataloging-in-Publication Data
Page, Jack
   Checkpoints: developing college English skills / Jack Page, Leslie Taggart. – 5ᵗʰ ed.
     p. cm.
   Includes bibliographical references and index.
   ISBN 0-321-10385-8
     1. English language—Rhetoric. 2. English language—Grammar. 3. College
     readers. I. Taggart, Leslie. II. Title.

PE1408.P245 2004
808'.042—dc21   2002043367

Please visit our Website at **http://www.ablongman.com/page**

ISBN 0-321-10385-8

2 3 4 5 6 7 8 9 10—CRK—06 05 04

For Ky, Joseph, Paul, Jimmy, and Michael

Brief Contents

Detailed Contents

Preface

Checkpoints is designed to help students gain the language skills needed to succeed in all college courses that require the ability to write with clarity and precision and to read with critical understanding. Of course, these skills will continue to be valuable after college, in the workplace, and in social and family life.

Throughout, *Checkpoints* emphasizes the need to express ideas and present information in clear, well-organized paragraphs. In the last four chapters, students learn to build on these paragraph skills in writing short essays. With accessible readings and an abundant variety of high-interest exercises and writing assignments, the text guides students through the acquisition and application of these skills.

A key feature of *Checkpoints* is its integration of a variety of interest-sustaining elements in each chapter. One of the most important of these is the reading that begins each chapter. The readings provide examples of writing strategies for students to emulate, as well as information and ideas that they may incorporate into their own writing. The follow-up questions under the headings Checking Meaning and Checking Ideas lead students to develop critical thinking skills by relating the topics to their own experiences, ideas, and knowledge. The readings also offer opportunities for improving oral communication skills through class discussions of significant contemporary issues.

A number of changes appear in this edition. Every chapter now presents three new writing topics as alternatives to the main writing assignment. A quarter of the readings that begin chapters are new. New coverage of using outside sources in writing (in MLA style) has been added to the Writing Resources. Emphasis continues to be given to an understanding of writing as a multistage *process*. For example, a new case study on revising and editing a paragraph is included, as Writing Resource G. Models and step-by-step guides for student writing are provided in every chapter.

Fundamentals Made Accessible

The integrated coverage of grammar allows instructors to teach sentence-level skills in the context of the whole piece of writing. Each chapter covers a separate area of grammar or mechanics and includes extensive exercises and quizzes. This instruction is designed to be accessible to students who need help with fundamentals and is presented concisely in a conversational, nontechnical way. Each brief unit of instruction is followed by a Spotcheck exercise to test understanding. Several related units are then reviewed in a Doublecheck exercise. All the material is reviewed in an Editing Check. Finally, a Checkpoint quiz tests mastery of the entire section. Further opportunities to reinforce this learning are afforded by the quizzes in the Instructor's Manual.

Checkpoints is a flexible text. An answer key for all odd-numbered items in Spotcheck, Doublecheck, and Editing Check exercises permits independent work by students and opens up class time for freewriting, group writing, revision, and other activities. Instructors who want to assign work to be turned in can rely on even-numbered items for which no answers are given. Additional suggestions for using the text will be found in the Instructor's Manual. The Instructor's Manual contains answers to Checkpoint quizzes, answers and background material for the readings, and two extra quizzes on grammar or mechanics for each chapter, with answers. A set of overhead transparency masters on grammar and style provides opportunities for varied presentation of material.

Features of the Fifth Edition

- *Writing Topic Banks.* To supplement the major writing assignment, a bank of three new writing topics in every chapter provides a diverse collection of assignments from which to choose. The first alternative topic draws on students' personal experiences and knowledge in an entirely print-based assignment. The second topic calls for exploring on the Internet, sometimes with suggestions for visiting specific websites and other times detailing types of searches to be made based on the writer's interests and skills. The third assignment calls for writing about media—everything from books to magazines to movies to music.

- *New readings.* A quarter of the readings are new to this edition. New narrative, comparison/contrast, opinion, and mixed-mode essays add fresh perspectives on ability and disability, gun laws, cures for poverty, and immigrants' experiences in the United States.

- *Using Outside Sources in Writing.* This new Writing Resource provides a straightforward introduction to using and citing outside sources in writing. Numerous examples from contemporary writers, all in MLA style, demonstrate the concepts. Basic Works Cited formats for books, articles, and online sources are shown and discussed, and a sample Works Cited page is annotated with general format guidelines. A section at the end discusses two tricky situations that can lead to plagiarism: cutting and pasting from the Web and paraphrasing the source too closely.

- *Expanded coverage of the writing process.* Throughout the book, the process of writing is emphasized. Chapter 1 gives an overview of the writing process. Other chapter writing assignments lead students through prewriting, drafting, and revising strategies. Journal writing topics precede each reading. In addition, a new case study, Revising and Editing a Paragraph, is given in the Writing Resources section. Three drafts of a paragraph are reprinted, with the writer's comments in between showing the decisions that led to revision. Editing is shown as a separate activity; the revised paragraph is shown with the writer's notes to herself and handwritten corrections.

The Longman Ancillary Package

A complete **Instructor's Manual/Answer Key** to accompany *Checkpoints* is available. Please ask your Longman sales consultant for ISBN 0-321-10386-6.

For additional Internet-based activities, be sure to visit this book's Companion Website, *Checkpoints Online,* at http://www.ablongman.com/page.

In addition to the instructor's manual, many other skills-based supplements are available for both instructors and students. All of these supplements are available either free or at greatly reduced prices.

For Additional Reading and Reference

The Dictionary Deal

Two dictionaries can be shrinkwrapped with this text at a nominal fee. *The New American Webster Handy College Dictionary* is a paperback reference text with more than 100,000 entries. *Merriam Webster's Collegiate Dictionary,* Tenth Edition, is a hardback reference with a citation file of more than 14.5 million examples of English words drawn from actual use. For more information on how to shrinkwrap a dictionary with your text, please contact your Longman sales representative.

Penguin Quality Paperback Titles

A series of Penguin paperbacks is available at a significant discount when shrinkwrapped with this text. Some titles available are Toni Morrison's *Beloved,* Julia Alvarez's *How the Garcia Girls Lost Their Accents,* Mark Twain's *Huckleberry Finn, Narrative of the Life of Frederick Douglass,* Harriet Beecher Stowe's *Uncle Tom's Cabin,* Dr. Martin Luther King, Jr.'s *Why We Can't Wait,* and plays by Shakespeare, Miller, and Albee. For a complete list of titles or more information, please contact your Longman sales consultant.

Penguin Academics: *Twenty-Five Great Essays, Fifty Great Essays,* and *One Hundred Great Essays,* edited by Robert DiYanni

These alphabetically organized essay collections are published as part of the "Penguin Academics" series of low-cost, high-quality offerings intended for use in introductory college courses. All essays were selected for their teachability, both as models for writing and for their usefulness as springboards for student writing. For more information on how to shrinkwrap one of these anthologies with your text, please contact your Longman sales consultant.

100 Things to Write About

This 100-page book contains 100 individual assignments for writing on a variety of topics and in a wide range of formats, from expressive to analytical. Ask your Longman sales representative for a sample copy. ISBN 0-673-98239-4

Newsweek Alliance

Instructors may choose to shrinkwrap a 12-week subscription to *Newsweek* with any Longman text. The price of the subscription is 59 cents per issue (a total of $7.08 for the subscription). Available with the subscription is a free "Interactive Guide to *Newsweek*"—a workbook for students who are using the text. In addition, *Newsweek* provides a wide variety of instructor supplements free to teachers, including maps, Skills Builders, and weekly quizzes. For more information on the *Newsweek* program, please contact your Longman sales representative.

Electronic and Online Offerings

The Longman Writer's Warehouse

The innovative and exciting online supplement is the perfect accompaniment to any developmental writing course. Developed by developmental English instructors specially for developing writers, The Writer's Warehouse covers every part of the writing process. Also included are journaling capabilities, multimedia activities, diagnostic tests, an interactive handbook, and a complete instructor's manual. The Writer's Warehouse requires no space on your school's server; rather, students complete and store their work on the Longman server, and are able to access it, revise it, and continue working at any time. For more details about how to shrinkwrap a free subscription to The Writer's Warehouse with this text, please consult your Longman sales representative. For a free guided tour of the site, visit http://longmanwriterswarehouse.com.

The Writer's ToolKit Plus

This CD-ROM offers a wealth of tutorial, exercise, and reference material for writers. It is compatible with either a PC or Macintosh platform, and is flexible enough to be used either occasionally for practice or regularly in class lab sessions. For information on how to bundle this CD-ROM FREE with your text, please contact your Longman sales representative.

The Longman Electronic Newsletter

Twice a month during the spring and fall, instructors who have subscribed receive a free copy of the Longman Developmental English Newsletter in their e-mailbox. Written by experienced classroom instructors, the newsletter offers teaching tips, classroom activities, book reviews, and more. To subscribe, send an e-mail to BasicSkills@ablongman.com.

iSearch Guide for English, by H. Eric Branscomb and Linda R. Barr

A guide to online research. Featuring the Longman Internet Guide and access to the Research Navigator™ Database, the *iSearch Guide* gives students and instructors instant access to thousands of academic journals and periodicals any time from any computer with an Internet connection. With helpful tips on the writing process, online research, and finding and citing valid sources, starting the research process has never been easier! Free when packaged with this textbook. Please consult your Longman representative.

For Instructors

Electronic Test Bank for Writing

This electronic test bank features more than 5,000 questions in all areas of writing, from grammar to paragraphing, through essay writing, research, and documentation. With this easy-to-use CD-ROM, instructors simply choose questions from the electronic test bank, then print out the completed test for distribution. CD-ROM: ISBN 0-321-08117-X; Print version: ISBN 0-321-08486-1

Competency Profile Test Bank, Second Edition

This series of 60 objective tests covers ten general areas of English competency, including fragments; comma splices and run-ons; pronouns; commas; and capitalization. Each test is available in remedial, standard, and advanced versions. Available as reproducible sheets or in computerized versions. Free to instructors. Paper version: ISBN 0-321-02224-6

Diagnostic and Editing Tests and Exercises, Sixth Edition

This collection of diagnostic tests helps instructors assess students' competence in Standard Written English for the purpose of placement or to gauge progress. Available as reproducible sheets or in computerized versions, and free to instructors. Paper: ISBN 0-321-19647-3; CD-ROM: ISBN 0-321-19645-7

ESL Worksheets, Third Edition

These reproducible worksheets provide ESL students with extra practice in areas they find the most troublesome. A diagnostic test and post-test are provided, along with answer keys and suggested topics for writing. Free to adopters. ISBN 0-321-07765-2

Longman Editing Exercises

Fifty-four pages of paragraph editing exercises give students extra practice using grammar skills in the context of longer passages. Free when packaged with any Longman title. ISBN 0-205-31792-8; Answer key: ISBN 0-205-31797-9

80 Practices

A collection of reproducible, ten-item exercises that provide additional practices for specific grammatical usage problems, such as comma splices, capitalization, and pronouns. Includes an answer key, and free to adopters. ISBN 0-673-53422-7

CLAST Test Package, Fourth Edition

These two 40-item objective tests evaluate students' readiness for the CLAST exams. Strategies for teaching CLAST preparedness are included. Free with any Longman English title. Reproducible sheets: ISBN 0-321-01950-4

TASP Test Package, Third Edition

These 12 practice pre-tests and post-tests assess the same reading and writing skills covered in the TASP examination. Free with any Longman English title. Reproducible sheets: ISBN 0-321-01959-8

Teaching Online: Internet Research, Conversation, and Composition, Second Edition

Ideal for instructors who have never surfed the Net, this easy-to-follow guide offers basic definitions, numerous examples, and step-by-step information about finding and using Internet sources. Free to adopters. ISBN 0-321-01957-1

Using Portfolios

This supplement offers teachers a brief introduction to teaching with portfolios in composition courses. This essential guide addresses the pedagogical and evaluative use of portfolios, and offers practical suggestions for implementing a portfolio evaluation system in a writing class. ISBN 0-321-08412-8

The Longman Instructor Planner

This all-in-one resource for instructors includes monthly and weekly planning sheets, to-do lists, student contact forms, attendance rosters, a gradebook, an address/phone book, and a mini almanac. Ask your Longman sales representative for a free copy. ISBN 0-321-09247-3

For Students

Researching Online, Fifth Edition

A perfect companion for a new age, this indispensable new supplement helps students navigate the Internet. Adapted from *Teaching Online,* the instructor's Internet guide, *Researching Online* speaks directly to students, giving them detailed, step-by-step instructions for performing electronic searches. Available free when shrinkwrapped with this text. ISBN 0-321-09277-5

Learning Together: An Introduction to Collaborative Theory

This brief guide to the fundamentals of collaborative learning teaches students how to work effectively in groups, how to revise with peer response, and how to co-author a paper or report. Shrinkwrapped free with this text. ISBN 0-673-46848-8

A Guide for Peer Response, Second Edition

This guide offers students forms for peer critiques, including general guidelines and specific forms for different stages in the writing process. Also appropriate for freshman-level course. Free to adopters. ISBN 0-321-01948-2

Ten Practices of Highly Successful Students

This popular supplement helps students learn crucial study skills, offering concise tips for a successful career in college. Topics include time management, test-taking, reading critically, stress, and motivation. ISBN 0-205-30769-8

[FOR FLORIDA ADOPTIONS] *Thinking Through the Test,* by D. J. Henry

This special workbook, prepared specially for students in Florida, offers ample skill and practice exercises to help student prep for the Florida State Exit Exam. To shrinkwrap this workbook free with your textbook, please contact your Longman sales representative. Available in two versions: with answers and without answers. Also available: Two laminated grids (one for reading, one for writing) that can serve as handy references for students preparing for the Florida State Exit Exam.

The Longman Student Planner

This daily planner for students includes daily, weekly, and monthly calendars, as well as class schedules and a mini-almanac of useful information. It is the perfect accompaniment to a Longman reading or study skills textbook, and is available free to students when shrinkwrapped with this text. ISBN 0-321-04573-4

The Longman Writer's Journal

This journal for writers, free with any Longman English text, offers students a place to think, write, and react. For an examination copy, contact your Longman sales consultant. ISBN 0-321-08639-2

The Longman Researcher's Journal

This journal for writers and researchers, free with this text, helps students plan, schedule, write, and revise their research project. An all-in-one resource for first-time researchers, the journal guides students gently through the research process. ISBN 0-321-09530-8

[NEW] *The Longman Writer's Portfolio*

This unique supplement provides students with a space to plan, think about, and present their work. The portfolio includes an assessing/organizing area (including a grammar diagnostic test, a spelling quiz, and project planning worksheets), a before and during writing area (including peer review sheets, editing checklists, writing self-evaluations, and a personal editing profile), and an after-writing area (including a progress chart, a final table of contents, and a final assessment). Ask your Longman sales representative for ISBN 0-321-10765-9.

The Longman Series of Monographs for Developmental Educators

Ask your Longman sales consultant for a free copy of these monographs written by experts in their fields.

#1: The Longman Guide to Classroom Management

Written by Joannis Flatley of St. Philip's College, the first in Longman's new series of monographs for developmental English instructors focuses on issues of classroom etiquette, providing guidance on dealing with unruly, unengaged, disruptive, or uncooperative students. Ask your Longman sales representative for a free copy. ISBN 0-321-09246-5

#2: The Longman Guide to Community Service-Learning in the English Classroom and Beyond

Written by Elizabeth Rodriguez Kessler of California State University–Northridge, this is the second monograph in Longman's series for developmental educators. It provides a definition and history of service-learning, as well as an overview of how service-learning can be integrated effectively into the college classroom. ISBN 0-321-12749-8

Acknowledgments

Reviewers making important contributions to this edition were Ashley S. Bonds, Copiah-Lincoln Community College; Valerie Russell, Valencia Community College; Nicholas Schevera, College of Lake County; and P. E. Zaccardo, Phoenix College.

Checkpoints

Chapter 1

The Writing Process

READING PRECHECK

Russell Baker had a low opinion of the writing assignments he was given in his high school English classes. But one day he wrote an essay on how to eat spaghetti without making a mess. His teacher, Mr. Fleagle, praised it, and young Russell found himself on the path to becoming a widely admired writer. The story told here is from Baker's autobiography, *Growing Up,* which won a Pulitzer Prize.

> **JOURNAL TOPIC:** How have your own English class experiences influenced your feelings about writing?

The Art of Eating Spaghetti
Russell Baker

[Mr. Fleagle] constantly sprinkled his sentences with "don't you see." It wasn't a question but an exclamation of mild surprise at our ignorance. "Your pronoun needs an antecedent, don't you see," he would say, very primly. "The purpose of the porter's scene,[1] boys, is to provide comic relief from the horror, don't you see."   1

Late in the year we tackled the informal essay. "The essay, don't you see, is the . . . ." My mind went numb. Of all the forms of writing, none seemed so boring   2

primly in a stuffy, formal manner

---
[1]From Shakespeare's play *Macbeth*

as the essay. Naturally we would have to write informal essays. Mr. Fleagle distributed a homework sheet offering us a choice of topics. None was quite so simpleminded as "What I did on my summer vacation," but most seemed to be almost as dull. I took the list home and dawdled until the night before the essay was due. Sprawled on the sofa, I finally faced up to the grim task, took the list out of my notebook, and scanned it. The topic on which my eye fell was "The Art of Eating Spaghetti."

dawdled wasted time

This title produced an extraordinary sequence of mental images. Surging up out of the depths of memory came a vivid recollection of a night in Belleville when all of us were seated around the supper table—Uncle Allen, my mother, Uncle Charlie, Doris, Uncle Hal—and Aunt Pat served spaghetti for supper. Spaghetti was an exotic treat in those days. Neither Doris nor I had ever eaten spaghetti, and none of the adults had enough experience to be good at it. All the good humor of Uncle Allen's house reawoke in my mind as I recalled the laughing arguments we had that night about the socially respectable method for moving spaghetti from plate to mouth.

exotic uncommon or foreign

3

Suddenly I wanted to write about that, about the warmth and good feeling of it, but I wanted to put it down simply for my own joy, not for Mr. Fleagle. It was a moment I wanted to recapture and hold for myself. I wanted to relive the pleasure of an evening at New Street. To write it as I wanted, however, would violate all the rules of formal composition I'd learned in school, and Mr. Fleagle would surely give it a failing grade. Never mind, I would write something else for Mr. Fleagle after I had written this thing for myself.

4

When I finished it the night was half gone and there was no time left to compose a proper, respectable essay for Mr. Fleagle. There was no choice the next morning but to turn in my private reminiscence of Belleville. Two days passed before Mr. Fleagle returned the graded papers, and he returned everyone's but mine. I was bracing myself for a command to report to Mr. Fleagle immediately after school for discipline when I saw him lift my paper from his desk and rap for the class's attention.

reminiscence memory

5

"Now, boys," he said, "I want to read you an essay. This is titled 'The Art of Eating Spaghetti.'" And he started to read. My words! He was reading my words out loud to the entire class. What's more, the entire class was listening. Listening attentively. Then somebody laughed, the entire class was laughing, and not in contempt and ridicule, but with openhearted enjoyment. Even Mr. Fleagle stopped two or three times to repress a small prim smile.

6

repress hold back

I did my best to avoid showing pleasure, but what I was feeling was pure ecstasy at this startling demonstration that my words had the power to make people laugh. In the eleventh grade, at the eleventh hour, as it were, I had discovered my calling. It was the happiest moment of my entire school career. When Mr. Fleagle finished he put the final seal on my happiness by saying, "Now that, boys, is an essay, don't you see. It's—don't you see—it's of the very essence of the essay, don't you see. Congratulations, Mr. Baker."

7

calling life's work, profession

FRED BASSET/Alex Graham

Copyright © Tribune Media Services. Reprinted with permission.

Checking Meaning and Style

1. In Russell Baker's story, he has Mr. Fleagle saying "don't you see" again and again. What is the effect of this repetition? Does the expression fit in with the description of Mr. Fleagle as "prim"?
2. Young Russell didn't intend to use his essay on spaghetti in his English class. Why did he write it ? (Paragraph 4) Why did he end up turning it in? (Paragraph 5)
3. What experience did he base the essay on? (Paragraphs 3–4)
4. Would you say the style of this selection is easy or hard? Are most of the words everyday words or uncommon words? Does this match your idea of "good writing"?

Checking Ideas

1. How often did you write essays in high school? What were some of your favorite topics?
2. Did you ever write something, in school or out, "for your own joy"? Explain.
3. Baker wanted to become a professional writer. Why should other people—you, for example—bother to improve writing skills?
4. Many government agencies and large corporations provide their employees with classes in writing skills. What does that suggest about American schools and about job success?

Writing as Process

This text is designed to help you acquire the writing skills necessary for success in college. Of course, language skills will help you in other ways—for example, in your social and family life and on the job. For now, it will be helpful to recognize that writing is not a single act. It is a process. It is a series of steps that result in a composition—whether a term paper in history or a job application letter—that is well thought-out, carefully organized, and technically correct. These steps usually should include the following:

Prewriting—This is a way of getting and arranging your ideas before you start the actual writing. Prewriting methods include brainstorming, asking how and why, keeping a journal, clustering, and freewriting. These techniques will be discussed in chapters to come.

First draft—The first effort rarely should be the final effort. Your composition will go through several more stages before it is ready to be handed in or put in the mail.

Revising—Go over the first draft carefully. When possible, set it aside for several hours or a day; you can then examine it with a fresh eye. Ask yourself if the style is suitable for your topic and your audience—not too formal or informal. Are there errors in spelling or grammar? Are the sentences clear and well put-together? Is the composition well organized? Does each paragraph have a topic sentence that states the main idea of the paragraph? Is there a thesis sentence that sums up the essay as a whole? Are the ideas adequately developed?

Asking for help—Show your paper to a friend or to a classmate working on the same assignment. That step might provide an unbiased opinion that may reveal weak spots that you overlooked. Be willing to collaborate with others.

Second draft—Complete the revision. Correct the weaknesses that you have discovered. This means rewriting the composition.

Final copy—Copy the last revision to produce a polished composition that you are willing to submit as your best work.

Proofreading—Give the paper one last check. Did a misspelled word slip past you? Did you hit the wrong key on the keyboard? Did the computer's spell-checker fail to inform you that you wrote *there* instead of *their*?

Prewriting: Brainstorming

We have all probably found ourselves in this uncomfortable situation: We are supposed to write something—a job application, a request for a raise, a letter to the landlord, a term paper. The blank piece of paper in front of us seems matched by the blank spot in our brain where all the words and ideas are supposed to come from. Finally, we finish the letter or squeeze out the five-hundredth word required for the English class paper. But we think there must be an easier way. And there is.

One way to make writing easier is to do some *prewriting* first. In the kind of prewriting called *brainstorming,* you jot down whatever ideas about your subject pop into your mind. You don't worry about grammar, spelling, or sentence structure. You don't even worry if the ideas are good or not. You just let them roll out on the paper.

Let's say you want to write an application for a part-time job in a downtown sporting goods store. Without stopping to judge your ideas, jot down a list of the reasons you should get the job. You might end up with something like this:

like sports
good worker
worked 3 summers in sales—Smith's Stationery
neat
punctual
honest
played basketball, tennis in high school
played Little League baseball
taking weight training in college
20 years old
6 feet tall, 165 pounds
sing in church choir
familiar with cash register, making change
some computer skills
2 sisters, 1 brother

Looking over your list, you notice that some items are about your general qualities and job skills. Others are about special skills that qualify you for a job in sporting goods sales. Still others don't seem important to your application, so you cross them out. Then you rearrange the others in a list similar to this:

general qualifications
    good worker
    pleasant personality
    neat
    punctual
    honest
    20 years old
    worked 3 summers in sales at Smith's Stationery
    familiar with computerized cash register
special qualifications
    like sports
    played basketball and tennis in high school
    played Little League baseball
    taking weight training in college

You leave out the points that don't seem relevant: your family, your height and weight, the church choir.

Now with most of your work done, you are ready to write your letter. Of course, it is all right to add details that come to you as you write. Here's what you might end up with:

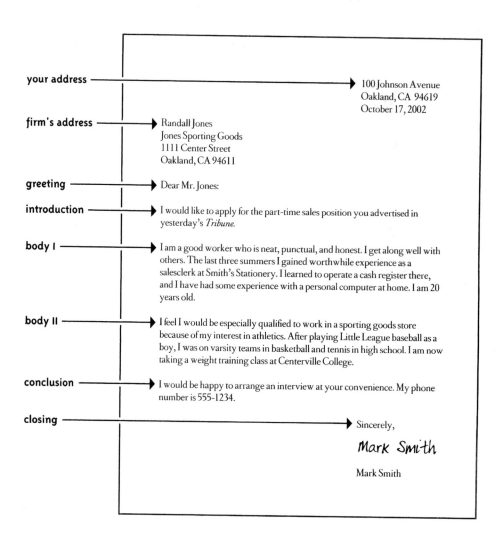

your address → 100 Johnson Avenue
Oakland, CA 94619
October 17, 2002

firm's address → Randall Jones
Jones Sporting Goods
1111 Center Street
Oakland, CA 94611

greeting → Dear Mr. Jones:

introduction → I would like to apply for the part-time sales position you advertised in yesterday's *Tribune*.

body I → I am a good worker who is neat, punctual, and honest. I get along well with others. The last three summers I gained worthwhile experience as a salesclerk at Smith's Stationery. I learned to operate a cash register there, and I have had some experience with a personal computer at home. I am 20 years old.

body II → I feel I would be especially qualified to work in a sporting goods store because of my interest in athletics. After playing Little League baseball as a boy, I was on varsity teams in basketball and tennis in high school. I am now taking a weight training class at Centerville College.

conclusion → I would be happy to arrange an interview at your convenience. My phone number is 555-1234.

closing → Sincerely,

Mark Smith

Mark Smith

Writing Assignment:
A Job Application Letter

Think of a job you might enjoy doing and would be qualified to do. Brainstorm that topic. Make a list of your experiences and interests that relate to that job. Then, as in the prewriting example list, cross out unrelated items and arrange the rest in some helpful order.

Your general qualifications: _____

_____

_____

_____

_____

Your specific qualifications: _____

_____

_____

_____

_____

Using the list, write a job application letter. Pick a job that you might actually be interested in. Make the letter as interesting and convincing as you can. Follow the overall format of the model letter.

Writing Topic Bank

An Important Experience

Think about a personal experience that was so interesting or important that you may want to tell your grandchildren about it some day.

1. Make a list of the details of the event. For example, who was there? What happened? When? Where?
2. Write down the reason why the experience was important.
3. On your list of details, circle the ones that directly relate to the reason the experience was so important.
4. Write your draft, using only the details you have circled.

Exploring Topics on the Internet

What topics do you want to know more about? Are you curious about a place, a person, an idea, an activity, or an object?

1. Brainstorm a list of things you are curious about. Choose one to find out about.
2. Go online to Yahoo (www.yahoo.com), Lycos (www.lycos.com), Google (www.google.com), or any other search engine, and type in different words and phrases to try to find the information you want.
3. Explore the links that may lead you to the information you want.
4. When you are finished, write about what you have learned.

Writing About Media

Think about a song whose lyrics (words) you know. What is your main impression of the song?

1. Write down the lyrics or read them if they are already available.
2. Which lyrics seem to lead to your main idea about the song?
3. Write a paragraph that explains your impression and gives several examples from the song that relate to it.

Spelling Troublemakers

Probably because the words sound alike, people often have trouble with little words like *its* and *it's* and *their*, *there*, and *they're*. Since the words come up so often in everyday writing, it's worth knowing how to get them right.

Its, It's

Let's take *its–it's* first. Here's a simple rule to guide you: Use *it's* only as a short form or contraction of *it is* or *it has*. The apostrophe (') means one or more letters have been left out.

> It's [It is] time to go home.

> It's [it has] been a week since the lawyer called.

Use *its* without an apostrophe when you don't mean *it is* or *it has*.

> The dog wagged *its* [not *it is*] tail when the burglar entered the house.

> The car lost *its* [not *it is*] headlight in the collision.

Its is an example of a possessive pronoun. Some other pronouns that show possession and do not take an apostrophe are:

| his | hers | ours | theirs | yours |

SPOTCHECK 1–1   Underline the correct word in parentheses. Remember to use *it's* only if you mean *it is* or *it has.*

1. A one-cent piece doesn't have the word "penny" on (its/it's) face.

2. Neither does the coin have "penny" on (its/it's) reverse side.

3. (Its/It's) unlawful for the face of any living person to appear on a United States coin or stamp.

4. Wear a hat when (its/it's) cold. Your body loses 80 percent of (its/it's) heat through the head.

5. (Its/It's) been more than 80 years since women were first allowed to vote in the United States.

They're, Their, and There

They're is a contraction of *they are*. Notice that the apostrophe goes where the letter *a* has been left out.

They're [They are] building a theater on the corner of First and Elm streets.

Kyle and Lauren said they're [they are] in the same biology lab.

Their is a possessive pronoun. It shows ownership.

The Mustang convertible is their car.

Their three sons are in the Navy.

There shows location (not *here*) and is also a frequent sentence starter: *There is . . . There are . . .*

The deer was standing right over there.

There was no way to solve the puzzle.

 **SPOTCHECK 1–2** Fill in the blanks with *they're, their,* or *there.*

[1]The Changs are selling _____ house. [2]_____ planning to build a new one in Kenwood. [3]_____ son and his family live _____.

[4]_____ may be a delay while _____ house is in escrow. [5]But before long, _____ sure _____ new home will be _____ in Kenwood.

SPOTCHECK 1–3 Write sentences using each of the words in parentheses.

1. (its) _____

2. (it's) _____

3. (there) _____

4. (their) _____

5. (they're) _____

DOUBLECHECK 1–1 Underline the correct word in parentheses.

[1]Americans seem to be tiring of (they're/their/there) long commutes to and from (they're/their/there) sprawling suburban neighborhoods. [2](They're/Their/There) choosing instead to live, work, and shop in planned communities that are sprouting up around the country. [3]Looking at the increase in the number of new homes in planned communities, (it's/its) clear that (they're/their/there) is a real attraction to (they're/their/there) picture-perfect settings. [4]Each planned community has (it's/its) own homeowners' association that is responsible for (it's/its) upkeep. [5]When moving to a planned community, home buyers must agree to follow (it's/its) rules.

[6](They're/their/there) can be rules that define anything from the color of (they're/their/there) house to the size of (they're/their/there) trees. [7]Developers of planned communities say that (it's/its) the strict regulation that attracts (they're/their/there) customers to these communities because (they're/their/there) hoping that the careful maintenance will help keep (it's/its) property value high.

More Troublemakers

Here are some more often-used words that cause many people problems. Be sure you can use them correctly.

a—an	Use *an* before a word that begins with the sound of a vowel (*a, e, i, o, u*): an apple, an opportunity, an hour (silent *h*). Use *a* before a word that begins with the sound of any other letters (called *consonants*): a book, a Chevrolet, a university (the *u* sounds like *y*).
a lot	Notice that it is two words—<u>not</u> *alot*.
are—or—our	*Are* is a verb: They *are* happy. *Or* separates two possibilities: Sara *or* Cathy will drive the van. *Our* is a word showing ownership: That is *our* house on the corner.
have—of	Don't use *of* for *have:* They should *have* (not *of*) phoned first.
hear—here	*Hear* is what you do with your ear. We *hear* a bird singing. *Here* means "this place": Bring the book *here*.
than—then	Use *than* in comparisons: Juanita is taller *than* Carol. *Then* refers to time: If I had known *then* what I know now, I wouldn't have bought the TV set.
there's—theirs	*There's* is a shortened form of *there is: There's* a full moon tonight. *Theirs* shows ownership: That poodle is *theirs*.
to—too—two	*To* is a preposition: Robert is going *to* college. *Too* means *also*: Besides the ketchup, bring some mustard, *too*. *Too* can mean "excessively": Sam is *too* tired to study. *Two* is a number: The Coles own *two* cars.

were—we're—where	*Were* is a verb: The cats *were* frisky.
	We're is a short form of *we are*: We will leave when *we're* ready.
	Where indicates place: That is *where* Antonio lives.
you're—your	*You're* is a short form of *you are*: Let us know if *you're* uncomfortable.
	Your shows ownership: Is that *your* basketball?

Still more "Troublemakers" are taken up in Writing Resource C at the back of the book.

✓ SPOTCHECK 1–4   **Underline the correct words in parentheses:**

¹(Are/Our/Or) you going to the lake in (are/or/our) car (are/or/our) in Franklin's? ²We should (have/of) planned ahead. ³I (hear/here) that Judith forgot her swim suit. ⁴I have mine (here/hear) in my tote bag. ⁵Monica is more excited (than/then) Karen about the trip. ⁶But Karen will be excited (to/too/two) when she arrives at the lake. ⁷(Were/Where) are Dave and Mary? ⁸They (were/where) supposed to roast the hotdogs. ⁹(You're/your) supposed to bring ice for the soft drinks. ¹⁰Let's use this picnic table over (hear/here). ¹¹(Than/Then) everything will be just about perfect.

✓ DOUBLECHECK 1–2   **Write sentences using the words in parentheses:**

1. (than) _____

2. (we're) _____

3. (too) _____

4. (there's) _____

5. (your) _____

6. (hear) _____

7. (an) _____

8. (our) _____

9. (too) _____

10. (you're) _____

DOUBLECHECK 1–3   In each sentence, underline the correct word in parentheses.

¹The human brain is almost (to/too/two) amazing to be believed. ²(Its/It's) unlikely that a computer will ever do all that the brain can do. ³The brain tells us what is happening in (are/or/our) world by processing messages from the eyes, ears, nose, and skin. ⁴It controls bodily functions (to/too/two), such as the beating of the heart. ⁵The brain stores information and memories, so (there's/theirs) a chance of learning and benefiting from experience. ⁶Without a developed brain, the human species might (have/of) disappeared, as the dinosaurs did.

⁷By the time you were about fifteen, (your/you're) brain had reached (its/it's) full size. ⁸By (than/then) it weighed about three pounds. ⁹The brain of a genius is not necessarily bigger (than/then) that of an average person. ¹⁰(Theirs/There's) no direct relationship between human intelligence and the size of the brain. ¹¹The brains of large animals, such as elephants, weigh more (than/then) those of humans, but (there's/theirs) are smaller in relation to body weight. ¹²The animal with the largest brain in proportion to (its/it's) size is the ant.

¹³(You're/Your) brain is not a single organ like your liver. ¹⁴Each of (it's/its) many parts has special functions. ¹⁵(Your/You're) using different sections when speaking (are/or/our) driving a car, for example.

EDITING CHECK 1   Edit the following paragraph to correct the eleven troublemaker errors. One error has been corrected as an example.

¹The "Star-Spangled Banner" is ~~are~~ ^our^ national anthem. ²Its had that honor since 1931. ³It was ~~than~~ that Congress chose it. ⁴Your perhaps aware that the song was written by a man named Francis Scott Key. ⁵However, alot of people don't know that Key was a lawyer as well as a song writer. ⁶During the War of 1812 with England, Key boarded a British ship to arrange a exchange of a prisoner. ⁷While he was their, he could here the bombardment of Fort McHenry in Maryland. ⁸The next morning, he could see "by the dawn's early light" that the United States flag, "spangled" with stars, was still flying over the fort. ⁹Key could of returned to land just to write his official report. ¹⁰However, he wrote a poem to. ¹¹The poem was published in a Baltimore newspaper, and it's words where soon made into a popular song. ¹²When the anthem is sung before sports events these days, not many of the singers know that it's melody was borrowed from an English drinking song.

✓ **CHECKPOINT 1**   Write the correct word in parentheses in the blank at the left.

_____ 1. (Are/Or/Our) chorus is getting better all the time.

_____ 2. (Were/Where) you at the concert last night?

_____ 3. (You're/Your) going to be sorry if you missed it.

_____ 4. You can (hear/here) us again in two weeks.

_____ 5. (Theirs/There's) going to be another performance.

_____ 6. But you really should (<u>have</u>/of) heard us last night.

_____ 7. We sang better last night (than/then) we ever had before.

_____ 8. There was a large turnout (to/too/two).

_____ 9. When (are/or/our) you going to sing with us?

_____ 10. (Its/It's) good that you are a tenor.

_____ 11. (Their/There/They're) always in demand.

_____ 12. In fact, we could use (to/too/two) or three tenors right now.

_____ 13. (Their/There/They're) voices are especially important in the folk songs.

_____ 14. Soon we expect to be accompanied by (a/an) organ as well as a piano.

_____ 15. (Than/Then) we will have a richer sound.

Wordcheck: Definitions

A dictionary is one of the most valuable tools a writer can have. A dictionary exercise called a "Wordcheck" will be found at the end of each chapter of this text. Each will take up one of the many helps a dictionary can provide. (An overview of dictionary use is found in Writing Resource A.)

We probably open a dictionary most often to find out what an unfamiliar word means. But then a problem may come up. The word may have more than one meaning. Suppose you come across this sentence in your reading:

The burglar <u>rifled</u> the bedroom dresser before taking my season tickets to the Dodgers games.

You know that a rifle is a kind of firearm. Does the sentence mean the burglar shot at the dresser? No. The dictionary tells us that *rifle* is also a verb meaning "to search with intent to steal." When more than one meaning is given for a word, we need to decide which one fits the context, that is, the other words surrounding the word in question.

Use the context to guess the meanings of the underlined words. Then, look up the words in a dictionary.

1. Because of vacations, the office had only a skeleton staff.

   Definition: _____

2. In the photo, my grandfather wore a handsome handlebar.

   Definition: _____

3. Fred wouldn't dance the polka, but Jason was game.

   Definition: _____

4. Montague's affected manner of speaking irritated Mrs. Oglethorpe.

   Definition: _____

5. Molly was ahead in the first game, forty to love.

   Definition: _____

6. Ginny pinch-hit in the accounting department when Francoise had her baby.

   Definition: _____

GO ELECTRONIC!

For supplemental readings, exercises, and Internet activities, visit
Checkpoints Online at
http://www.ablongman.com/page

Chapter 2

Paragraphs with Topic Sentences

READING PRECHECK

This essay, which discusses the values emphasized during the Muslim holy month of Ramadan, is a helpful example of effective writing. Notice that the first paragraph ends with a sentence that states the main idea of the entire essay; notice also that each of the next four paragraphs begins with a *topic sentence* (underlined) that says what point will be made in that paragraph.

JOURNAL TOPIC: What values or principles are especially important in your own life?

Lessons Learned During Ramadan
Ameena El Jandali

abstain do without

The holy month of Ramadan ended a couple of days ago. As Muslims throughout the world have abstained from food and drink between sunrise and sunset for the past 30 days, many of the things that were taken for granted have taken on special value and meaning.   1

bounties benefits

Among the obvious, of course, are the dual blessings of food and drink. We   2
are so accustomed to having these in abundance that we rarely think twice about the fact that they are bounties that millions are deprived of. We forget that in countless countries, meat, milk, or sugar are not staples, but luxuries, afforded only to the rich. We forget that throughout the world, including [the United States], there are millions of people who cannot sleep at night from pangs of hunger or

15

remorse sadness

gnawing cold. We forget, not only to share what we have with those less fortunate, but to feel remorse for their plight, and thankfulness for our own good fortune.

Fasting in Ramadan was also a month-long lesson in discipline and self-control. In today's world in which the rule is "if it feels good, do it," Ramadan is an opportunity to practice that long lost art of abstinence, sacrifice, and endurance. Brainwashed into believing that we cannot function without our morning coffee, midday candy bar, or constant train of snacks, many of us find incomprehensible the idea of going without food or drink for over 12 hours. That Muslims fast, not to lose weight or for medical reasons, but for a higher spiritual cause is what makes fasting in Ramadan possible for people who in normal circumstances cannot miss a meal.

Ramadan is not only a time to exert control over our physical side, but over the mental and spiritual as well. While negative thoughts and ill behavior toward others should be avoided year round, in Ramadan special effort is made to eschew such destructive vices as back-biting, cursing, arguing, or lying. Combined with the emphasis on generosity and sharing in Ramadan, the outlook of the fasting person should be on doing good toward others, while improving one's own shortcomings.

eschew give up
back-biting mean gossip

Ramadan is a time for Muslims to remember the less fortunate, not merely in thoughts or prayers, but with financial support . . . . Even here, in the bastion of democracy and freedom, poverty, homelessness, and hunger are affecting growing numbers of the population . . . . But in Ramadan, even rich Muslims experience the pangs of hunger and the taste of thirst. At least in the month of Ramadan, they walk in the shoes of their less fortunate brethren.

bastion fortress

In today's competitive and self-centered world, Ramadan is a time to remember qualities and people we tend to forget. Let us learn from the lessons of Ramadan, the lessons of thankfulness, sharing, and caring . . . .

Checking Meaning and Style

1. What is the main point of the essay? In what paragraph is it expressed?
2. How do the first sentences of Paragraphs 2 to 5 help the reader?
3. What "blessing" is mentioned in Paragraph 2?
4. What lesson does Ramadan teach, according to Paragraph 3?
5. What kinds of controls does the holy month emphasize? (Paragraph 4)
6. What kind of charity is emphasized in Paragraph 5?
7. How are Americans "brain-washed"? (Paragraph 3)

Checking Ideas

1. Would an observance similar to Ramadan be good for all Americans, regardless of their religious affiliation?
2. Would most Americans be willing to meet the requirements of Ramadan? Would you?
3. What views expressed in the essay do you agree or disagree with?

Writing Paragraphs with Topic Sentences

For good reasons, most writing is divided into paragraphs, as in "Lessons Learned During Ramadan." Breaking up a composition into paragraphs helps a reader follow the flow of the writer's ideas. This is true because a traditional paragraph discusses only one idea. That means a new paragraph alerts the reader that a new idea is coming up. Another reason for paragraphs is that they help writers organize their thoughts.

We can recognize the beginning of a paragraph because it is usually indented. That is, it starts a half-inch or so from the left margin, as in the following model paragraphs. However, material that is typewritten or word processed is sometimes written in block form: a new paragraph is shown by an extra space between paragraphs, and there is no indenting.

Analyzing Paragraphs with Topic Sentences

"Lessons Learned During Ramadan" is a well organized piece of writing. What can we learn from it? We notice that the last sentence of the first paragraph states the general idea or thesis of the entire selection—that things often taken for granted assume new meaning for Muslims during a month of fasting. The next four paragraphs give details to support or develop that idea. Notice that each paragraph begins with a *topic sentence* (underlined). That sentence states the main idea of the paragraph. The other sentences give details that support or develop the main idea.

The models that follow will help make the topic sentence approach clear.

Model Paragraph with Topic Sentence 1

Just as is true today, early advertising tried to take advantage of Americans' insecurities. Magazines were full of troubling questions like these: "Do You Make These Mistakes in English?" "Will Your Hair Stand Close Inspection?" and "Did Nature Fail to Put Roses in Your Cheeks?" A former golf champion was shown blaming the decline in his game on his failure to use the right toothpaste. New health and social problems were discovered: halitosis ("Even Your Best Friends Won't Tell You"), iron-poor blood, vitamin deficiency, and body odor. Some ads promised to ease insecurities. Smoker's cough could be cured by smoking a certain brand of cigarettes ("Not a Cough in a Carload"). Another cigarette brand claimed to be "Just What the Doctor Ordered."

The topic sentence says the paragraph will discuss early efforts to sell products by raising doubts in people about their own health or popularity. The idea is developed with specific examples.

Model Paragraph with Topic Sentence 2

Scientists studying satellite data have recently learned that lightning strikes are not evenly distributed over the Earth's surface. You are more likely to be struck by lightning in Florida or Central Africa than you would be on the ocean or at the polar ice caps. One factor that increases the likelihood that lightning will strike an area on the globe is the presence of two air masses pushing moist air upward between them. An example of this occurs when westward breezes from the Atlantic Ocean and eastward breezes from the Gulf of Mexico meet over Florida. The presence of warm air close to the Earth's surface also influences how often lightning strikes. The ocean surface doesn't warm up as quickly as the land surface does, so lightning strikes occur less frequently there.

The topic sentence says the paragraph will discuss how lighting strikes some places more than others. The other sentences then describe the various reasons this is so.

SPOTCHECK 2–1   Support each topic sentence with sentences of your own.

1. Mr. Wrigley was showing his age. _____

   _____

   _____

   _____

   _____

2. The house next door was badly run-down. _____

   _____

   _____

   _____

3. Mrs. Lindley is active in the community. _____

   _____

   _____

   _____

   _____

Topic Sentences and Paragraph Unity

A well-written paragraph is unified. That means it deals with only one idea or topic and doesn't wander into other matters. The reading on Ramadan demonstrates a useful way to gain paragraph unity: to start each paragraph with a topic sentence that says what the paragraph will be about. The other sentences *develop* or *support* the topic sentence with examples and specific details. Although the topic sentence can appear anywhere in the paragraph (or merely be implied), starting the paragraph with a topic sentence is the helpful approach that will be emphasized in this text.

Here is an example of a paragraph that lacks unity and does not stick to the topic sentence (underlined). Which sentences should be left out?

¹Cats have stirred strong feelings in people for thousands of years. ²Ancient Egyptians treated cats almost like gods, and someone who killed a cat could be punished with death. ³People who like cats often don't like dogs, and vice versa. ⁴In Europe in the Middle Ages, cats became associated with witchcraft and black magic and were persecuted by the Christian church. ⁵In the nineteenth century, sentimental Victorians restored the cat as a household favorite. ⁶It is clear that cats are minor gods in many American homes today. ⁷We spend more money on cat food than on baby food. ⁸Birds and fish are also popular in many homes.

Checking sentences 3 and 8 against the topic sentence, we see they have gotten off the track and should be omitted.

SPOTCHECK 2–2

Two of the sentences in this paragraph do not stick to the topic sentence (underlined). In the blanks that follow the paragraph, write the numbers of sentences that violate the unity of the paragraph.

¹The ancient Egyptians were pioneers in the use of eye makeup. ²By 4000 B.C., they were emphasizing the eyes as the facial feature that most clearly revealed inner thoughts and feelings. ³The Egyptian queen Cleopatra was famed for her beauty. ⁴Green eye shadow was a favorite cosmetic. ⁵Made from a copper ore, it was used on both the upper and lower eyelids. ⁶A paste made from a variety of substances outlined the eyes and darkened the eyebrows and lashes. ⁷"Eyebrow pencils" were made of sticks of wood, metal, or ivory. ⁸Both men and women used an eye glitter made from crushed beetle shells. ⁹The ancient Egyptians are also famous for their huge pyramids, which were used as tombs for royalty.

_____   _____

Topics and Topic Sentences

The topic of a paragraph is what it is about. You could write a paragraph about volleyball, movies, or your Uncle Fred. Each one could be a topic for a paragraph. But you wouldn't have a topic sentence until you gave the topic a focus, until you said something about your topic that leads you into the paragraph. Notice how the three topics just mentioned could become parts of topic sentences:

Playing volleyball with the other guys from the accounting department has helped me get along better at the office.

Now you can give specific details and examples: how you can join in your teammates' conversations during coffee breaks, how the boss complimented you on your improved spiking ability, and so on.

Movies are getting more and more violent.

Now discuss some films you have seen recently that illustrate that idea.

Of all my relatives, Uncle Fred is the most generous.

Now discuss the way he is helping you attend college, the birthday presents he gives the family, and his contributions to charity.

Be sure your topic sentence leads easily into a discussion of the topic. If you only state facts, there will be nothing to discuss. Avoid "So what?" sentences that lead nowhere, such as these:

Our office volleyball team plays the first and third Saturdays of each month at Ocean Beach. (So what?)

My uncle Fred lives on Maple Street. (Who cares?)

 **SPOTCHECK 2–3** In the blanks at the left, write *good* for effective topic sentences that could lead to fully developed paragraphs; write *weak* for those that seem to lead nowhere.

_____ 1. My writing skills have improved since I started reading more books and magazines.

_____ 2. Mayor Johnson wants to improve the city's park system.

_____ 3. Denver, Colorado, is at an altitude of one mile.

_____ 4. Denver's mile-high altitude affects visiting athletes.

_____ 5. There are three boys and three girls in my family.

Narrowing the Topic of the Topic Sentence

Be sure that your topic sentence isn't too broad, that it doesn't try to cover too much ground. Narrow the topic so it can be discussed in a worthwhile way in the few sentences of a paragraph.

(too broad)   The weather in California is sometimes uncomfortable.

(better)   The weather in San Francisco is surprisingly chilly in July.

(too broad)   Dogs are devoted pets.

(better)   My grandfather's dog Fifi is a devoted pet.

SPOTCHECK 2–4   Rewrite the topics at the left twice. Each time make them less broad and more suitable for discussion in a single paragraph.

Example: work   office work   computer programming

1. books   _____   _____

2. sports teams   _____   _____

3. buildings   _____   _____

4. relatives   _____   _____

5. politicians   _____   _____

Being Specific

Having narrowed your topic, be sure what you say about it is specific, not general or vague.

(vague)	Marlene appeals to me.
(specific)	Marlene is good-looking and rich.
(vague)	My Mustang is a better car than Fred's Toyota.
(specific)	My Mustang is faster than Fred's Toyota.
(vague)	Radio station KXYZ has good programs.
(specific)	Radio station KXYZ plays the kind of country and western music that I like.
(vague)	New Orleans is an interesting city.
(specific)	New Orleans has many outstanding restaurants.
(more specific)	New Orleans is a good place to find Cajun cooking.

SPOTCHECK 2–5   In the blanks at the left, write *weak* for topic sentences that are broad or vague. Write *good* for the others.

_____ 1. Mr. and Mrs. Howell are helpful neighbors.

_____ 2. Baseball is one of America's favorite sports.

_____ 3. The woman at the checkout counter is nice.

_____ **4.** My new pickup truck costs a great deal in loan payments, insurance, and maintenance.

_____ **5.** Most of the "romance" novels sold at supermarkets are poor.

✓ **SPOTCHECK 2–6**

Turn the following topics into topic sentences by saying something specific about each one. Ask yourself if each sentence would lead easily into a full paragraph.

Example: Watching professional football on TV <u>takes up too much of my time in the fall</u>.

1. My favorite holiday _____

_____

2. Elementary school _____

_____

3. My first love _____

_____

4. Poetry _____

_____

5. Cousins _____

_____

Prewriting: Keeping a Journal

If you were learning to play the guitar, the more you practiced the better you would get. In the same way, the more you practice writing the more you will improve. One way to get in some extra practice is to keep a journal. Journal writing can also be a way to explore a topic before writing a paragraph or an essay.

A journal is a notebook in which you jot down thoughts about whatever has interested you that day or in the past few days. (Entries should be made at least several times a week, ideally at the same time each day, such as at bedtime.) A loose-leaf or spiral notebook would do nicely. In addition, you might want to carry a smaller pad or a piece of paper during the day to make reminders of ideas and experiences.

Your journal might include such things as how you felt when you got back your latest math quiz or your feelings about the math instructor or the person who sits next to you in class. Did you have a disagreement with a friend or family member or enjoy a movie or TV show? What are your goals in life—job, money, family? Include something that was especially significant or interesting that your sociology instructor said about the causes of poverty, or the joke she told that you might want to use some day. How did you feel about the man playing the trombone in the subway? And so on.

Tennis great Arthur Ashe suggested that keeping a journal would help players improve their game. Some of his ideas in *Arthur Ashe on Tennis* might also help us improve our writing and, perhaps, our lives. His advice:

WRITE IT DOWN

A notebook should be an integral part of your equipment. When you are learning the game, keep notes on your lessons. So many things pop up that if you record your learning process in diary form, you will be amazed at how much valuable information you will gather. Then when you go out to practice, pull out your notebook and devise a plan of how to use the time you have allotted.

Once you begin to play matches, use your notebook to keep track of how you do in competition. At the end of a match put your thoughts down in writing. First, record the basics of the match, such as the opponent and the score. Then write a brief rough summary of such critical factors as double faults, return of serve errors, and ad[vantage] points lost. Don't worry about compiling a precise tally; the notes are merely to remind you of the areas of your game that need work.

SPOTCHECK 2–7   Write a short journal entry on one of the topics that will appear in the next writing assignment: relatives, animals, or stores.

_____

_____

_____

_____

_____

_____

Writing Assignment:
A Paragraph with a Topic Sentence

To get ready for your next assignment, first write a topic sentence for each of the broad subjects listed below. Narrow the topic to one particular example—one relative or one sports event, for example. Then make a specific point about it. You may find ideas in your journal writing in Spotcheck 2–7.

Example: *kids* My brother's two-year-old son was the center of attention at Sunday's family reunion.

1. relatives _____

   _____

2. animals _____

   _____

3. stores _____

   _____

Now write a paragraph of five to ten sentences that begins with one of the topic sentences you just wrote.

 Writing Topic Bank

Protecting the Environment

What can an ordinary person do to protect the environment? Think about the everyday activities you engage in and the choices you make about how to do them. Consider how other people you know act to protect or damage the environment.

1. Write your ideas in a journal entry.
2. How can these ideas be summed up in a single sentence? Use this as the topic sentence.
3. Organize your ideas and write them in a paragraph.

Exploring Sports on the Internet

Go to the sports page of a major news website, such as CNN (www.cnn.com), the New York Times on the Web (nytimes.com), or the Los Angeles Times (www.latimes.com). Examine the statistics of a favorite player or team. Write a

WRITING CHECKLIST

 Use the brainstorming technique discussed in Chapter 1 or the journal writing discussed in this chapter to find details to develop your paragraph.

 Start with a topic sentence that makes clear the main point of the paragraph.

 Be sure your paragraph is unified, with all sentences sticking to the topic sentence.

 If you have a chance, discuss the assignment and your paragraph with a classmate.

 In this and all other writing assignments in this text, observe the guidelines for manuscript preparation below.

topic sentence that makes a specific point about the player or team. Now write a paragraph that includes details that support your point.

Writing About Media

What is the best (or worst) movie you have seen recently? Write a topic sentence that names the movie and describes how good (or bad) it was. Then write a paragraph that gives several specific examples of its good (or bad) points.

Manuscript Preparation

Procedure for Papers Written with Word Processors

1. Use standard white paper, 8 ½ by 11 inches.

PEANUTS® by Charles M. Schulz

PEANUTS reprinted by permission of United Feature Syndicate, Inc.

2. Double-space the lines.
3. Be sure your ink cartridge is fresh enough to print clearly.
4. Leave a margin of 1 inch on all four sides.
5. Number each sheet in the upper right-hand corner, using the word processor's page numbering system. Before the page number, write your last name. Be sure the pages are in order.
6. Follow the instructor's suggestions for placement of your full name, the instructor's name, the course name, and the date.

Procedure for Handwritten Papers

1. Use a pen (never a pencil) with blue-black or black ink. Write as neatly and clearly as you can.
2. Use standard lined notebook paper. Avoid the spiral-bound kind that leaves a ragged edge when you tear a sheet out. Or use unlined white paper with a lined guide sheet underneath.
3. Write on every other line.
4. Write on only one side of the paper.
5. Follow items 4–6 in the word processing instructions.
6. Other instructions

_____

_____

_____

_____

Sentence Sense: Identifying Subjects and Verbs

When we write acceptably, we write in *sentences.* We do that most of the time without thinking about it. But sometimes we may write something that looks like a sentence—that starts with a capital letter and ends with a period—but isn't really a sentence. Here is an example:

Walking to school at 7 a.m. in a blizzard.

Since a complete sentence needs a subject and a verb, we need to be able to recognize these sentence parts. Recognizing subjects and verbs isn't worth much in itself. But if you can do it, you will be able to deal later with some very real problems in writing: sentence fragments, run-together sentences, lack of subject-verb agreement, inconsistencies in person and tense, and errors in punctuation. Those matters make up a large part of the rest of the course, so give subjects and verbs your full attention.

Finding the Subject

The <u>subject</u> tells *who* or *what* the sentence is about. The underlined words in the following sentences answer the question "who?" or "what?"

<u>Janice</u> arrived early.

<u>Tijuana</u> is south of San Diego.

<u>Glass</u> breaks.

<u>We</u> always sing before supper.

The subject is often a noun or a pronoun. A *noun* is the name of a person, place, or thing (*Janice, Tijuana, glass*). A *pronoun* is a word that takes the place of a noun. *We* is an example of a pronoun. Other examples are *he, she, it, you, they.*

The words underlined in the examples just given are the *simple subjects* of their sentences. A *complete subject* is the simple subject plus words that describe it. In the following example, the complete subject is underlined once and the simple subject (*computer*) twice.

<u>The third <u>computer</u> from the end of the row</u> needs repair.

In this textbook, the words *the subject* refer to the simple subject.

SPOTCHECK 2–8   Underline the subject in each sentence. Ask who or what the sentence is about.

1. The average person can see 93 million miles—when looking at the sun.

2. Air conditioning was invented to control humidity, not temperature.

3. George Ferris invented the Ferris wheel in 1893.

4. Jupiter, the largest planet, is three times bigger than Earth.

5. Less snow falls at the South Pole than in parts of the United States.

Finding the Verb

There are two kinds of verbs.

1. *Action verbs* tell what the subject *does* (or did, or will do).

Geese <u>fly</u> south in the winter.

Luana's brother <u>attended</u> Yale University.

2. *Linking verbs* connect the subject to words that say something about the subject.

> Marcia <u>was</u> overjoyed at getting the job.

> Robert <u>seems</u> tired tonight.

The verb *was* links the subject, *Marcia,* to information about the subject: that she was overjoyed. The verb *seems* links the subject, *Robert,* to the description *tired.*

One group of linking verbs contains forms of the verb *to be*:

am   is   are   was   were   been

Another group of linking verbs contains words such as these:

seem   appear   look   become   feel   taste   smell

Some of these words can be either linking or action verbs.

> Rudy <u>looked</u> happy. **(linking verb)**

> Rudy <u>looked</u> at the magazine. **(action verb)**

 **SPOTCHECK 2–9**

Underline the verbs. In the blanks, indicate whether they are action verbs or linking verbs.

_____ 1. Many birds <u>eat</u> twice their weight each day.

_____ 2. Today's blue whales <u>are</u> bigger than the biggest dinosaurs.

_____ 3. Lobsters <u>look</u> red only after boiling.

_____ 4. Dolphins and monkeys have better <u>memories</u> than elephants.

_____ 5. Ants <u>live</u> on every continent except Antarctica.

 **DOUBLECHECK 2–1**

Draw one line under the subject and two lines under the verb in each sentence.

1. French soldiers <u>fought</u> an odd battle in World War I.

2. German soldiers <u>threatened</u> to cross the Marne River.

3. The river <u>was</u> only thirty miles from the French capital, Paris.

4. The French cause <u>seemed</u> lost.

5. The army <u>needed</u> reinforcements at the front immediately.

6. The reinforcements arrived in time—and in style—as passengers in the taxicabs of Paris.

Crossing Out Prepositional Phrases

Often it is easier to find the subject if you cross out all *prepositional phrases*. First, here are some common prepositions:

about	beside	of
above	between	on
according to	by	over
across	during	through
after	for	to
among	from	toward
around	in	under
at	into	upon
before	near	with

Prepositions are usually followed by a noun or pronoun called the *object of the preposition*. A preposition and its object form a *prepositional phrase*. Examples:

into the house   on top of Old Smoky   among the many paintings

 **SPOTCHECK 2–10**

Use eight different prepositions to form prepositional phrases with these words.

Example: near the window

1. _____ midnight

2. _____ the neighbors

3. _____ Chicago

4. _____ the ground

5. _____ your help

6. _____ the books

7. _____ the telescope

8. _____ the two cars

Here is how to find the sentence subject by first crossing out all the prepositional phrases.

~~Behind the house~~, Mr. Olson was asleep ~~in a hammock~~.

After we cross out the two prepositional phrases, *behind the house* and *in a hammock*, it is clear that the subject is *Mr. Olson*.

> **IMPORTANT** *A word in a prepositional phrase is never the subject of the sentence.*

SPOTCHECK 2-11   Cross out the prepositional phrases and underline the subject.

> Example: ~~In the office,~~ the <u>president</u> stood ~~near his desk.~~

1. In Germany in 1910, the world's first airline service used dirigibles, not airplanes.

2. After *Gone With the Wind*, Margaret Mitchell never wrote another book.

3. For American taxpayers, no taxes were withheld from paychecks until 1943, during World War II.

4. Between 1800 and 2000, world population grew from 1 billion to over 6 billion.

5. After forty-one days in New York's Museum of Modern Art, a painting by Henri Matisse was discovered to be upside-down.

Finding the Subject: More Tips

The subject usually appears at the beginning of the sentence, but it may appear somewhere else.

> Flitting from flower to flower was a <u>hummingbird</u>. (The usual word order: A hummingbird was flitting from flower to flower.)

Although it often starts a sentence, *there* is not the subject.

> There were three books lying on the table. (*Books* is the subject of the verb *were lying.*)

A sentence can have more than one subject.

> The <u>oil</u> and the <u>filter</u> should be changed.

In sentences that express commands, the unwritten but understood subject is *you.*

> [You] Close the door on your way out.

Sometimes it is easier to find the subject if you pick out the verb first.

> In the spring, the poppies on the hillside ***appear*** first. (What appear? Poppies.)
>
> verb

SPOTCHECK 2-12   Draw a line under each subject.

1. College athletes have little chance of joining a professional team.

2. In football, for example, only one player in 100 has a chance of turning professional.

3. There is only one chance in 500 of succeeding in the National Basketball Association.

QUICKCHECK ON SUBJECTS

✓ Every complete sentence requires a subject.

✓ The subject tells who or what the sentence is about.

✓ The subject usually appears at the beginning of the sentence, but it may appear elsewhere.

✓ A word in a prepositional phrase is never the subject.

✓ In commands, the unwritten but understood subject is *you.*

4. Even then, the average <u>sports</u> career is short—4.2 years in football and 3.2 years in basketball.

5. [You] Remember these statistics when dreaming about sports instead of doing homework.

6. Less likely than other <u>students</u> to complete a degree are college athletes.

Finding the Verb: More Tips

If the subject performs more than one action, there will be more than one verb.

The car <u>swerved</u> and <u>hit</u> a tree.

The verb may consist of more than one word. The main verb may have one or more *helping verbs.*

The hikers <u>had</u> <u>walked</u> ten miles before noon.

Here are some examples of helping verbs with forms of the verb *work.*

can work	does work
is working	has been working
might have been working	would have worked
had worked	will work
will have worked	will be working

NOTE A word ending in *-ing* cannot be the verb without one or more helping verbs. A verb preceded by *to (to work)* is an *infinitive* and cannot be the verb.

Sometimes the verb is broken in two by words that are not part of the verb. Such words include *never, always, just, only,* and *not* (and its contraction *n't*).

Mr. Ochoa <u>had</u> never <u>seen</u> a redwood tree.

The fire <u>hadn't</u> <u>been</u> <u>started</u> in the fireplace when we arrived.

Sometimes the verb has an *object*—the person or thing that receives the action of the verb. The object of a verb is never the subject of a sentence.

        verb   **object**
The landlord <u>raised</u> the <u>rent</u> twice this year.

 **SPOTCHECK 2–13**   Underline the verb or verbs in each sentence.

1. The Barbie doll first appeared in 1958 and achieved instant popularity.

2. It was invented by Ruth Handler for the Mattel toy company.

3. Before Barbie, American dolls usually had resembled infants.

4. Noticing her daughter's fondness for full-figured paper cutout dolls, Mrs. Handler developed a shapely adult doll.

5. As a full-sized person, Barbie would have a 39-23-33 figure.

6. A large wardrobe and other accessories for Barbie soon were offered.

7. Taking his place with Barbie on toy store shelves in 1961 was Ken.

8. Barbie and Ken were named after the Handlers' daughter and son.

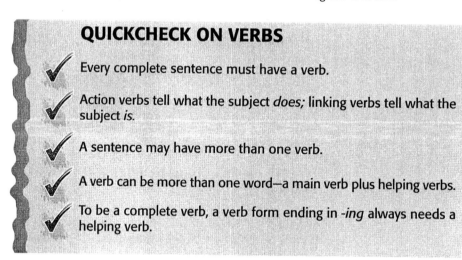

QUICKCHECK ON VERBS

✓ Every complete sentence must have a verb.

✓ Action verbs tell what the subject *does;* linking verbs tell what the subject *is.*

✓ A sentence may have more than one verb.

✓ A verb can be more than one word—a main verb plus helping verbs.

✓ To be a complete verb, a verb form ending in *-ing* always needs a helping verb.

 **DOUBLECHECK 2–2**   In the following paragraph, draw one line under the subject and two lines under the verb. Finding the subject may be easier if you cross out prepositional phrases first.

[1]Education in Japan is different in many ways from education in the United States.

[2]For one thing, only 7 percent of Japanese students drop out. [3]In the United States, the

dropout rate is about three times higher. [4]The quality of the Japanese education system is often credited for Japan's success in technological fields. **5**For many Japanese, education has been the only path to social and economic status. **6**Starting in the first grade, Japanese schools stress hard work, endurance, and concentration. **7**These same <u>values</u> are reinforced in the students' homes. **8**The status of a Japanese woman depends in large part on the success of her children in school. **9**Nearly half of the high school students attend tutoring centers after school. **10**They worry about passing the difficult college entrance exams. **11**Four hours of sleep at night is common for serious students. **12**Surprisingly, Japanese colleges often receive low marks from some American observers. **13**Americans sometimes have been critical of the emphasis in Japanese schools on memorizing facts. **14**Too much emphasis on learning facts may hamper creativity.

CHECKPOINT 2　　　**Enter the subjects and verbs of each sentence in the blanks.**

_____　1. Apple trees first grew in Russia and then came to America with European settlers.

_____

_____　2. European grapes didn't thrive in the cold winters of the northern Atlantic coast.

_____

_____　3. Apple cider was the most popular beverage in the New England colonies.

_____

_____　4. Both George Washington and Thomas Jefferson grew apple orchards.

_____

_____　5. American's early pioneers traveled westward to get land of their own.

_____

_____　6. On the frontier, Johnny Appleseed sold apple trees to these westward travelers.

_____

_____ 7. Before the Industrial Revolution, most Americans lived on farms.

_____

_____ 8. Each family reserved part of their land for an apple orchard.

_____

_____ 9. Yeast converts the sugar in apple cider to alcohol.

_____

_____ 10. During the Temperance Movement, millions of apple trees were destroyed in an effort to reduce alcohol use.

_____

Wordcheck: Pronunciation

Let's suppose you aren't quite sure how to pronounce the word *psychology*. Looking it up in a dictionary, you will find something like this right after the entry for the word:

(sī-kŏl´-ə-je)

The accent mark (´) after *kŏl* means that syllable gets emphasized in speaking. Other pronunciation marks are explained at the bottom of one of the two pages you see when you open the dictionary. The upside down *e* (ə) in the third syllable is pronounced *uh*, like the *a* in *ago* or *around*.

Using a dictionary, copy the pronunciations of the following words. Use the key words at the bottom of the dictionary page to practice pronouncing the words. If more than one pronunciation is given, the first one is used more often.

| theater | ask | nuclear |
| Mozart | | pronunciation |

GO ELECTRONIC!

For supplemental readings, exercises, and Internet activities, visit *Checkpoints Online* at
http://www.ablongman.com/page

Chapter 3

Paragraphs with Specific Details

READING PRECHECK

Mary E. Mebane grew up on a farm in the South and went on to become a university professor. In this excerpt from her autobiography, *Mary*, we see how she uses specific details to make a portrait of her mother.

> **JOURNAL TOPIC:** The portrait suggests why the daughter wanted a different life for herself. In your journal, write a paragraph or two about the kind of life you would find most satisfying.

Nonnie
Mary E. Mebane

structured highly organized

Nonnie led a structured, orderly existence. Before six o'clock in the morning, she was up, starting her day. First she turned on WPTF and listened to the news and the weather and the music. Later, when WDNC in Durham hired Norfleet Whitted, the first black announcer in the area, she listened first to one station, then to the other. Some mornings it would be "They Traced Her Little Footprints in the Snow," and other mornings it would be black gospel-singing and rhythm-and-blues. Then she would make a fire in the wood stove and start her breakfast. She preferred some meat—fried liver pudding or fatback, or a streak-of-fat streak-of-lean—and made a hoecake of bread on top of the stove, which she ate with either Karo syrup or homemade blackberry preserves, occasionally with watermelon-rind preserves that she had canned in the summer. Then she would drink her coffee, call me to get up, and leave the house in her blue uniform, blue apron, and blue

1

cap—it would still be dark when she left on winter mornings—and go to catch her ride to the tobacco factory. . . .

My mother worked as a cutter, clipping the hard ends of each bundle of tobacco before it was shredded to make cigarettes. At noon she ate lunch she had brought from home in a brown paper bag: a biscuit with meat in it and a sweet potato or a piece of pie or cake. Some of the women ate in the cafeteria, but in her thirty years at the Liggett and Myers factory, she never once did. She always took her lunch. Then she worked on until closing time, caught her ride back to Wildwood, and started on the evening's activities. First she had supper, which I had finished preparing from the morning. After I got older we sometimes had meat other than what had to be prepared in a "pot." It would be my duty to fry chicken or prepare ham bits and gravy. **2**

After supper, she'd read the Durham *Sun* and see to it that we did the chores if we hadn't done them already: slop the hogs, feed the chickens, get in the wood for the next day. Then we were free. She'd get her blue uniform ready for the next day, then listen to the radio. No later than nine o'clock, she would be in bed. In the morning she would get up, turn on the radio, and start frying some fatback. Another day would have started. **3**

Saturdays were work days, too, the time for washing, ironing, going to the garden, preparing Sunday dinner (no one was supposed to work on the Sabbath), so we ran the chicken down in the yard and Nonnie wrung its neck or chopped its head off with the ax. Sometimes we went to town on Saturday but not often, for Nonnie went to town every day. Sometimes, at lunchtime, she'd go down to Belk's, and always on Friday she went to the A&P on Mangum Street and bought her groceries; then she'd stop at the Big Star in Little Five Points if she had heard that there was a particularly good buy on something. So the Saturday-in-town ritual that is so much a part of the lives of most country children was not mine at all. I myself sometimes went to Brookstown several times a week when my father was alive, because that is where he went to get trash, sell vegetables, and visit his relatives. **4**

Sunday afternoons she would go to see her friends or they would come to see her. She would say, "I believe I'll go up to Miss Angeline's a little while." Or it would be Miss Pauline's or Claudia's. And she would stay until about dusk and come home, listen to the radio, then go to bed, ready to start Monday morning again. **5**

In the spring and summer after work, my mother would plant in her garden: tomatoes, string beans, okra, and she'd sow a turnip patch. Then, every day after work, she'd go over to the garden on the hill to see how it was doing. On Saturdays she'd get her buckets if it was time for us to go berry picking. And on hot summer evenings, if the peaches man had been around, she'd can them after work because they wouldn't keep until Saturday, the day she did most of her canning. **6**

This was her routine—fixed, without change, unvarying. And she accepted it. She more than accepted it, she embraced it; it gave meaning to her life, it was what she had been put here on this earth to do. It was not to be questioned. **7**

ritual   something always done the same way

baffled   unable to understand

To Nonnie this life was ideal; she saw nothing wrong with it. And she won-   **8**
dered in baffled rage why her daughter didn't value it but rather sought something
else, some other rhythm, a more meaningful pattern to human life.

Checking Meaning and Style

1. How does the first sentence help organize the entire selection?
2. Each of the first six paragraphs is about one part of Nonnie's life. The first paragraph describes how she got ready to go to work. What is each of the others about?
3. How does the content of the last two paragraphs differ from that of the first six?
4. The writing is almost always specific rather than general or vague. What are the specific details that make Paragraph 1 interesting?
5. How does Mary E. Mebane feel about her mother's life? Does she want the same kind of life for herself? Where does she say this?

Checking Ideas

1. How do you feel about Nonnie's life? What are its good points? Its bad points?
2. Would you want your own life to be different from hers? In what ways? At home? At work? In social life?
3. Nonnie's life is described as "structured" and "orderly." How would you describe it?
4. What, in your opinion, is necessary for a "meaningful" life?

Analyzing Writing That Uses Specific Details

The late-night TV host Johnny Carson used to open his show with a line like "Boy, was it hot today!" His studio audience always shouted back, "How hot was it, Johnny?" Carson then replied with a witty comeback.

There's a lesson for writers in that exchange. People aren't satisfied with generalities. They want specific details. They want to know not just that it was hot but that the thermometer hit ninety-five, that downtown office workers waded in the courthouse fountain at lunch time, that freeway traffic was snarled by overheated cars.

Using specific details is one of the best ways of developing the general idea of a topic sentence. Specific details help make a paragraph interesting, convincing, and clear, as they do in the selection "Nonnie." Mary Mebane is not content to say the children had to do some chores after supper. She is specific: slop the hogs, feed the chickens, get in the next day's wood. The daughter is specific about the kinds of things her mother grew in the garden: tomatoes, string beans, okra, turnips.

Being Specific

Writing that doesn't get down to specifics—writing that is general or vague—is uninteresting and often unclear.

(vague)	Susan <u>can't be trusted</u>.
(specific)	Susan <u>borrowed my reggae album two weeks ago and hasn't returned it</u>.
(vague)	Jeff has a new <u>dog</u>.
(specific)	Jeff has a new <u>attack-trained Chihuahua</u>.
(vague)	Kevin lives in a <u>big house</u>.
(specific)	Kevin lives in a <u>fourteen-room mansion that has six bathrooms, four garages, and an indoor swimming pool</u>.

SPOTCHECK 3–1 Fill in the blanks so that vague words are on the left and the most specific words are on the right.

Example:

animal	farm animal	cow
1. magazines	weeklies	_____
2. countries	_____	Nigeria
3. _____	indoor sports	basketball
4. cars	foreign cars	_____

SPOTCHECK 3–2 Rewrite these sentences to make the vague words (underlined) more specific. Your sentences probably will be longer than the originals.

Example:

My parents are <u>nice</u>.
My parents <u>give me money whenever I want it</u>.

1. The new office building is <u>tall</u>.

   _____

2. Marly's two-year-old boy is <u>cute</u>.

   _____

3. Joaquin usually carries a bunch of credit cards.

_____

4. Cynthia bought her dress at a department store.

_____

5. The little girl was unhappy.

_____

Prewriting: Clustering

Clustering is another type of brainstorming that many writers find useful. Clustering helps you organize your thoughts and produce the details that make your writing interesting. This is how clustering works: First, choose a word or phrase as the starting point. Put it in the middle of a blank page and circle it. Let your mind make connections with the topic word. Write your new ideas down, forming a web all around the center word. Put ideas that seem related near each other. When done, use the cluster as an outline of your paragraph (or essay). Here is an example that will help you with your next writing assignment, a portrait of a person.

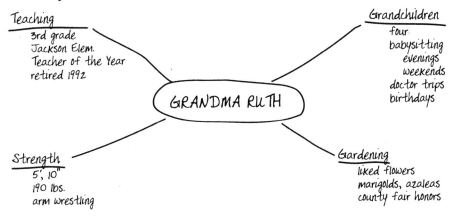

The following paragraph could be written from the "Grandma Ruth" cluster. The topic sentence is underlined.

Model Paragraph with Specific Details 1

Grandma Ruth played an important part in the lives of many children. She taught third grade at Jackson Elementary School for thirty-five years, retiring in 1992. The city had honored her as Teacher of the Year in 1985.

After retiring, she devoted much of her time to her four grandchildren. She spent many evenings and weekends babysitting them when the parents wanted to go to a movie or attend an out-of-town event, such as a church retreat. Sunday dinner was always held at Grandma's, even though her small house was overflowing when everyone attended. If both of a child's parents were at work, Grandma could be counted on to drive the child to a doctor's or dentist's appointment. She never forgot a birthday. It's no wonder that so many people appreciated Grandma's role in their lives.

The cluster items about her stature and her gardening activities have been left out because they don't develop the topic sentence idea—that she was important to many children.

Another use of clustering would be to choose one of the topics in the cluster and put that in the center of a new cluster. That way you could have a more detailed paragraph on, for example, her teaching years.

To prepare for the next writing assignment, study this portrait of a Marine drill sergeant.

Model Paragraph with Specific Details 2

Drill Sergeant Brogan was one of the most intimidating men I had ever met. His smile had the same effect as an ax-killer's smile; it screamed, "I'm dangerous!" Standing six-feet-five, he had a Mr. Universe build. His growling, snarling voice earned him the nickname "The Bear," and his eagle eyes never missed a recruit's slightest misstep. To top it all, his mind was quicker than a mainframe computer.

Notice that the topic sentence says what the focus of the portrait will be—that the sergeant was "intimidating." Note, too, how specific details show that the sergeant was indeed intimidating.

Writing Assignment: A Portrait of a Person

With "Nonnie" and the model paragraphs in mind, write a one-paragraph portrait of a person you know well. Begin with a topic sentence that focuses on one quality of the person. For example, if your topic sentence says

Mrs. Schaffer always dresses in the latest fashions.

you would discuss only Mrs. Schaffer's clothing, not her favorite TV shows or how many children she has.

Notice how each of these sample topic sentences could lead to a limited, unified paragraph.

I can never count on my husband to do anything on time.

My neighbor loves to listen to loud music, unfortunately.

When I was in the hospital, my nurse, Miss Haversham, was very helpful.

WRITING CHECKLIST

 Use a topic sentence to provide a focus for the paragraph.

 Use the prewriting technique of clustering to develop and organize your paragraph.

 Use specific details to make your writing interesting and clear.

 If possible, collaborate with a classmate when revising the paragraph.

 Proofread the final draft, looking especially for troublemakers.

In this and all writing assignments, remember to revise your work, as demonstrated in the example on page 42.

Writing Topic Bank

Your Best (or Worst) Quality

What is your best (or worst) quality? Write a paragraph that describes this quality and gives examples of it. Make sure the topic sentence clearly states the quality and that the other sentences in the paragraph discuss only that one quality.

Exploring Art on the Internet

Visit an art museum online. For example, you might visit one of the special online exhibits at the Museum of Modern Art (http://www.moma.org/docs/online projects/index.htm) or the permanent collection of the Art Institute of Chicago (http://www.artic.edu/aic/collections/index.html). There is a list of art museums at the Art Museum Network site under "Museums" (http://www.artmuseum network.org/). Or, if you would like to explore the art of a particular artist, use a search engine to locate examples of the artist's work. Select a piece of art that you have a strong reaction to. Write a paragraph about your reaction and the details of the work that sparked it.

Writing About Media

What character in a book or movie do you like? Why do you like him or her? Write a paragraph that gives details about the person that makes him or her likable.

REVISION CHECKLIST

Here are some questions you might ask about a paragraph written for this class:

 Does it have a <u>topic sentence</u> that says clearly what the paragraph is about?

 Is it <u>unified</u>? Do all the other sentences stick to the topic?

 Is it adequately <u>developed</u> with specific details to make it interesting and convincing?

 Does it contain errors in spelling, punctuation, grammar, or sentence construction? (Many of these problems will be discussed in later chapters.)

Writing Process: Revising the Paper

Even skilled writers like the author of "Nonnie" usually have to do their "assignments" more than once. In other words, they need to *revise* their work to make it as effective as possible. The famous novelist Ernest Hemingway said he wrote the last page of *A Farewell to Arms* thirty-nine times before he was satisfied. Even if you don't keep up with Hemingway, you should expect to go over your writing more than once. Look on your first effort as a *rough draft,* not the final product.

If time permits, let your first draft sit for a while. When you come back to it, your opportunities for making improvements will stand out more clearly. (*Revision* literally means "seeing again.") It may not be necessary, but be prepared to perform major surgery: to cut, add, change.

Compare this draft of a paragraph describing a person with the revised version that follows. Weaknesses in the original are underlined, with margin comments. Problems indicated in the margin will be covered in later chapters.

vague topic sentence
comma splice
sentence fragment

punctuation, spelling
parallel structure
lacks unity

Nonnie <u>was my mother.</u> She listened to the same radio programs each morning as she had breakfast, then she put on her blue uniform and caught a ride to her job at the tobacco factory. <u>Cutting the hard ends off tobacco leaves.</u> She always took her lunch to work. After supper she read the Durham *Sun,* and made sure the <u>childern</u> completed their chores. Saturdays were her days for washing the clothes, ironing, and <u>she worked</u> in the garden. Sunday afternoons she would visit her friends. She was content with this routine. <u>Her neighbor, Claudia, worked in a general store.</u>

Here is a revised version:

> Nonnie, my mother, lived a structured life. She listened to the same radio programs each morning at breakfast. Then she put on her blue uniform and caught a ride to her job at the tobacco factory, where she cut off the hard ends of tobacco leaves. She always took her lunch to work. After supper, she read the Durham *Sun* and made sure the children completed their chores. Saturday was her day for washing the clothes, ironing, and working in the garden. Sundays she visited her friends. She was content with this routine.

Sentence Sense: Avoiding Fragments

In the last chapter you learned how to recognize subjects and verbs. Now you can put that knowledge to good use as we move on to writing sound sentences, a skill that lies at the heart of effective writing.

A complete sentence has three characteristics:

1. A sentence has a <u>subject</u> (that tells who or what the sentence is about).

2. A sentence has a <u>verb</u> (that tells what the subject does or that links it to words that describe the subject).

3. A sentence <u>expresses a complete thought</u> (makes sense by itself).

Fragments are pieces of sentences that look like sentences because they start with a capital letter and end with a period, but they are not sentences unless they meet the three tests just listed. An example:

The man on the white horse.

The man on the white horse is a fragment. It has a subject, *man*. (You know *horse* isn't the subject because it is the object of the preposition *on*. The object of a preposition is never the subject of a sentence.) But *The man on the white horse* is not a sentence because it lacks a verb (what did the man *do?*) and because it is incomplete (it does not make sense by itself).

The man on the white horse waved.

When we add the verb *waved*, the words express a complete thought and become an acceptable sentence.

Remember that an *-ing* word is not a complete verb.

(fragment) The politician <u>speaking</u> for two hours.

Such verbs need helping verbs such as *is*, *was*, and *has been*.

(complete sentence) The politician <u>has been speaking</u> for two hours.

SPOTCHECK 3–3

The following paragraphs contain fragment errors. At the end of each paragraph indicate which "sentences" are really fragments. Then indicate whether the fragments lack a subject, a verb, or both. Finally, rewrite the error to correct the error.

A. [1]Americans drink more soda pop than water, says the publication *Beverage Industry*. [2]The average American drank 42.1 gallons of soft drinks in a recent year. [3]Compared to 41.2 gallons of water. [4]Americans also drank more beer (23.9 gallons per person) than milk (20.3 gallons).

Fragment _____   lacks: **S**   **V**   **Both**

B. [1]Dogs may be man's best friend, but cattle are more useful. [2]Cattle provide half of the world's meat. [3]Ninety-five percent of its milk and 80 per cent of its leather. [4]Cattle are especially important in the United States. [5]The average American consumes 291 pounds of beef a year. [6]With 5 percent of the world's population, Americans consume about 35 percent of its beef.

Fragment _____   lacks: **S**   **V**   **Both**

C. [1]In all of human history, there have been about 250 different alphabets. [2]About fifty still in use today, including our own ABCs. [3]Of the fifty alphabets, half are in one country. [4]India.

Fragment _____   lacks: **S**   **V**   **Both**

Fragment _____   lacks: **S**   **V**   **Both**

D. [1]A diamond is the hardest substance on earth. [2]Twice as hard as the next hardest substance, corundum. [3]Nothing on earth can chip it except another diamond. [4]It is surprising to learn that the atomic structure of a diamond is the same as that of coal, one of the softest substances. [5]Both being composed of carbon.

Fragment _____   lacks: **S**   **V**   **Both**

Fragment _____   lacks: **S**   **V**   **Both**

E. [1]A bicycle is a good choice if one wants cheap transportation. [2]A good bike costs far less than a car. [3]Uses muscle power instead of expensive and polluting gasoline. [4]It also promotes good health.

Fragment _____   lacks: **S**   **V**   **Both**

SPOTCHECK 3–4

In the blanks indicate which sentences are really fragments and show whether they lack subjects, verbs, or both.

A. [1]*I Love Lucy* was the most popular TV show of its day. [2]A program that still can be seen on cable reruns. [3]President Eisenhower once postponed an address to the nation rather than run against *Lucy*. [4]Department stores that were open on the night of the program installed TV sets to hold their customers. [5]The first issue of *TV Guide* featured Lucy (Lucille Ball) on the cover.

Fragment _____   lacks: **S**   **V**   **Both**

B. [1]The amazing Brazilian soccer player known as Pele scored 1,281 goals during his career. [2]He played from 1956 until his retirement in 1977. [3]Finished his career playing for the New York Cosmos of the North American Soccer League. [4]A French magazine named him the "Athlete of the Century."

Fragment _____   lacks: **S**   **V**   **Both**

C. [1]The first table tennis games were played by English university students in 1879. [2]They hit a champagne cork over books stacked in the middle of a table. [3]Balls made of rubber and then celluloid replaced the cork. [4]With a net taking the place of the books.

Fragment _____   lacks: **S**   **V**   **Both**

D. [1]The Chinese language is made up almost entirely of one-syllable words. [2]There are only 405 syllables in Chinese. [3]The same word, therefore, may have several different meanings. [4]The meaning depending on how the syllable is pronounced. [5]The word *wan* can mean "to bend," "to finish," "late," or "ten thousand."

Fragment _____   lacks: **S**   **V**   **Both**

E. [1]Learning to write in the Chinese language is very difficult. [2]With some 3,000 characters to be memorized for a basic vocabulary. [3]Elementary pupils in China spend half their time learning the language. [4]Typing in Chinese seems nearly impossible. [5]Typewriters having 2,200 keys.

Fragment _____   lacks: **S**   **V**   **Both**

Fragment _____   lacks: **S**   **V**   **Both**

✓ **SPOTCHECK 3–5**   **Add subjects or verbs or both to turn these fragments into complete sentences.**

Example: reading a book.

The third grader was reading a book. _____

1. a gift from Uncle Alonzo

_____

2. the gas station attendant

_____

3. during the final exam

   _____

4. since turning twenty-one

   _____

5. a large hole in the road

   _____

Joining Sentence Parts

A sentence fragment is often really a part of the sentence in front of it or behind it. Study these examples:

> We set out for the fairgrounds. Hoping to watch the fireworks.

The underlined fragment can be corrected by making it part of the first sentence.

> We set out for the fairgrounds, hoping to watch the fireworks.

Another example:

> Arriving at the corner at 10:31. We missed the bus.

> **(joined)** Arriving at the corner at 10:31, we missed the bus.

(Put a comma after fragments that lead up to the words that could be a sentence by themselves—for example, "We missed the bus." There will be more on commas in Chapter 10.)

✓ **SPOTCHECK 3–6**   **Get rid of sentence fragments by joining them to neighboring sentences. Change punctuation and capital letters as needed.**

> **Example:** In Egypt stands the Great Pyramid of the pharaoh Cheops. The largest stone structure in the world.

1. Covering thirteen acres of desert. It is as tall as a forty-story building.

2. It is made up of about 2.5 million stone blocks. Some weighing 70 tons each.

3. Hundreds of thousands of workers toiled for twenty years. To build a monument considered one of the wonders of the world.

4. The workers hauled the blocks upward with ropes made of reeds. And with their own muscle power.

5. Fifty centuries after being built. The pyramid still inspires awe in the viewer.

EDITING CHECK 3   Edit the following paragraph to correct the seven sentence fragment errors. Supply needed subjects or verbs, or join each fragment to a neighboring sentence. The first error has been corrected as an example. (There is more than one way to correct the sentences.)

¹Helen Keller provides an inspiring example. ²~~Of~~ ^{of} a person who overcame great physical handicaps. ³She was made deaf and blind by illness. ⁴Before the age of two. ⁵With the help of a teacher, Anne Sullivan. ⁶Helen learned to communicate by spelling out words on a person's hand. ⁷She learned to speak by the time she was sixteen. ⁸As a result of her own hard work and Miss Sullivan's patience. ⁹Graduating from Radcliffe College in 1904 with honors. ¹⁰She began working to improve conditions for the blind. ¹¹Writing books, lecturing, and appearing before legislative bodies. ¹²Two movies tell of her life. ¹³*The Helen Keller Story* and *The Miracle Worker.*

QUICKCHECK ON FRAGMENTS

✓ A sentence must have a subject and a complete verb, and it must express a complete thought.

✓ A fragment can often be corrected by joining it to a neighboring sentence.

✓ Any fragments in your writing may stand out more clearly if you look over your paper by starting at the last sentence and reading toward the first.

CHECKPOINT 3   In the blank spaces, write *C* if the word group is a complete sentence. Write *F* if it is a fragment.

_____ 1. Department stores transformed shopping in America.

_____ 2. They provided a greater range of goods than earlier stores.

_____ 3. Along with new levels of comfort and excitement.

_____ 4. The first department store was opened in 1846 by an Irish immigrant, Alexander Stewart.

_____ 5. Who named the store, fittingly, the Marble Dry-Goods Palace.

_____ 6. It seeming to wide-eyed shoppers a true palace.

_____ 7. The store was a big success.

_____ 8. Soon the store covered an entire block on Broadway in New York City.

_____ 9. Having a staff of more than 2,000.

_____ 10. The open interiors of the store were made possible by the development of cast-iron construction.

_____ 11. Starting in 1856, elevators enabled shoppers to browse through several floors of merchandise without puffing up stairs.

_____ 12. The escalator introduced around 1896.

_____ 13. At first, a nurse might be stationed at the top of the "movable stairway" to assist panicky passengers.

_____ 14. Today, unconcerned passengers zipping on elevators to the top of the 103-story Empire State Building in New York.

Wordcheck: Spelling

You can improve your spelling by looking up any words you are unsure of and by listing (and studying) words misspelled in your college papers. If the dictionary gives two spellings for a word, the first one—or the one with a definition—is probably preferred.

In these pairs, underline the preferred word.

thru	through	theater	theatre
cigaret	cigarette	ax	axe
gray	grey	donut	doughnut

GO ELECTRONIC!

For supplemental readings, exercises, and Internet activities, visit *Checkpoints Online* at
http://www.ablongman.com/page

Chapter 4

The Description Paragraph

READING PRECHECK

Descriptive writing gives us a clear picture of a person, a place, or an event. In this reading, we experience the sights, sounds, and smells of a place most of us will never get to visit. A sports reporter takes us into the trainer's room of a professional football team, the San Francisco 49ers, and we are reminded of what risks the players are willing to take in their well-paid work. Notice especially the descriptive details in Paragraphs 1, 2, 9 and 10.

> JOURNAL TOPIC: What sacrifices would you be willing to make to keep a job? What sacrifices would you *not* make?

Selling Off Pieces of Their Bodies
Joan Ryan

NASA National Aeronautics and Space Administration

The machine looks like something from NASA. While his 49er teammates practiced yesterday afternoon, cornerback Marquez Pope sat inside the sealed chamber, an oxygen mask over his face. The atmospheric pressure inside is equal to 33 feet under water. The theory is that pressurized oxygen is absorbed on a cellular level, speeding up the body's metabolism and thus speeding up healing. Pope sat for more than hour, feeding oxygen to two deep thigh bruises. **1**

On a table nearby, special teams player Anthony Lynn lay with half a dozen electrodes taped to his leg and ankle, sending electric currents into his muscles. As he read a supermarket tabloid to pass the time, the muscle above his knee twitched like a ruptured fish. He didn't notice. **2**

NFL National Football League

To grasp the depth of the Faustian bargain[1] that players make with the NFL, spend an afternoon in the trainer's room of any pro team. The career-threatening injury to fullback William Floyd's knee last Sunday pointed up with frightening clarity what every player knows: He has sold more than his skills to the NFL. He has sold his body. 3

Offensive tackle Steve Wallace prays before every game. "God, give me luck," he says. Most players push the thought of injury from their heads. "It's like crime. It's always something that happens to other people," linebacker Gary Plummer said. But Wallace says he can't help but think about it. "Every time you hit the field, you know there is the possibility the you might not walk tomorrow," he said. 4

When Plummer hyperextended his neck against the Saints on Sunday, his family feared, as they watched the head-on collision with running back Mario Bates, that he had broken his neck. Not until he was asked about the hit did Plummer voice his own concerns. "I'm lucky that my neck wasn't lower or I could have ended up like Christopher Reeve,[2]" he said. 5

Plummer hasn't missed a game since 1987 despite a laundry list of injuries: pinched nerves in his neck that occasionally numb his arm, sprained ankles, sprained knees, dislocated fingers, fractured wrist. He had two four-inch pins inserted into his broken thumbs during surgery on a Tuesday and played on Sunday. The surgery left him barely able to turn a key in a lock or palm a basketball, and he knows his hands will only get worse as arthritis eventually sets in. 6

"But that's the tradeoff," he said. By next year, he'll have his house in Fremont, two houses in San Diego and 20 acres of land in Fremont completely paid off. (He says his kids' schooling is already paid off, and because of prudent investments, he won't have to work for the rest of his life) 7

He no longer can tolerate anti-inflammatory drugs for more than two days a week because too many pills cause blood in his urine. He takes the anti-inflammatory on Friday and Saturdays so he will feel good on Sunday. And the rest of the week? "It's just willpower now," he said. "I don't think I can put into words the pain and agony it takes to get there." 8

testament to evidence of

The 49ers trainer's room is a testament to that pain. The players go through at least 80 bags of ice, six cases of athletic tape and Lord knows how much Bufferin, Tylenol, Advil, Motrin and other pain relievers to get through each day's practice. On one counter sit two pump-action bottles of Flexall 454 pain-relieving gel, both the size of Clorox bottles. Inside a cabinet over the sink are bottles of Chi Da, a liniment a man in Sacramento concocts from Chinese herbs. There are more than a dozen electronic stimulator machines: ten training tables; hundreds of rolls of tape and bandages; three whirlpools, two filled with ice water to stem swelling after practice. . . . 9

(An NFL player shouldn't calculate the cost of his beautiful home and expensive cars in dollars and cents or even in sweat and hard work) Make no mistake. He pays for his lifestyle by selling off pieces of his body. The only question, during the course of a career, is how many pieces. And he never knows on which Sunday he'll receive the frightening answer. 10

---

[1]In German legend, Faust sold his soul to the devil in exchange for magical powers.
[2]"Superman" star who was paralyzed in a fall from a horse

Checking Meaning and Style

1. What injury was Marquez Pope treating? (Paragraph 1)
2. What injury threatened to end the career of William Floyd? (Paragraph 3)
3. What did Steve Wallace pray for before each game? (Paragraph 4)
4. List three injuries suffered by Gary Plummer. (Paragraph 6)
5. What was Plummer's "payoff"? (Paragraph 7)
6. What specific pain relievers are mentioned in Paragraph 9?
7. What is writer Joan Ryan's attitude toward the pay-injury tradeoff that players make? (Paragraph 10)

Checking Ideas

1. How much money would you insist on to endure life-long discomfort or pain?
2. Besides money, what benefits do professional athletes receive?
3. What kinds of sacrifices do other people make to keep their jobs?
4. Gary Plummer "doesn't have to work for the rest of his life." What would you do if you were so rich that you didn't have to work?

Analyzing Descriptive Writing

The reading "Selling Off Pieces of Their Bodies" contains several paragraphs of descriptive writing. We see and feel Marquez Pope and the pressure inside the sealed chamber as he treats thigh bruises. We see and feel Anthony Lynn's muscle twitch "like a ruptured fish." We see the trainer's room with its bags of ice, cases of athletic tape, and the huge bottles of pain relievers. We hear the players describe the risks they take on the playing field. It is almost as if we are in the trainer's room ourselves.

These paragraphs are examples of *descriptive* writing. Description brings writing to life by appealing to our senses—sight, sound, touch, smell, and taste.

Study the use of descriptive details in the two model paragraphs that follow.

Model Descriptive Paragraph 1

Last week I arrived at work with a small head cold; by the time I left I felt like I had the Hong Kong flu. Usually I don't mind helping the workers on the construction site with their hammering and sawing. Because of my cold, however, the buzzing of the electric saw vibrated my head as if a fly were in my ear. The strong smell of damp wood cleared my sinuses at first, but later it only stuffed them up. The sawdust in my nostrils felt like an itch that I just couldn't scratch the right way. The hammering was no better. Since the rooms had no furniture, the pounding was amplified at least ten times. It was as though someone was using my head as a drum. By the time I got home, I was in no condition for school or work the next morning.

LUANN / Greg Evans

LUANN reprinted by permission of United Feature Syndicate, Inc.

Notice how the sensory details (underlined) enable us to suffer along with a student describing the start of a bad cold. The description lets us *hear* the buzzing of the saw and the hammering; *see* and hear the unfurnished, echoing room; *feel* the itch in the nose and the stuffed-up sinuses, the head vibrating as if a fly were in the ear, the head being pounded like a drum; and *smell* the damp wood.

Another student describes the day when, as a six year old, she got too friendly with a bee. Underline the words and phrases that bring her experience to life.

Model Descriptive Paragraph 2

When I was six years old I decided, against my mother's advice, that I could pet bees. The sun was warm on my back and the bees were buzzing around the sweet-smelling flowers of the lemon tree. Some of the bees were sitting so still that I just had to touch one. The bee felt soft and furry, and I could feel its "buzziness." Then I let out the loudest yell I could make. I thought my finger was going to explode. My mother yelled out the back door, "I told you so!" She pulled out the stinger and put ice on my finger. The cold ice dulled the pain, and I knew that I was going to live.

Writing Assignment: A Descriptive Paragraph

Write a paragraph using specific descriptive details on one of these topics:

1. A room in your house or apartment

2. Your car

3. An unpleasant experience

4. A favorite recreation spot

5. A person whose looks you like

Writing Topic Bank

New Technology

What do you like (or dislike) about some recent technological development, such as cellular phones, phone answering machines, personal digital assistants, laptop computers, or automatic bank teller machines? State your position and describe the features or uses of the technology that you like or dislike.

Exploring History on the Internet

The American History Museum of the Smithsonian Institution has an exhibit online called "Within These Walls." The exhibit provides words, photos, sketches, and audio details about five families who lived in the same Massachusetts house through different periods of American history. Start your visit at this web address: http://americanhistory.si.edu/house/. Explore the various materials related to one or more of the families. What is the museum's purpose in providing so much description? Do all the details offered on the site add up to a clear picture? Write a paragraph to share your thinking.

Writing About Media

Study the photograph below. In addition to what you see, imagine what sounds, smells, tastes, and textures are part of the scene. Write a paragraph that describes the scene in vivid detail.

WRITING CHECKLIST

 Use the clustering prewriting technique—perhaps using separate clusters for sight, sound, and smell, for example—to come up with descriptive details that appeal to the senses.

 Use a topic sentence that makes clear what impression you want to create, as in these examples:

> Anyone who looks at my room knows at once that I enjoy sports. (Picture the tennis racket on the dresser, the high-tops under the bed, the posters of sports heroes, and so on.)

> Johnathan has the kind of looks that make women sigh.

> The park across from my house is a good place to relax.

> I still remember the wonderful smells in my grandmother's kitchen at Thanksgiving.

 When revising the first draft, be sure the descriptive details are strong and interesting.

 Check especially for sentence fragment errors and the kinds of problems marked in recent papers.

 Proofread the paper before turning it in.

Writing Process: Writing a Summary

A good way to test your understanding of a reading is to write a brief summary of the material, putting the main ideas in a few sentences. This practice sharpens both your reading and writing skills. Follow these steps:

1. Identify and make a note of the main ideas of the reading. (Help in doing this can be found in Writing Resource B, "Reading in College," at the back of the text.)
2. Jot down the most important details that explain or support those ideas.
3. Write the summary, using the main idea and supporting details. It should be no longer than half the length of the original material and will probably be less.

4. In the first sentence, give the title and author of the work you are summarizing.
5. Omit your opinion of the material summarized.

Model Summary Paragraph

In "Selling Off Pieces of Their Bodies," Joan Ryan discusses the damage to their bodies that professional athletes often endure. After a visit to the trainer's room of the San Francisco 49ers, she says a player knows that he has sold more than his skills; "he has sold his body." She mentions a fullback whose knee injury may end his career. A lineman admits that he prays before each game to be lucky enough to escape serious injury. Ryan lists the electronic devices, the tapes, and the pain relievers that help the players get ready for the next game. Although the athletes earn huge salaries and can afford beautiful homes and expensive cars, Ryan suggests the price they pay may be too high.

You try it. Summarize the reading "The Art of Eating Spaghetti" in Chapter 1.

_____

_____

_____

_____

_____

_____

Sentence Sense: Avoiding Clause Fragments

The sentence fragments we looked at in the last chapter were made up of *phrases*. Phrases are groups of related words that do not contain both a subject and a verb. These are phrases:

Covering thirteen acres of desert. (no subject, no complete verb)

Before the age of two. (no subject, no verb)

Now we're going to look at another kind of word group—the *clause*. A clause *does* contain a subject and verb. Here are some examples of clauses:

The <u>pyramid</u> [subject] <u>covered</u> [verb] thirteen acres of desert.

She became deaf and blind before the age of two.

If you think those clauses look a lot like sentences, you're right. They meet the three tests of the sentence: (1) each has a subject; (2) each has a verb; and (3) each expresses a complete thought—makes sense by itself.

So a clause is the same thing as a sentence? Sometimes it isn't. Look at these clauses:

Because **Cinderella left** the party.

While **Robinson Crusoe lived** on an island.

Each one is a clause because it has a subject and a verb. But neither one is a sentence because neither one expresses a complete thought. Each needs more words to finish the idea.

Because Cinderella left the party, the prince was sad.

While Robinson Crusoe lived on an island, Mrs. Crusoe worked crossword puzzles at home.

Without the added words, each is an example of our enemy the fragment.

So we now have two kinds of clauses. *Independent clauses* are complete in themselves and can stand alone as sentences. *Dependent clauses* depend on other words to complete their meaning.

IMPORTANT *Every complete sentence must contain at least one independent clause.*

Test yourself on the following examples by marking the independent clauses *Ind* and the dependent clauses *Dep.*

_____ 1. Alicia arrived early at work yesterday.

_____ 2. Because Alicia arrived early at work yesterday.

_____ 3. Mrs. Ng admired the roses.

_____ 4. Although Mrs. Ng admired the roses.

_____ 5. The store has a sale.

_____ 6. Whenever the store has a sale.

All six are clauses because they have subjects and verbs. Examples 1, 3, and 5 are independent clauses. They are complete sentences and make sense by themselves. Examples 2, 4, and 6 are dependent clauses. They depend on other words to complete their meaning. They are sentence fragments.

What is it that turns the complete sentences into sentence fragments? It is just one word in each case: *because* in 2, *although* in 4 , and *whenever* in 6. Since they turn independent clauses into dependent clauses, we will call such words *dependent words*. (They are sometimes called *subordinating conjunctions*.)

Here is a longer list of dependent words. Study it carefully.

after	in order that	whenever
although	since	where
as	so that	wherever
as if	than	whether
because	that	which
before	though	whichever
even if	unless	while
even though	until	who
ever since	what	whom
how	whatever	whose
if	when	why

SPOTCHECK 4–1 Fill in the blanks with the dependent word that best completes the meaning of the sentence.

1. _____ the 1876 Centennial Exposition was held in Philadelphia, the unfamiliar telephone and the banana were the most popular exhibits.

2. _____ many of us are on diets, the average American eats about sixteen pounds of candy a year.

3. Ice cream actually makes us feel warmer _____ it contains so many calories.

4. Early experiments with electric vehicles took place in Europe _____ an electric cart was built in 1887.

5. _____ his team loses, the coach locks himself in his office for several hours.

SPOTCHECK 4–2 In the blank spaces that follow the paragraph, write the numbers of "sentences" that are actually fragments and the dependent word that makes each a fragment.

[1]Two Latin-American poets who won worldwide praise were Octavio Paz and Pablo Neruda. [2]Who both won the Nobel Prize in literature. [3]Paz was born in 1914 in Mexico City. [4]Where he founded a literary journal at age 17 and published his first book of poetry at 19. [5]He wrote many of his best-known works. [6]While he served in Mexico's diplomatic corps in such places as France, Switzerland, and India. [7]These works include a book of essays, *El Laberinto de la Soledad (The Labyrinth of Solitude)*.

[8]Which is considered his masterpiece. [9]Pablo Neruda (1904–1973), a Chilean, also served in the diplomatic corps, representing Chile as ambassador to France. [10]Like Paz, Neruda began to write poetry at an early age. [11]When he was still in his teens. [12]Although both writers were enormously influential in Latin America. [13]Their admirers were found throughout the world.

No.	Dependent Word	No.	Dependent Word
2	Who	8	Which
12	Although	9	as
6	While	11	When

Joining Fragments

You can usually correct a dependent-word fragment by joining it to the sentence in front of it or behind it.

> When his computer stopped working. **(fragment)** The engineer was glad the warranty hadn't expired.

> **(corrected)** When his computer stopped working, the engineer was glad the warranty hadn't expired.

The fragment has been added to the sentence following it.

> Nate will gain weight. Unless he stops eating so much. **(fragment)**

> **(corrected)** Nate will gain weight unless he stops eating so much.

The fragment has been added to the sentence in front of it.

Notice that a comma separates the two clauses in the first example but not in the second. Here's a guide: Use a comma if the dependent clause comes first; don't use a comma if the independent clause comes first.

Another way to correct this kind of fragment is simply to get rid of the dependent word.

> When the police chief bought an antique Colt revolver. **(fragment)**

> **(corrected)** The police chief bought an antique Colt revolver.

 **SPOTCHECK 4–3** Make complete sentences by adding an independent clause before or after these dependent clauses. Underline the dependent words. Remember to use a comma when the dependent clause comes first.

1. Although the CD was expensive, I bought it. _____

_____

2. _____

   Mr. Brown was happy because his wife was having a baby.

3. Whenever Macy's has a sale, _there is no parking space._

   _____

4. _____

   The president arrived as the program started.

5. Since the riot in the park, _it has not been the same_

   _____

Are you sure the words you added are independent clauses? Would they make complete sentences by themselves?

Who, Which, That

Sometimes a dependent word is the subject of the dependent clause. Words often used that way are *who, which,* and *that.*

   Mr. Munson is a friend <u>who</u> can be trusted.

The subject of the dependent clause is the dependent word *who.* The verb is *can be trusted.* (The independent clause is *Mr. Munson is a friend.* Remember that every sentence must have at least one independent clause.)
   Sometimes the dependent clause is in the middle of the sentence.

   A friend <u>who can be trusted</u> is valuable.

The dependent clause, *who can be trusted,* interrupts the independent clause, *A friend is valuable.*
   Sometimes the dependent word *that* is left out.

   (correct) The officials assumed that the queen would be present.

   (also correct) The officials assumed the queen would be present.

SPOTCHECK 4–4 These sentences use *who, which,* and *that* to introduce dependent-word clauses. Underline the entire dependent clause.

   Example: Rosanne, <u>who works harder than anyone else,</u> should be paid more.

   1. April 15, <u>which is the day taxes are due,</u> should be a national holiday.

2. A specialist is a person <u>who knows more and more about less and less.</u>

3. *The Star-Spangled Banner* has several verses <u>that hardly anybody knows.</u>

4. In 1986, <u>which was named "The Year of Peace" by the United Nations,</u> five million people died in thirty-six wars and armed conflicts.

5. The only international sport <u>that was invented in the United States</u> is basketball.

The *Who-Which* Choice

Use *which*, not *who*, to start a clause about animals or things.

> Sandra was feeding her horse, which [not *who*] had a sore leg.

Use *who*, not *which*, to start a clause about people.

> On the bus were the teachers who [not *which*] were attending the conference.

Whose may be used with people, animals, or things.

> All photos <u>whose</u> colors are fading should be protected from light.

> Any American <u>whose</u> passport is valid can travel abroad.

Use *which* and commas for dependent clauses that are not essential to the meaning of the sentence.

> *Rocky III,* *which* I have seen three times, will be on TV again tonight.

Use *that* with dependent clauses that are essential to the meaning of the sentence.

> A movie *that* I have seen three times will be on TV again tonight. (no commas)

That may also be used to refer to unnamed people.

> Where is the taxi driver *that* was supposed to here fifteen minutes ago?

 **SPOTCHECK 4–5**   **Underline the correct word in parentheses.**

1. Mrs. Emory saved the calendar pages (which / that) had birthdays marked.

2. Beneath the freeway, (which / that) was very noisy with traffic, was a homeless camp.

3. It was the Biology Club (who / which / that) won the state prize.

4. Drivers (which / that) run red lights are a serious menace to themselves and others.

5. Mr. Janovich, (who / which / that) owns the corner grocery, has three daughters in college.

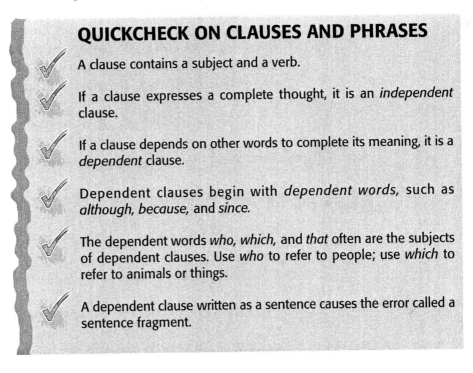

QUICKCHECK ON CLAUSES AND PHRASES

✓ A clause contains a subject and a verb.

✓ If a clause expresses a complete thought, it is an *independent* clause.

✓ If a clause depends on other words to complete its meaning, it is a *dependent* clause.

✓ Dependent clauses begin with *dependent words,* such as *although, because,* and *since.*

✓ The dependent words *who, which,* and *that* often are the subjects of dependent clauses. Use *who* to refer to people; use *which* to refer to animals or things.

✓ A dependent clause written as a sentence causes the error called a sentence fragment.

 **DOUBLECHECK 4–1** Write sentences using the dependent words in parentheses.

1. (while) _____

2. (if) _____

3. (whenever) _____

4. (because) _____

5. (which) _____

DOUBLECHECK 4–2 Seven of the sentences in this paragraph contain dependent clauses. Underline the dependent word in each.

¹Americans, who love pizza, spend $15 billion a year on that food. ²We eat 75 acres of pizza a day, which is enough to fill the Houston Astrodome more than eight times. ³While the average American eats 22.5 pounds of pizza a year, the average Chicago resident eats 30 pounds. ⁴Wherever you go in this country, you are likely to find a pizza restaurant. ⁵A restaurant that serves pizza has more than 38,000 competitors in America. ⁶Although it may surprise you, there are more restaurants specializing in pizza than in hamburgers. ⁷Would you believe that 11 percent of

restaurants feature pizza and 8.5 percent hamburgers? [8]Of every ten pizza orders, six are for thin crust and four for thick crust or deep-dish.

✓ EDITING CHECK 4 Edit these paragraphs on the martial arts to correct the fragments in them. (The first fragment has been corrected as an example.) The fragments may be either phrases or clauses. Correct them by adding subjects and verbs or by joining the fragments to neighboring sentences.

[1]The term *martial arts* covers a variety of fighting methods based on ancient Asian combat skills. [2]The martial arts are practiced today for a number of reasons, including self-defense, physical fitness, and sports competition. [3]Styles, techniques, and teaching methods vary. [4]Even within a given branch of martial arts, such as karate. [5]Although adherence to ancient traditions is usually emphasized.

[6]Although the exact origins are uncertain. [7]The Asian styles of the martial arts seem to have come to China from India and Tibet. [8]Where they were used by monks for exercise and protection against bandits. [9]The arts flourished in Japan. [10]Although Japan was among the last of the Asian nations to learn them. [11]For a time, practice of martial arts was restricted to the Japanese warrior class, but the peasants practiced in secret.

[12]Martial arts can be divided into two categories. [13]Those that use weapons and those that don't. [14]In the weaponless methods, such as karate and kung fu, the contestant depends on kicks and hand and arm blows. [15]As well as various holds, chokes, and twists, to subdue an opponent. [16]In one of the branches using weapons, kendo, based on ancient Japanese sword-fighting. [17]Contestants today use bamboo swords cased in leather.

[18]T'ai chi is the most gentle of the martial arts. [19]Slow, graceful movements that bear little resemblance to the original blows and blocks on which the movements are based. [20]Used today for conditioning and flexibility. [21]Some use it as a form of meditation.

CHECKPOINT 4 At the end of the following paragraph, write the numbers of any sentence fragments. Then write the dependent words contained in the fragments. The fragments may be more obvious if you give the paragraph a second reading, starting with the last sentence.

¹Icebergs are huge chunks of ice floating in the ocean. ²They are made of frozen fresh water. ³That breaks off from glaciers. ⁴The icebergs in the North Atlantic come from Greenland. ⁵Which is an island almost entirely covered by a sheet of ice hundreds of feet thick. ⁶Because icebergs are made of fresh water, sailing ships used to replenish their drinking water supply from pools formed on the ice. ⁷Of course, icebergs are a danger to ships. ⁸One of the greatest sea disasters occurred in 1912. ⁹When the ocean liner *Titanic* sank after hitting an iceberg. ¹⁰While it was on its first trans-Atlantic trip. ¹¹An estimated 1,517 people lost their lives. ¹²The danger to ships is less today. ¹³Because the United States Coast Guard keeps a lookout for icebergs.

No.	Dependent Word
___	_____
___	_____
___	_____
___	_____
___	_____

Wordcheck: Spelling Compound Words

Is this the correct spelling of *good bye?* Is it two words, one word, or one hyphenated word? Your dictionary will tell you. (It's hyphenated: *good-bye; good-by* is also acceptable.)

Should the following be written as one word, two words, or hyphenated? Write in the correct forms where appropriate.

1. self conscious
2. sea bird
3. week end
4. brother in law
5. south paw
6. fire arm
7. early bird
8. two thirds

GO ELECTRONIC!

For supplemental readings, exercises, and Internet activities, visit *Checkpoints Online* at
http://www.ablongman.com/page

Chapter 5

The Narrative Paragraph

READING PRECHECK

Each of us can point to an event that had a major impact on how we feel about ourselves. In this essay, written as part of an application for admission to Stanford University, Jonathan Bailey describes his life-changing experience. As you read, notice how the author uses increasing detail to slow the pace of the story and focus the reader's attention on the critical moments.

> **JOURNAL TOPIC:** Has someone else's faith in your ability ever helped you overcome a problem or fear?

A Different Drummer
Jonathan Bailey

I was born a little bit different from everyone else. I have no fingers, only a thumb, on my left hand. Throughout much of my life I was ashamed of my physical distinction. I believed that people would judge my character based on what my hand looked like, and I feared rejection. One thing in particular helped to change my perspective: the drums. 1

When I was thirteen, as my stepmother and I stood in the kitchen talking, I began to tap on the table. My stepmother, who was once a musician, immediately noticed a good sense of rhythm in my counter-tapping endeavor and suggested we consider starting me on the drums. I was surprised that she would 2 even suggest such a thing. Drums required two hands—and I had only one. However, the very next day, the two of us were off to the music store to purchase a pair of drumsticks and a "practice pad." Six months later we purchased my drum set.

I'll never forget the first time I sat on the throne of my new drum set. My entire body shook with excitement. I had always wanted to play the drums, but I never believed I could. I thought my "disability" would stop me. Now, before me lay not just one drum, but an entire drum set, beckoning me to play. I cautiously picked up my drumsticks and, ever so gently, began tapping on first one, and then all of the drums and cymbals. Then I let loose. I sounded awful, but I didn't care. It was one of the most romantic experiences of my life. Never had I been so enveloped in a blanket of pulsating frequencies and tones. I was in love. My parents, however, were not, and we quickly agreed that I could continue playing the drums only if I took lessons. It was settled. I started my lessons and began to practice.

3

Drums were not only a source of pleasure and joy for me, they became the means by which I realized that I could use my left hand productively. By being able to play the drums, I discovered that my left hand could be used to produce something beautiful, something useful, and I realized its unique importance. Instead of hating my hand, I began to respect it—to respect me.

4

Through my drums, my hand and I have become one. Now, when I meet new people, I no longer fear that the first part of me a person sees will be my hand. That person may see my heart, as I share with him a poem I have just finished. Another person will see my mind, as I discuss with her Newton's Law of Universal Gravitation. Another will see me, sitting behind the fruit of my passion, the drums, driving a punk quartet or the school jazz band. And if that person does see my hand—what of it? It is with this hand that I make music. It is with this hand that I write a poem, or do a calculus problem, or stroke a kitten. What more could I possibly want? I am complete.

5

beckoning inviting

quartet a group of four musicians

Checking Meaning and Style

1. Aside from describing his hand, what other perspectives about himself does the author list in the essay? Why does he list them?
2. Write a sentence that sums up the main idea in the essay.
3. Who does Bailey credit for seeing more in him than he saw in himself?
4. How many words can you find in the story that describe feelings?

Checking Ideas

1. List at least one event that you believe changed your life.
2. When you meet new people, what do you hope they will notice about you? What do you hope they will ignore?

3. Why do you think that some people seem to focus on differences more than others do?

4. Bailey was an adolescent before he was able to put his "difference" in perspective. Do you think that it's possible to create a society where that happens earlier in life? Why or why not?

Analyzing Narrative Writing

Writing that tells a story, that tells "what happened," is called *narration*. In "A Different Drummer," Jonathan Bailey tells the story of his experience growing up with a physical distinction and then learning that it didn't matter as much as he thought. The story is told in order, from beginning to end, the usual narrative order. As in Bailey's narrative, a story will often help make a point. The point of Bailey's story is that he has changed his idea about how important his lack of fingers is. Before he learned to play the drums, he thought his fingerless hand would cause other people to judge him. Afterward, he realized his hand was only a part of who he was. His story makes up the entire essay. An essay will often contain briefer narratives, called anecdotes, that support the main idea of the essay.

Starting in childhood, we get much of our information and entertainment through stories. The child says, "Read me a story," and the parent gets out *Winnie the Pooh* for the umpteenth time. Stories continue to entertain us as we go through life—in books and magazines, on television, and at the movies.

We request stories of a different kind when we want to know "what happened." What happened in the crisis in the Mideast? What happened at the tenants meeting? What happened on Tom's date with Betsy last Saturday night? In such cases, we want a story that gives us information, although it may be entertaining too.

Don't be shy about using anecdotes from your own life in your writing. Let's say you are writing an essay on crime in your community. The essay will be more interesting and believable if you include a short account of the time you were mugged. Or if you want to make the point that holidays have become too commercialized, you could tell about an experience you had shopping at the mall when the season was in full swing.

After a topic sentence, tell your story in ordinary time order (chronologically); that is, start with what happened first and continue step-by-step to the end. Include details, but only those needed to make your point; don't go on and on.

In the two model paragraphs that follow, notice that each paragraph begins with a topic sentence (underlined).

Model Narrative Paragraph 1

Driving home from work can be a nightmare. Last week it took me forty-five minutes to get home, twice as long as it used to take. The freeway was packed. Although the posted speed limit was 55, I was lucky if I averaged 15. Everyone was riding the bumper of the car ahead. Conditions got no better after I left the freeway for the city streets. At traffic lights, I had to wait through two or three changes before I got my turn to cross. Finally, at home, when my wife asked, "Did you have a good day, honey?" I could only mutter and shake my head.

After announcing his topic—that the trip home from his job can be unpleasant—the writer tells the story of his experience on a bad day. Notice his use of specific details to make that point. Notice the step-by-step organization of the paragraph.

Model Narrative Paragraph 2

Children need to understand that frustration and failure are not only inevitable but often helpful. Over the weekend my husband and I tried to teach my daughter to ride her new bike. Each time one of us wasn't holding her up, she fell over. After falling again and again, she became frustrated and started to cry. I couldn't get her to try again. Then my neighbor talked to her, and she decided to give it one more attempt. My daughter ran over bushes and sprinklers. She tried to ride up walls. But by the end of the day she had a smile on her face that couldn't be wiped off. She had learned to ride her bike.

Children can learn from difficult experiences, says the parent, who then develops that idea with a story about the writer's own child.

Prewriting: Nonstop Writing

Before going on to the next writing assignment, let's look at one more way of brainstorming for ideas. This method is called *freewriting* or *nonstop writing*. In this method you put your pen to a blank paper, or your fingers to a keyboard, and then write without stopping for three minutes or so. If you can't think of anything new about a topic, you just repeat the last word until something new comes to mind. The important rule is to keep writing without stopping. Don't worry about such things as spelling or punctuation.

Nonstop writing puts you in touch with your thoughts and gives you some ideas to use in your first draft. Let's say Bill wants to write about a memorable experience or person. He starts his nonstop writing.

memorable memorable memories memories are hard to remember remember I always have a hard time remembering things I hate memorizing we always had to memorize poetry in school and recite it i used to race through my poem when it was my turn my turn didn't want to forget it so I raced through so fast the teacher probably couldn't understand a word of it once a teacher required the class to memorize the gettysburg address by lincoln and I remember I was able to say it in 30 seconds at home but in class she made me say it slowly no, I could only say it fast

Bill's nonstop writing put him in touch with a long-forgotten memory. After he finished, he read over the material and underlined the part he felt could be used—the lines about the Gettysburg Address experience. Now he had the information to write his first draft.

Practice nonstop writing on one of these subjects: college, politics, friends. Write for three minutes without stopping.

Writing Assignment: A Narrative Paragraph

With the earlier model paragraphs as examples, write a narrative paragraph—one that tells "what happened"—on one of the numbered topics below.

1. The first day I attended college classes
2. A funny or embarrassing incident
3. The day I learned how to drive (swim, dance, etc.)
4. The time I learned an important lesson

 Writing Topic Bank

Your College Major or Career Decision

What led you to choose the college major or career you did? Did particular events lead you to this choice? Write a paragraph telling the story of the events that led to your decision.

Exploring a Hobby on the Internet

Select a hobby or interest to explore on the Internet. Use any search engine you like (such as Lycos.com, Google.com, Yahoo.com, Dogpile.com) to find a website on the subject. Take notes as you explore the site so that you will remember which pages you looked at and in which order. Then write a paragraph about what happened—how you moved around the site and what you found on the different pages.

WRITING CHECKLIST

 Use prewriting techniques such as nonstop writing, brainstorming, and clustering to get ideas for your topic.

 State the point of your story in a topic sentence, as in these examples:

> Uncle Ed made a fool of himself at the family reunion last week.

> I'll never forget my embarrassment on my first date with Charlie.

 Develop the topic sentence with interesting details by explaining how or why Uncle Ed made a fool of himself or you got embarrassed.

 Start at the beginning of the story and continue step by step to the end. Include only those details that support your main point.

 Revise the paper as often as needed. Watch especially for sentence fragments and troublemakers.

 Proofread the final copy for such things as overlooked misspellings and punctuation errors.

Writing About Media

Have you ever heard a piece of music that immediately took you back in memory to an earlier time? What happened in that earlier moment of time? How does the music relate to it? Write a narrative of your experience.

Sentence Sense:
Avoiding Run-Together Sentences

This "sentence" is hard to read:

> Raymond was supposed to pick up Harry at 6:30 a.m. for the drive to the factory however, his alarm didn't go off as a result Raymond was an hour late Harry was understandably upset "there goes my chance for a foreman's job," he complained.

Of course it's hard to read. That's because the reader expects to see a *capital letter* at the beginning of each sentence and a *period* at the end. Without these guides, the reader quickly gets lost.

This version is easier to follow:

> Raymond was supposed to pick up Harry at 6:30 a.m. for the drive to the factory. However, his alarm didn't go off. As a result, Raymond was an hour late. Harry was understandably upset. "There goes my chance for a foreman's job," he complained.

The first example is full of <u>run-together sentences</u>, the result when two or more sentences are written as if they were one.

Sometimes no punctuation is used to separate the sentences, resulting in a <u>fused sentence</u> or <u>run-on</u>.

> It was snowing the road to the cabin was blocked.

Sometimes a comma is used, causing a <u>comma splice</u>.

> It was snowing, the road to the cabin was blocked.

A sentence, you will remember, has a subject and a verb and expresses a complete thought. Both *It was snowing* and *The road to the cabin was blocked* qualify separately as sentences.

Run-together sentences can be corrected in five ways.

1. Use a period and a capital letter to make two sentences.

> It was snowing. The road to the cabin was blocked.

2. Use a comma and one of these <u>connecting words</u> (coordinating conjunctions).

> for   and   nor   but   or   yet   so

(It's a good idea to memorize this short list. Just think of "FANBOYS," which contains the letters that start the words in the list.)

> It was snowing, <u>and</u> the road to the cabin was blocked.

Note that there is an independent clause (a sentence) on each side of the connector *and*.

SPOTCHECK 5–1 Correct these run-together sentences by adding one of the connecting words *for, and, nor, but, or, yet,* or *so* (FANBOYS) between the two independent clauses. The first sentence has been done as an example.

[1]It may be hard to believe, ~~but~~ today's hair dryer was based on a combination of

the vacuum cleaner and the milk shake blender. [2]Manufacturers noticed that hot air

came out of the vacuum's exhaust, _____so, yet_____ they soon advertised their machine as a two-in-one product. **³**With the hose attachment provided, buyers could

vacuum rugs, _____and_____ they could blow-dry their hair. **⁴**This was a popular but

awkward setup, _____so_____ the manufacturers looked for a better way. **⁵**They

found it in the newly developed milk shake mixer, _____but_____ its small, efficient

motor permitted a dryer that could be held in the hand. **⁶**The hand dryer was at first used

almost exclusively by women, _____and_____ it found new users in the 1960s when

men started wearing their hair long.

SPOTCHECK 5–2   Use the connecting words shown to write sentences containing two independent clauses. Use a comma after the first clause.

> **Example**: (yet) Timothy has a good job, yet he is always borrowing money.

1. (and) _____

   _____

2. (but) _____

   _____

3. (or) _____

   _____

4. (so) _____

   _____

3. Make one of the clauses dependent by using a <u>dependent word</u> such as *because, since, while,* and *unless*. (You may want to review the list of dependent words on page 57.)

> <u>Because</u> it was snowing, the road to the cabin was blocked.

SPOTCHECK 5–3   Correct these run-together sentences by changing one of the independent clauses into a dependent clause by using a dependent word. Be sure that the punctuation and capitalization are correct.

> **Although**
> **Example**: ∧Carlos had a full-time job, he got good grades.

Example: Carlos got good grades ~~because~~ ∧ he studied hard.

Because

1. ∧ The baseball game went into extra innings the Ellisons had to leave before the game ended.

2. I always seem to buy something I go into a bookstore to browse.

Because

3. ∧ She was late for class Deborah decided to skip breakfast.

about

4. The professor droned ~~on~~ the students grew restless.

5. Rex gets a raise he will buy a new bicycle.

SPOTCHECK 5–4

Use the dependent words shown to write sentences containing one independent clause and one dependent clause. (Put a comma after the dependent clause if it begins the sentence.)

Example: **(while)** The sun went down <u>while</u> we were fishing.

1. (when) When I was 5yrs old, I jump in the lake.

When my mother got pregant, she heated me.

2. (even though) I was late for class, I made it.

_____

3. (if) I was rich, I would go to the white house.

I had the money, I would go shoping.

4. (unless) you watch those dishes, you will be punish.

_____

5. (since) _____

_____

4. Use a <u>semicolon</u>. This mark suggests a closer relation between the two clauses than a period would.

It was snowing; the road to the cabin was blocked.

Be sure you always have an independent clause on *both sides* of the semicolon.

5. Use a semicolon and a <u>transitional word</u> or <u>phrase</u> that reflects the change (transition) from the first part of the sentence to the second.

It was snowing; therefore , the road to the cabin was blocked.

A period may be used instead of a semicolon. In that case, be sure to capitalize the next word. A comma is usually placed after the transitional word when the word comes at the beginning of the clause.

Following are some more examples of transitional words. You will notice that they have about the same meanings as the more common connecting words (*and, but,* etc.). The transitional words make your writing seem more formal, which may or may not be desirable.

Transitional words similar in meaning to *and:*

furthermore   moreover   also   besides   in addition

Transitional words similar in meaning to *but:*

however   instead   nevertheless   on the other hand

Transitional words similar in meaning to *so:*

therefore   consequently   thus   as a result

Some other transitional words:

still	first
meanwhile	second
even so	next
otherwise	then
for example	finally
in fact	

SPOTCHECK 5–5   Use a transitional word and semicolon to correct these run-together sentences.

Example: Wilson got into his car; however, it wouldn't start.

[1]Americans have great faith in education; ___and___ they believe it is the solution to most problems. [2]Education can help people "get ahead"; ___Furthermore,___ it produces citizens who can make intelligent decisions when they vote. [3]People tend to think of education as something that takes place in schools; ___instead___ we learn in many ways outside of school. [4]Many parents read to their small children, those children are likely to enjoy reading as adults. [5]Most experiences are "educational";

_____ television teaches us more than we may realize—some good and some not so good.

SPOTCHECK 5–6

Use a semicolon and the transitional words shown to write sentences containing two independent clauses.

Example: **(nevertheless)** Today is Steven's birthday; nevertheless, he plans to work until eight o'clock.

1. (in addition) _____

_____

2. (as a result) _____

_____

3. (nevertheless) _____

_____

4. (meanwhile) _____

_____

DOUBLECHECK 5–1

Each of the following sentences contains two clauses. Draw one line under the subject and two lines under the verb in each clause. In the blanks at the left, enter *RTS* for a run-together sentence or *C* for a correctly punctuated sentence.

Example: **C** The world's first airline service in 1910 didn't use airplanes; instead, it used airships or dirigibles.

_____ 1. The airships were also called zeppelins, the name honored the founder of the airline, the German Count Ferdinand von Zeppelin.

_____ 2. The dirigibles at first carried passengers between cities in Germany, but later they covered routes around the world.

_____ 3. When a giant airship named the Hindenburg exploded while landing at Lakehurst, New Jersey, in 1930, thirty-six of its ninety-two passengers were killed.

_____ 4. Passenger service on airships declined, but the ships continued to be used by the military as late as World War II.

_____ 5. Fans at sporting events can sometimes spot a dirigible flying over the stadium, it usually advertises a tire company.

DOUBLECHECK 5-2 Each of the following sentences contains two clauses. Draw one line under the subject and two lines under the verb in each clause. In the blanks at the left, write *RTS* for a run-together sentence or *C* for one that is correct.

_____ 1. If you are a typical American, you eat about 50 quarts of popcorn a year.

_____ 2. The Native Americans brought popcorn to the first Thanksgiving in 1621, the Pilgrims apparently liked it.

_____ 3. Popcorn is a good snack since one quart of dry-popped corn contains only one hundred calories.

_____ 4. Even if you add cooking oil and salt, it compares favorably with potato or corn chips.

_____ 5. Oil-popped popcorn has one-third the calories of potato chips, it has one-fourth the fat of potato chips.

DOUBLECHECK 5-3 Add connecting words (such as *but*), dependent words (such as *because*), and transitional words (such as *however*) to complete these paragraphs. The punctuation may provide a clue to which type to use.

[1]Bathing suits did not make an appearance until the middle of the 1800s _because_ recreational bathing was not popular before then; _however_ at that time doctors began to prescribe "the waters" for a variety of ailments. [2]Europeans flocked to the streams, lakes, and the ocean _where_ they sought relief from "nerves" or other disorders.

[3]Standards of modesty were different in those days, _so_ bathing suits covered more of the body than they do today. [4]Women wore knee-length skirts in the water; _in addition_ they wore bloomers and black stockings under the skirts. [5] _Since_ a wet bathing suit could weigh as much as the bather, the accent was on *bathing,* not swimming. [6] _If_ she wanted greater privacy, a

woman could use a "bathing machine" at the ocean. [7]Attendants would wheel her and the portable dressing room into shallow waters. [8] _After_ she had changed into a head-to-toe loose gown, she would step down a ramp into the surf _while_ the attendants shooed away any interested males.

[9]A Danish immigrant to the United States named Carl Jantzen revolutionized swim wear in 1915 _when_ he invented a knitting machine that yielded a stretchy fabric. [10]The fabric resulted in a body-clinging fit; _however_, swimsuits still had sleeves and reached to the knees. [11]Swimsuits became more revealing in the 1930s _when_ narrow straps and backless models paved the way for the two-piece suit. [12]It wasn't until 1946 that the bikini made its appearance. [13]World War II had recently ended, _and_ the United States was testing an atom bomb in the Pacific. [14]A French designer was about to introduce a skimpy swimsuit model, _but_ he didn't have a catchy name. [15] _Thus_ the atomic blast at Bikini Atoll on July 1, 1946, gave him the name for the "explosive" suit he displayed to the world four days later.

DOUBLECHECK 5–4

Correct each run-together sentence in three ways: (1) with a connecting word, (2) with a dependent word, and (3) with a semicolon and transitional word or phrase.

Example: Most Americans waste a large part of their lives, they spend five years standing in line.

1. _____ . . . their lives, for they spend . . . _____

2. _____ . . . their lives because they spend . . . _____

3. _____ . . . their lives; for example, they spend . . . _____

A. Lowell's sneakers are worn out, he will buy a new pair.

A1. _____but_____

A2. _____however_____

A3. _____

B. Fritz has a computer, he doesn't know how to operate it.

B1. _____

B2. _____

B3. _____

EDITING CHECK 5

Edit this paragraph to correct run-together sentences. Use one of the five methods listed in the Quickcheck on Run-Together Sentences that follows the paragraph. The first error has been corrected as an example.

[1]The Great Wall of China is remarkable, **for** it is the only human structure large enough to be seen from outer space. [2]The wall is about fifty feet high and sixteen feet wide at the top, it stretches for 1,500 miles. [3]It was built between 300 B.C. and 1646 as a fortification against enemies, it once had 40,000 watch towers. [4]The wall required 400 million cubic yards of material, that is enough to build a six-foot-high wall around the earth at the equator. [5]The wall's construction required an enormous number of laborers, when construction was at its peak, one-third of all Chinese males were required to work on the project. [6]Hundreds of thousands of workers died, their efforts did not succeed in keeping out invaders.

QUICKCHECK ON RUN-TOGETHER SENTENCES

✓ You can correct a run-together sentence in five ways.

1. Use a period and a capital letter.
2. Use a comma and a connecting word (*and, but*, etc.).
3. Use a dependent word (*although, because*, etc.).
4. Use a semicolon by itself.
5. Use a semicolon and a transitional word (*however, therefore*, etc.) with a comma after it.

✓ A comma cannot be used alone to separate two independent clauses. A semicolon or period is required.

✓ A semicolon must have an independent clause (sentence) on each side of it. You can test your use of a semicolon by asking if you could use a period instead. If not, the semicolon is wrong.

✓ Be sure you understand the differences between connecting words (*and, but*, etc.), transitional words (*however, therefore*, etc.), and dependent words (*since, although, because*, etc.). Study the punctuation that goes with each type.

 **CHECKPOINT 5**

In the blank to the left of each paragraph, write the number of the run-together sentence in that paragraph.

___2___ 1. ¹Automobiles were introduced in the 1890s. ²At first, they seemed very strange, in fact, they were displayed in circuses. ³Before cars, most long-distance travel was done in horse-drawn carriages, which explains why the first autos were called "horseless carriages."

___✓___ 2. ¹The first vehicles that could move themselves were built as early as the eighteenth century; however, they were powered by steam, not gasoline. ²A steam carriage in England in the 1830s reached a speed of 15 miles an hour, and some of the vehicles carried as many as 22 passengers. ³The success of steam-powered road vehicles worried the railroad people, they got laws passed limiting the use of steam carriages.

___/___ 3. ¹In the United States, cars powered by electric batteries were the most popular. ²They were cleaner and quieter than those powered by steam or gasoline, but they had major drawbacks, they couldn't go fast, and their batteries had to be recharged every 50 miles. ³Gasoline cars gradually replaced steam and electric cars.

___/___ 4. ¹Although the gasoline car originated in Europe with such men as Daimler and Benz, the first successful American car of that type is usually credited to two brothers, Charles and Frank Duryea. **²**That car was built in 1894, in 1895 the Duryeas started the first company to manufacture gasoline-powered cars. **³**Men such as Henry Ford and Ransom Eli Olds soon were also making cars.

_____ 5. **¹**The young car industry was helped in 1901 by the discovery of huge oil fields in Texas, in addition, mass production methods were introduced to make cars cheaper. **²**One no longer had to be rich to afford a car. **³**Not surprisingly, cars became a popular means of transportation.

_____ 6. **¹**The Olds Motor Works in Detroit had the first auto assembly line. **²**Parts for the cars were made at a variety of machine shops; they were then brought to a central factory to be assembled into cars. **³**This made the work go faster, production jumped from 425 cars in 1901 to 5000 cars in 1903.

_____ 7. **¹**Henry Ford wanted to make a car that almost everyone could afford, to do that he introduced the moving assembly line. **²**A conveyor belt moved the frame of the car through the plant while workmen on each side of the belt added parts brought to them on other conveyor belts. **³**This method cut the time needed to assemble a car from 12 1/2 hours to 1 1/2 hours.

_____ 8. **¹**By cutting assembly time, Ford was able to cut costs. **²**The famous Model T Ford dropped in price from $850 to less than $400, making it cheaper than any other car. **³**More than 15 million Model Ts were sold between 1908 and 1927, half the cars sold in America in that period were Fords.

Wordcheck: Word Origins

Many words have histories that are interesting in themselves and that sometimes help us remember a word's meaning. The dictionary lists a word's origin or derivation in square brackets [ ].

Look up the origins of these words:

1. sandwich
2. smog
3. bonbon
4. dandelion
5. sinister

GO ELECTRONIC!

For supplemental readings, exercises, and Internet activities, visit
Checkpoints Online at
http://www.ablongman.com/page

Chapter 6

The Process Paragraph

READING PRECHECK

The process of developing the jeans we all take for granted involved a number of steps. This reading analyzes that process and tells why jeans have become popular not only in this country but throughout the world.

> **JOURNAL TOPIC:** Would you rather wear jeans or get "dressed up"? Why?

The Jeaning of America — and the World
Carin C. Quinn

This is the story of a sturdy American symbol which has now spread throughout most of the world. The symbol is not the dollar. It is not even Coca-Cola. It is a simple pair of pants called blue jeans, and what the pants symbolize is what Alexis de Tocqueville[1] called "a manly and legitimate passion for equality . . . ." Blue jeans are favored equally by bureaucrats and cowboys; bankers and deadbeats; fashion designers and beer drinkers. They draw no distinctions and recognize no classes; they are merely American. Yet they are sought after almost everywhere in the world—including Russia, where authorities recently broke up a teen-age gang that was selling them on the black market for two hundred dollars a pair. They have been around for a long time, and it seems likely they will outlive even the necktie. 1

    This ubiquitous American symbol was the invention of a Bavarian-born Jew. His name was Levi Strauss. 2

ubiquitous found everywhere

---
[1]French statesman who toured the United States in 1831

81

He was born in Bad Ocheim, Germany, in 1829, and during the European political turmoil of 1848 decided to take his chances in New York, to which his two brothers already had emigrated. Upon arrival, Levi soon found that his two brothers had exaggerated their tales of an easy life in the land of the main chance. They were landowners, they had told him; instead, he found them pushing needles, thread, pots, pans, ribbons, yarn, scissors, and buttons to housewives. For two years he was a lowly peddler, hauling some 180 pounds of sundries door-to-door to eke out a marginal living. When a married sister in San Francisco offered to pay his way west in 1850, he jumped at the opportunity, taking with him bolts of canvas he hoped to sell for tenting.

3

mother lode a large vein of gold ore
rigors harsh conditions

It was the wrong kind of canvas for that purpose, but while talking with a miner down from the mother lode, he learned that pants—sturdy pants that would stand up to the rigors of the digging—were almost impossible to find. Opportunity beckoned. On the spot, Strauss measured the man's girth and inseam with a piece of string and, for six dollars in gold dust, had [the canvas] tailored into a pair of stiff but rugged pants. The miner was delighted with the result, word got around about "those pants of Levi's" and Strauss was in business. The company has been in business ever since.

4

When Strauss ran out of canvas, he wrote his brothers to send more. He received instead a tough, brown cotton cloth made in Nimes, France—called *serge de Nimes* and swiftly shortened to "denim" (the word "jeans" derives from *Génes,* the French word for Genoa, where a similar cloth was produced). Almost from the first, Strauss had his cloth dyed the distinctive indigo that gave blue jeans their name, but it was not until the 1870s that he added the copper rivets which have long since become a company trademark. The rivets were the idea of a Virginia City, Nevada, tailor, Jacob W. Davis, who added them to pacify a mean-tempered miner called Alkali Ike. Alkali, the story goes, complained that the pockets of his jeans always tore when he stuffed them with ore samples and demanded that Davis do something about it. As a kind of joke, Davis took the pants to a blacksmith and had the pockets riveted; once again, the idea worked so well that word got around; in 1873 Strauss appropriated and patented the gimmick—and hired Davis as a regional manager.

5

pacify calm down

appropriated took for himself

By this time, Strauss had taken both his brothers and two brothers-in-law into the company and was ready for his third San Francisco store. Over the ensuing years, the company prospered locally, and by the time of his death in 1902, Strauss had become a man of prominence in California. For three decades thereafter the business remained profitable though small, with sales largely confined to the working people of the West—cowboys, lumberjacks, railroad workers, and the like. Levi's jeans were first introduced to the East, apparently, during the dude-ranch craze of the 1930s, when vacationing Easterners returned and word spread about the wonderful pants with rivets. Another boost came in World War II, when blue jeans were declared an essential commodity and were sold only to people engaged in defense work . . .

6

dude ranch guest ranch for city residents

The pants have become a tradition, and along the way have acquired a history of their own—so much so that the company has opened a museum in San Francisco. There was, for example, the turn-of-the-century trainman who replaced a faulty coupling with a pair of jeans; the Wyoming man who used his jeans as a

7

towrope to haul his car out of a ditch; the Californian who found seve
an abandoned mine, wore them, then discovered they were sixty-three
and still as good as new and turned them over to the Smithsonian [Mu
a tribute to their toughness. Then there is the particularly terrifying st
careless construction worker who dangled fifty-two stories above the s
rescued, his sole support the Levi's belt loop through which his rope was hooked.

Checking Meaning and Style

1. Explain the title.
2. Why do jeans symbolize an American "passion for equality"? (Paragraph 1)
3. Who invented blue jeans? (Paragraph 2)
4. Why are today's pants called "jeans"? Why is the material called "denim"? (Paragraph 5)
5. Why were rivets added to the pants? (Paragraph 5)
6. Who, apparently, introduced jeans on the East Coast? Who was permitted to wear them during World War II? (Paragraph 6)

Checking Ideas

1. Is America still the "land of opportunity" that it was 150 years ago in Levi Strauss' day?
2. If you agree that Americans have a "passion for equality," how, besides wearing jeans, do we show it?
3. Do you wear jeans? Why or why not?

Analyzing Process Writing

To describe a process is to tell, step-by-step, how something is done: how to teach a dog to roll over, how to make catfish stew (first, catch a catfish), how you made a million dollars in real estate, how Hitler came to power. We have seen that several steps were involved in developing today's jeans:

1. Levi Strauss went to California with canvas to make tents for gold miners.
2. He turned to making the sturdy pants the miners said they needed.
3. The pants were a success, and Levi Strauss was in business.
4. When he ordered more canvas, he got "denim" instead.
5. The trademark rivets were added to strengthen the pockets to hold ore samples.

Study the organization of this step-by-step description of how to write a composition.

Model Process Paragraph 1

Effective writing is a step-by-step process. The <u>first step</u> is prewriting. You gather details to develop your topic by using such prewriting methods as list-making, clustering, and freewriting. <u>Now</u> you're ready to write—but not with the idea that this is a final step. You will write a *first draft* that you expect to improve in later drafts. If time permits, put the draft aside for a day or so. Then you will be able to look at it with a clearer eye. The next step is to revise the composition, to improve it in any way you can. Does it say what you wanted it to say? Is it interesting and convincing? Is it unified, or could some parts be left out? Are there sentence errors, such as fragments and run-together sentences? Are words chosen carefully and spelled correctly? Next, make a copy in which you eliminate any of the problems you found in the first draft. The last step is to proofread carefully the final copy, looking for such things as spelling and punctuation errors. The final result should make your readers say they have read something that is interesting and worthwhile.

Transition words, such as those underlined in the preceding paragraph, can be helpful in making the steps of a process clear. But don't overdo them; use them only when they help. Here are some more transitions:

to start with	the first step	second
the next step	after that	the last step

Prewriting: Asking How and Why

"The Jeaning of America—and the World" explains how and why jeans came about. Those questions can often be useful in obtaining details to develop a topic.

Let's say you're looking at this topic sentence:

Education and on-the-job training are increasingly necessary for job success.

Like most topic sentences, it is rather general. You need specific details to make the paragraph interesting and convincing. Ask yourself *why* the education and training are necessary. Then jot down ideas that answer that question. Remember, you are brainstorming, so don't worry if all the ideas are good. You can get rid of the bad ones later.

technological changes—new skills needed
jobs less secure these days
layoffs and downsizing, even for veteran workers
blue-collar jobs more complicated
college grads make more money—50 percent more

Then ask *how* the skill training might be obtained.

finish high school
go to college or trade school
look for on-the-job training opportunities
take night classes

These ideas should provide enough details for a paragraph. After crossing out any that don't fit and rearranging the others, you might write a paragraph like the following.

Model How-and-Why Paragraph

✓ More than ever, education and training throughout a worker's life are important to job success. Changes in technology can make old skills obsolete. Downsizing and layoffs may mean the need to enter another line of work. Continued education usually produces bigger paychecks; the average college graduate earns nearly 50 percent more than the average high school graduate. Blue-collar workers need solid math and communication skills as jobs grow more complex and workers take part in the teams that are used more and more in factories. Clearly, a person should get as much schooling as he or she can. Beyond that, job applicants might do well to join a company that offers on-the-job training when new skills are needed. Formal education should continue, too. For example, night classes at the local community college can keep a worker up-to-date or provide skills in a new field.

Sometimes, only one of the how-why questions will work. If, for example, the boss asks for a memo on *why* you should get a raise, you will leave it to the boss to worry about *how* to pay for it. In a process paragraph, emphasis will be on *how* the process takes place.

Writing Assignment: A Process Paragraph

Write about a process that can be described in one paragraph. Write on one of these subjects or one that is similar.

1. How to do something around the house (not a recipe)

2. How to get an "A"

3. How you do something on your job

4. How something is made (cheese, a baseball, etc.)

5. How to do something in sports or with a hobby

6. How to become a citizen of the United States

The topic sentence of a process paragraph usually says something about the process: that it is easy, hard, fun, worthwhile, and so on. Here are three examples:

Changing the wallpaper in your kitchen is not an easy task, but the job can be simplified if you follow these steps.

A bill follows a complex path in Congress before it becomes a law.

A major league ballplayer probably has been playing the game at least since he was six.

To help you get started, do the following outline. First, write a topic sentence for your process paragraph. Then describe the necessary steps. If a transition word or phrase would help make the process clear, enter it where indicated.

1. Topic sentence _____

   _____

2. The first step _____

   _____

   Transition word or phrase? _____

3. The second step _____

   _____

   Transition word or phrase? _____

4. The third step _____

   _____

   Transition word or phrase? _____

5. The fourth step _____

   _____

Your process may have more than four steps.

Writing Topic Bank

Becoming a Smart Consumer

Throughout your life, you will likely have to purchase many goods. For example, you might want to buy a house, a car, or a CD player, and you will certainly need to buy clothes and food. How can a person become a smart consumer?

WRITING CHECKLIST

 Use whatever prewriting techniques seem useful: listing, clustering, asking how and why, etc.

 Start with a topic sentence that leads easily into the steps of the process.

 Be sure each step is described clearly and that all necessary steps are included.

 Revise the paragraph as needed, watching especially for troublemakers, sentence fragments, and run-together sentences.

 Proofread the final copy.

Write a paragraph that gives the steps a person should follow to make wise purchases.

Exploring Health Information on the Internet

Visit WebMD (http://webmd.lycos.com/health-e-tools). Select one of the Anatom-E-Tools, which are animated diagrams that show how various heart and spine problems develop. Watch one of the animations several times, selecting "Labels" at the top right of the diagram so you know which parts of the body are being shown. Write a paragraph that explains in simple terms how the problem develops.

Writing About Media

Suggest a process that parents could use to decide whether their children should see a particular movie. You might find it helpful to think about the children you know. How can a parent decide whether a movie is appropriate for a child to see? Write a how-and-why paragraph.

Sentence Sense: Using Verbs Correctly

Verbs change their form to show changes in time. Most verbs are *regular;* that is, they show past time in a consistent way, by adding *-ed* or *-d* to the present-time form.

Present Time	Past Time
jump	jumped
dance	danced
hope	hoped

But that isn't true of all verbs. Look at the verbs in these past-time sentences:

Angela <u>knowed</u> the words to all the Top 40 songs.

Mrs. Greene <u>losed</u> her wedding ring in the potato salad.

Obviously, adding *-ed* or *-d* to *know* or *lose* just results in embarrassing errors. They are *irregular* verbs. Their past-time forms are made in irregular or inconsistent ways. Those sentences should have been written this way:

Angela <u>knew</u> the words to all the Top 40 songs.

Mrs. Greene <u>lost</u> her wedding ring in the potato salad.

To avoid mistakes with irregular verbs, we have to memorize the past-time form and the past participle for each one. The past participle is the form used with the helping verbs *has, have,* and *had.*

Present time	Today Viola <u>sings</u>.
Past time	Yesterday Viola <u>sang</u>.
Past participle	Viola <u>has sung</u> all week long.

Unfortunately, the list of irregular verbs is rather long (the following list is not complete).

Present	Past	Past Participle (used with the helping verbs *has, have, had*)
arise (s)[2]	arose	arisen
become (s)	became	become
begin (s)	began	begun
bite (s)	bit	bitten
blow (s)	blew	blown
break (s)	broke	broken
bring (s)	brought	brought
burst (s)	burst	burst
buy (s)	bought	bought
catch (es)	caught	caught
choose (s)	chose	chosen
come (s)	came	come
dive (s)	dived or dove	dived
do (does)	did	done
draw (s)	drew	drawn
dream (s)	dreamed or dreamt	dreamed or dreamt

---

[2]Present-time verbs add an *-s* or *-es* if the subject is *he, she,* or *it.*

Present	**Past**	**Past Participle (used with the helping verbs *has, have, had*)**
drink (s)	drank	drunk
drive (s)	drove	driven
eat (s)	ate	eaten
fall (s)	fell	fallen
feed (s)	fed	fed
feel (s)	felt	felt
fight (s)	fought	fought
find (s)	found	found
fly (flies)	flew	flown
forget (s)	forgot	forgotten
get (s)	got	got or gotten
give (s)	gave	given
go (goes)	went	gone
grow (s)	grew	grown
hear (s)	heard	heard
hide (s)	hid	hidden
hurt (s)	hurt	hurt
keep (s)	kept	kept
know (s)	knew	known
lay (to place)	laid	laid
lead (s)	led	led
leave (s)	left	left
let (s)	let	let
lie (to recline)	lay	lain
lose	lose (s)	lost
make (s)	made	made
meet (s)	met	met
pay (s)	paid	paid
prove (s)	proved	proved or proven
ride (s)	rode	ridden
ring (s)	rang	rung
run (s)	ran	run
say (s)	said	said
see (s)	saw	seen
send (s)	sent	sent
shake (s)	shook	shaken
shoot (s)	shot	shot
shut (s)	shut	shut
sing (s)	sang	sung
sink (s)	sank or sunk	sunk
slide (s)	slid	slid
sit (s)	sat	sat
speak (s)	spoke	spoken
spend (s)	spent	spent

Present	Past	Past Participle (used with the helping verbs *has, have, had*)
spring (s)	sprang or sprung	sprung
steal (s)	stole	stolen
swim (s)	swam	swum
take (s)	took	taken
teach (es)	taught	taught
tell (s)	told	told
think (s)	thought	thought
throw (s)	threw	thrown
wear (s)	wore	worn
win (s)	won	won
write (s)	wrote	written

To see if any of the irregular verbs are a problem for you, cover the past and past participle columns and test yourself. Make up sample sentences for the present, past, and past participle forms. The sentences don't have to make a lot of sense to serve your purpose. For example:

Today I <u>write</u> a letter. Yesterday I <u>wrote</u> a letter. I <u>have written</u> two letters.

Today Mrs. Enseña <u>wears</u> a suit. Yesterday she <u>wore</u> a dress. She <u>has worn</u> different outfits every day this week.

Put a check beside any verbs you had trouble with; then practice them again and again until the correct forms seem natural. Errors in verbs show up conspicuously in both speaking and writing, so time spent on these problems will be time well invested.

> **NOTE** Present-time verbs are used not only to express an action going on right now but also to express an action that continues from the past into the present and future.

Alta <u>sings</u> in the chorus at her college.

 **SPOTCHECK 6–1**

Use all three forms of the verbs in italics—present, past, and past participle (in that order). Remember that the present-time verb ends in -s if the subject could be *he, she,* or *it.* The past participle is always used with one of the helping verbs *has, have,* or *had.*

Example: Six-year-old Billy likes to *draw.* He <u>draws</u> whenever he gets a chance. He <u>drew</u> a Corvette for his dad's birthday. He <u>has drawn</u> since he was two years old.

1. Baby birds quickly learn to *fly.* They _____ within days of being

   hatched. A baby robin _____ for the first time this morning in my yard. By October it will have _____ to a warmer location.

2. Some people *eat* more than is good for them. For example, Tom

_____ between meals. He _____ two doughnuts this

morning during coffee break at work. By bedtime he usually has

_____ a candy bar or two.

3. It is discouraging to *forget* what one has learned in class. I _____

the forms of irregular verbs if I don't review them frequently. In a test yesterday,

I _____ the past participles of *forget* and swim. I'm afraid I have

also _____ the difference between *lie* and *lay.*

4. Jacqueline likes to *go* dancing. She _____ almost every Saturday

night. Last week she _____ to a club called the Top Hat. She didn't

like the band; she says she has _____ there for the last time.

5. It is easy to *hurt* oneself skiing. Amahl and Jake usually _____ them-

selves at least once each season. Curtis _____ his ankle at Heavenly

Valley last weekend. Jake has _____ his arm three times in two winters.

✓ **SPOTCHECK 6–2** **In the blanks, write the correct form of the verbs in parentheses. The first one has been done as an example.**

¹Sandra (buy) <u>bought</u> a new motorcycle yesterday. ²She had (gave)

_____ the purchase a good deal of thought. ³Finally, she (throw)

_____ aside all her doubts. ⁴The salesman at the cycle shop (tell)

_____ her she should buy a helmet, too. ⁵He mentioned statistics that a

state automobile association had (bring) _____ out on motorcycle safety.

⁶Riding a motorcycle has (become) _____ much more dangerous than

driving a car. **7**For every mile they have (ride) _____, cyclists are five times more likely than motorists to have had an accident. **8**Cycle accidents have (win) _____ the unhappy distinction of being sixteen times more likely than auto accidents to result in death. **9**In recent years several hundred persons have (go) _____ to their deaths in California motorcycle accidents. **10**After hearing these figures, Sandra (begin) _____ to think she should at least wear a helmet while riding her bike.

SPOTCHECK 6–3   Write in the correct form of the verbs shown in parentheses.

1. (teach) Mr. Tam has _____ at Castlemont High School for fifteen years.

2. (sing) Louis and Besonda have _____ together on a local television program.

3. (fly) Charles Lindbergh _____ alone across the Atlantic Ocean in 1927.

4. (eat) Cathy had already _____ the bowl of mixed nuts by the time the guests arrived.

5. (drink) Meanwhile, her husband had _____ all the soda.

6. (speak) Monica and Mark have not _____ to each other since the college dance.

7. (see) Marilyn _____ the movie six times.

8. (write) Have you _____ your sociology term paper yet?

9. (spend) Corporations have _____ large sums to get their products displayed in movies.

10. (pay) A cigarette manufacturer is said to have _____ actor Sylvester Stallone $500,000 to use its brands in five films.

SPOTCHECK 6–4   Write sentences using the verb forms in parentheses. Use helping verbs where needed.

1. (seen) _____

_____

2. (became) _____

_____

3. (rang) _____

_____

4. (known) _____

_____

5. (driven) _____

_____

Past Participles as Adjectives

Sometimes the past participle is used not as a verb but as an *adjective*, a word that describes a noun or a pronoun. In those cases it will come after a linking verb or before a noun.

The runner was exhausted. (after the linking verb *was*)

The stolen car was soon recovered. (before the noun *car*)

 **SPOTCHECK 6–5**   Underline past participles used as adjectives.

1. The mayor looked excited when the news came.

2. A frightened rabbit hurried across the road.

3. Two grown men were swinging in the playground.

4. The speaker seemed annoyed at the interruption.

5. The shopper thought the clerk was prejudiced.

Three Verbs to Watch Out For

Three irregular verbs that sometimes cause trouble are *be*, *have*, and *do*. Be sure you are familiar with the forms of each.

Present Time (*be*)		Past Time (*be*)	
Singular	**Plural**	**Singular**	**Plural**
I am	we are	I was	we were
you are	you are	you were	you were
he (she, it) is	they are	he (she, it) was	they were

Present Time (have)		Past Time (have)	
Singular	**Plural**	**Singular**	**Plural**
I have	we have	I had	we had
you have	you have	you had	you had
he (she, it) has	they have	they had	they had

Present Time (do)		Past Time (do)	
Singular	**Plural**	**Singular**	**Plural**
I do	we do	I did	we did
you do	you do	you did	you did
he (she, it) does	they do	he (she, it) did	they did

 **SPOTCHECK 6–6**   Underline the standard verb form in parentheses.

1. The albatross is a bird that (have has) a reputation for bringing bad luck.

2. From the fifth century to the ninth, the average life span (be / was / were) thirty-six years.

3. Despite its name, the College of William and Mary (do / does / did) not admit women students for 255 years, until 1918.

4. Libya (be / is / are) the only country with a flag of a single color—green.

5. Nepal is the only country that (have / has) a nonrectangular flag.

6. Country music (have / has) gained many new fans in recent years.

7. Rob usually (does / do) the 100 meters in around ten seconds.

8. However, yesterday he (do / did / done) it in over eleven seconds.

9. The MacGees (have / has) a boat.

10. Yesterday you (be / was / were) late for your music class.

Verb Endings

The *-s* and *-ed* endings of regular verbs sometimes get dropped (or added) when they shouldn't be.

No: John hope to get a job at the foundry.

Yes: John hoped (or hopes) to get a job at the foundry.

No: Cindy always play the piano at our parties.

Yes: Cindy always <u>plays</u> the piano at our parties.

No: The restaurant advertises <u>home-cook</u> meals.

Yes: The restaurant advertises <u>home-cooked</u> meals.

Following are the standard forms for a typical regular verb. If any of them don't "sound right," they are worth practicing until they do.

Present Time		Past Time	
Singular	**Plural**	**Singular**	**Plural**
I work	we work	I worked	we worked
you work	you work	you worked	you worked
he (she, it) works	they work	he (she, it) worked	they worked

Notice that the past-time forms are all the same and that the only change in the present-time forms is the *-s* added in the singular ("he <u>works</u>").

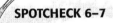

SPOTCHECK 6–7　　Underline the correct form in parentheses.

1. Ming (commute / commutes) eighteen miles to work each day.

2. Austin (say / says) he won't attend the Homecoming game.

3. Felix was (suppose / supposed) to usher at church last Sunday.

4. Vernal's mother-in-law (ask / asked) him to wash her car.

5. Ali (know / knows) the way to San Jose.

DOUBLECHECK 6–1　　Orville and Wilbur Wright invented the first practical airplane. As an exercise, change the underlined words in the following paragraph to give all the credit to Wilbur. Change the subjects and verbs from the plural to the singular, as in the first sentence. Put all the verbs in the *present tense.*

　　　　　　　<u>Wilbur Wright</u>　　　　　<u>introduces</u>
[1]<s>Orville and Wilbur Wright</s> <s>introduce</s> the age of air travel when, in 1803, <s>they</s>　<u>he</u>

<u>makes</u>
<s>make</s> the first successful powered flight. [2]Without even finishing high school, <u>the two</u>

<u>bicycle makers</u> <u>discover</u> complicated principles of aerodynamics that make flight

possible. [3]On that historic day, on a beach in Kitty Hawk, North Carolina, <u>they</u> <u>fly</u> a

homemade, twelve-horsepower craft for twelve seconds. [4]<u>They</u> <u>travel</u> 120 feet. [5]After

that first flight, <u>they</u> <u>complete</u> three more on the same day, December 17, 1903, the

longest trip covering 852 feet. [6]Then <u>the brothers</u> <u>watch</u> in dismay as a gust of wind blows the flimsy craft along the beach, wrecking it. [7]Undiscouraged, <u>they</u> <u>build</u> another model. [8]At first, <u>they</u> <u>receive</u> little attention for the historic accomplishment. [9]Today, however, <u>they</u> <u>are</u> honored by a national memorial near Kitty Hawk.

EDITING CHECK 6

Edit the following paragraphs to correct verb errors. Use *past-time* verbs in the first ten sentences. Then switch to *present-time* verbs in the last ten sentences.

[1]Elizabeth Cochrane ~~be~~ ^{was} her name in the small Pennsylvania mill town where she grew up. [2]But she have a different name—Nellie Bly—when she became famous as a daring newspaper reporter around 1900. [3]Her remarkable story start when she read in a Pittsburgh newspaper an editorial titled "What Girls Are Good For." [4]She be angry at its sneering attitude toward women. [5]The teenager felt she just have to answer the editorial. [6]Her letter so impress the editors that they offered her a job.

[7]The first stories she do for the newspaper were about divorce, a touchy subject one hundred years ago. [8]Under the by-line "Nellie Bly," she also expose inhuman conditions in the city's slums, sweatshops, and jails. [9]Sales of the newspaper went up, but some of the city's most prominent citizens do not approve of the stories. [10]Nellie's editors urge her to take a "vacation."

[11]She gets a job in Mexico, where her stories about corruption ~~be~~ ^{are} embarrassing to the officials, who ask her to leave. [12]What she do next is get a job on Joseph Pulitzer's *New York World* by promising an exposé on conditions at the city's insane asylum on Blackwell's Island. [13]After she acts crazy at a rooming house, she be taken to Blackwell's Island for ten days. [14]Her newspaper stories describe the asylum as "a human rat hole," cause a sensation, and make Nellie a celebrity. [15]For other stories, she pose as an immigrant girl to expose cheating by employment agencies and gets arrested for theft to write about abuse of female prisoners. [16]Another time she throw

herself off a Hudson River ferry to see how fast its rescue squad reacts. **¹⁷**Nellie be inspired to perform her greatest stunt by the publishing of Jules Verne's novel *Around the World in Eighty Days.* **¹⁸**Not yet 22, she set out in 1889 to beat the globe-circling record of Verne's traveling hero, Phileas Fogg. **¹⁹**She send back stories to a fascinated nation from exotic points around the world. **²⁰**And she do it—completing the journey in seventy-two days.

Were you careful to use past-time verbs in the first ten sentences and present-time verbs in the last ten?

✔ **CHECKPOINT 6** — **In the blank at the left of each sentence, write the correct form of the verb in parentheses:**

_____ 1. All the domino players (bring) their own sets yesterday.

_____ 2. Cesar (run) two miles before breakfast.

_____ 3. Her history class hadn't yet (begin) when Lily got there.

_____ 4. Minh and Rudy (shoot) a game of pool after work Tuesday.

_____ 5. How much has Yuko (spend) on books this term?

_____ 6. I wonder where all the cookies (go) that I bought yesterday.

_____ 7. Timmie said he had no idea where they had (go).

_____ 8. If Lynn had (know) that Pierre was the capital of South Dakota, she would have had a perfect score on the test.

_____ 9. She knew it last week, but by test time she had (forget).

_____ 10. The estimated value of the average housewife's labor has (rise) to $60,000 a year.

_____ 11. The Swiss have (fight) in no wars since 1515.

_____ 12. In 1650, the world (have) half as many people as live in China today.

_____ 13. Some parts of Canada (lie) farther south than some parts of California.

_____ 14. President Andrew Johnson was (teach) to read and write at age seventeen by the woman he would later marry.

_____ 15. Was it Emerson who (say), "Money often costs too much"?

Wordcheck: Verb Forms

There is ice on the pond. You want to write that the pond behind the barn has . . . *froze? frozen?* Your dictionary lists the past time and past participle forms of irregular verbs. It will tell you that *frozen* (the past participle of *freeze*) is the form of *freeze* to use with the helping word *has.* The forms are printed in boldface (dark) type in the dictionary.

Look up the past-time and past participles of these verbs:

1. shake   _____   _____

2. put   _____   _____

3. swear   _____   _____

4. forgive   _____   _____

5. sink   _____   _____

GO ELECTRONIC!

For supplemental readings, exercises, and Internet activities, visit
Checkpoints Online at
http://www.ablongman.com/page

Chapter 7

The Cause and Effect Paragraph

READING PRECHECK

Speeding bullets had joined speeding cars on the Southern California freeways when this story appeared in the *Los Angeles Times*. The article analyzes the problem of drivers who take out their frustrations and anger by attacking other motorists. What *causes* this behavior? What are its *effects*?

JOURNAL TOPIC: How do you handle *your* frustrations while driving or as a passenger in a car or bus?

Road Warriors of the Freeways
Lonn Johnston

Los Angeles—Barreling along the freeway at about a mile a minute, Harold Harvey Hawks pulled out a 12-gauge shotgun and fired. Later, he told police that he just meant to scare the driver of a van who had flashed his bright headlights, thrown a can, and cut him off.   **1**

Hawks received the maximum term of 17 years to life for the shot he fired that killed a passenger in the van—Patricia Dwyer, an off-duty Corona policewoman whose husband was driving. "Two hotheads met on the freeway and neither one of them would give in," summed up jury forewoman Joyce Beck, after jurors found Hawks guilty of second-degree murder.   **2**

It was the first in a recent spate of Southern California freeway shootings—a new kind of urban warfare that California Highway Patrol officials and others fear may be a trend. "It's a war out there," said Dr. Ange LoBue, director for medical affairs at College Hospital in Cerritos and a psychiatrist specializing in stress man-   **3**

spate   sudden increase
urban   found in cities

99

agement. "For most people, the most stressful place in Southern California is the freeway."

California Highway Patrol officer Matt Clark of Santa Ana compares the freeways to psychological experiments in which rats crowded into a box become violently aggressive. "People are going crazy out there," he said. "And it's getting worse." 4

consensus agreement

Although no one keeps statistics on such things, there is a broad consensus that violent confrontations on the freeway are rising, according to state CHP spokesman Kent Milton. The reasons, say those who study driver aggression, are as complicated as a rush-hour commute: 5

Cars offer anonymity, a feeling of power, and the chance to escape, lowering inhibitions to aggressiveness. "It's the private bubble that brings out Mr. Hyde," said Raymond W. Novaco, a professor at the University of California at Irvine who studies freeway driver stress and anger. 6

Traffic congestion is worsening because freeway construction has not kept pace with population growth. Rush hour has become creep hour. As driver frustrations and blood pressures rise, Novaco said, "there is a highly significant decrease in tolerance." 7

condones accepts or allows

"American society increasingly condones violence," said Arnold Goldstein, director of the Center for Research on Aggression at Syracuse University in New York. In advertising and television, for example, we see "great levels of displayed violence but fewer and fewer restraints," he said. "So now if someone cuts you off on the freeway, instead of yelling or an obscene gesture, the violence of the response may escalate to actual physical injury—in some cases with a gun." 8

escalates increases
homicidal murderous

Freeway killings have only recently grabbed the public's attention, but homicidal thoughts have been a commuting companion of frustrated motorists for some time, according to one study. In a survey of Salt Lake City drivers, 12 percent of the men and 18 percent of the women reported that, at times, they "could gladly kill another driver." 9

lethal able to cause death

Indeed, the sometimes-lethal game of high-speed freeway leapfrog—with drivers cutting each other off, tailgating, and flashing lights—continues much as before, said Ken Daily, a 20-year CHP veteran who works in the San Capistrano office. "It's nothing new, just now they have weapons." 10

Experts say that cars can bring out the worst in people. "For some, a car is incredibly important territory. You're the master, you're on your own turf. A person feels dominant," said Albert Mehrabian, professor of psychology at the University of California at Los Angeles. Combine dominance with feelings of discomfort and anxiety and you have the perfect conditions for hostility and aggression, Mehrabian said. 11

deindividuation loss of personal self by identifying with a group

The anonymity offered by cars creates a behavior called deindividuation, a concept that emerged in studies of mobs and riots. LoBue of College Hospital compared the behavior to that of soldiers in battle. "It's like war," he said. "You can kill because you don't know your adversary." 12

Inhibitions for aggression are lowered further when people see an opportunity to be aggressive and escape, said Novaco of UC Irvine. And what better way to escape than in a car? 13

cathy® 　　　　　　　　　　　　　　　　　　　　　**by Cathy Guisewite**

To lower stress while driving, therapists recommend deep-breathing exercises, **14** changing the car's environment by turning on air conditioning and relaxing music, and being aware of one's feelings while on the road. "It's a lot easier to interrupt troublesome inner states early on," Novaco said.

Also, therapists recommend driving with someone else to reduce aggressive **15** reactions and allowing enough time to get there. "Some people are adrenaline junkies," LoBue said. "They wait until the last minute to get into a car to get that adrenaline rush."

Checking Meaning and Style

1. The article discusses the effects of freeway violence as well as the causes of that violence. Where do the paragraphs dealing with the effects of violence end and the causes begin?
2. Can you explain the sentence "[A car is the] private bubble that brings out Mr. Hyde"? (Paragraph 6)
3. What three things encourage violence in driving? (Paragraph 6)
4. What two things condition Americans to accept violence? (Paragraph 8)
5. "Cars can bring out the worst in people." What two explanations are given in paragraph 11?
6. According to therapists, what can a person do to lower stress while driving? (Paragraphs 14 and 15)
7. What is the meaning of the reference to rats in Paragraph 4?

Checking Ideas

1. You probably haven't seen any shootings, but have you seen other kinds of aggressive or hostile driving behavior that could cause injury or death? If so, what kinds?
2. What freeway behaviors or conditions irritate you most?
3. Do you agree that cars can "bring out the worst" in people? How do you feel while driving in heavy traffic?
4. Would you be more likely to make a rude gesture to another motorist than to a person you encountered on a sidewalk? Explain.

5. Could the "safety" of being rude or worse in a car also help explain the anonymous, abusive comments often heard on radio talk shows or seen on computer "chat room" screens? Discuss.

Analyzing Cause and Effect Writing

What causes some people to shoot at other motorists on the freeway? That is the question reporter Lonn Johnston set out to answer in his newspaper story. His task was similar to one that you may expect to face in your college writing. Your instructors may call on you to analyze a subject in terms of cause and effect: What caused World War I? What are the causes of the high divorce rate in America? What were the effects of the invention of electric lights? What are the effects of television viewing on students' grades?

Johnston first presents the effects or results of freeway violence: specific cases of death or injury. But most of his article deals with what causes this crazy behavior.

The student paragraphs that follow discuss causes of student dropout.

Model Cause and Effect Paragraph 1

Two reasons why many students drop out of college are that they hang around with the wrong crowd, or they have to go to work to support their family. If they associate with students who go to school just to socialize, they are likely to neglect their studies and possibly could fail their courses. Their friends may encourage them to cut classes to "hang out." If they fall behind in their classes, they may drop out altogether. Other students drop out because they are the only ones to support their families. They may have done well in school, but now they need to work full-time.

The writer announces that the topic will be causes of student drop-out. Two causes are then discussed: neglect of studies and need to hold a job.

Model Cause and Effect Paragraph 2

My friend Al had to drop out of college to support his family. Al's father has been unemployed since the local steel mill shut down. His mother quit her job as a nurse years ago because of back trouble. His two brothers are still in elementary school, and his sister is in high school. Even though Al had been working from 4 p.m. to midnight at a filling station and his father receives unemployment insurance, the family was having trouble making house payments. So Al added a 2-to-6 job stocking shelves at a supermarket. He tried to continue his classes, too. However, when he found that he was coming to classes unprepared and often dozing off, he decided to postpone his college education until the family finances improved.

The second paragraph is better than the first because it has a narrower focus. It takes up just one reason for dropping out. Presenting a fuller discussion of that one reason makes the paragraph more interesting and worthwhile. Don't try to cover too much ground in a single paragraph.

Writing Assignment:
A Cause and Effect Paragraph

Write a paragraph in which you analyze the causes or effects (not both) of something. Start with a topic sentence that may look similar to one of these.

> Reciting the Gettysburg Address in elementary school made me realize something about myself. (effect)

> The slow pace is one reason I enjoy baseball. (cause)

> A major cause of teen drug use is pressure from friends. (cause)

> My life has been wonderful (miserable) since I met Lulu. (effect)

Develop the topic sentence with at least a half-dozen sentences of explanation or examples.

Topics for Writing

Subjects emphasizing <u>cause</u>

1. Why I bought the kind of car (bicycle, motorcycle) I did
2. Why I chose to attend this college
3. Why I am a Democrat (vegetarian, jogger)

Subjects emphasizing <u>effect</u>

4. How my life has changed since I quit smoking (started drinking, joined the debate club)
5. How driving affects my emotions and behavior
6. How friends make my life better (worse)
7. How my bad habit has affected me

 Writing Topic Bank

Writing About an Activity

What activity (for example: jogging, studying, parenting, shopping) is important to you? Write a paragraph explaining why you chose to start doing that activity (cause), or write a paragraph describing how doing that activity has changed you (effect).

WRITING CHECKLIST

 You might try writing nonstop or asking how and why—or both—to develop your topic. Asking why you chose this college (what caused your decision), you might come up with a list like this one:

close to home

low tuition

friends attending

chance to play football

good music department

 Start with a true sentence, not a fragment. The seven suggested Topics for Writing on page 103 begin with a dependent word—*why* or *how*—and are dependent clause fragments.

 Be sure your paragraph sticks to the causes or effects of your subject.

 When revising your first drafts, look especially for sentence fragments, run-together sentences, and verb errors.

 Ask a classmate or a friend to read the paper and to tell you if it seems well organized, interesting, and convincing.

 Remember to proofread the final copy for overlooked mistakes.

Exploring the News on the Internet

Go to a news website, such as the Washington Post (www.washingtonpost.com), USA Today (www.usatoday.com), or the Christian Science Monitor (www.csmonitor.com).

1. Choose a news headline that emphasizes the cause of something and rewrite it to emphasize the effect. For example: "Flood Kills Three in East Overshoe" might be rewritten: "Three Die in East Overshoe Flood." Write a short paragraph describing the news item with an emphasis on effect.

2. Next, choose a news headline that emphasizes effect and rewrite it to emphasize the cause. For example: "Increased School Dropout Rate Blamed on New Dress Code" might be rewritten: "New Dress Code Leads to Increased School Dropout Rate." Write a short paragraph describing the news items with an emphasis on cause.

Writing About Media

What causes a person to hate a particular kind of music? Think of someone you know who strongly dislikes one kind of music, such as country music, opera, rock and roll, or rap. Ask that person what he or she hates about it. Try to figure out which reason is the most important, or if you can't, just choose one reason. Then write a paragraph to explain that reason in detail.

Affect and *Effect*

This is a good time to look at the difference between the words *affect* and *effect*. *Affect* is an action verb meaning "to influence."

> The medicine affected Chauncey's score on the algebra exam.

Effect is a noun meaning "result."

> Did the medicine have an effect on Chauncey's score on the algebra exam?

Sentence Sense:
Making Subjects and Verbs Agree

Subjects and verbs must *agree*. That means that singular (one-item) subjects need singular verbs, and plural (more than one item) subjects need plural verbs.

Usually we don't have problems with subject-verb agreement:

> Mary attends college. (subject and verb both singular)

> The Olson boys attend college. (subject and verb plural)

A complication to keep in mind: A plural subject usually ends in *-s* (*boys*), while a singular verb often ends in *-s* (*attends*).

Here are some other situations to consider.

1. Subjects joined by *and* are usually plural.

> Latanya and David have [not *has*] announced their engagement.

> Swimming and walking are [not *is*] good exercise.

2. When subjects are joined by *either . . . or* or *neither . . . nor*, the verb agrees with the nearer subject.

> Either Jim or his parents are meeting the plane. (The plural verb *are meeting* agrees with the nearer subject, *parents*.)

> Neither the Smiths nor their daughter has reservations. (The singular verb *has* agrees with the nearer subject, *daughter*.)

Or rewrite the sentence:

The Smith's don't have reservations. Neither does their daughter.

 **SPOTCHECK 7–1** Underline the correct verb in parentheses. It may help to underline the sentence subject first.

[1]Anagrams and Scrabble (is / are) word games. [2]Either Terrie or Jonathan (promise / promises) to bring the games to tonight's party. [3]Of course, neither Naomi nor Richard (expects / expect) to attend the party because of final exams coming up. [4]And neither Jeffrey nor his parents (enjoys / enjoy) word games. [5]They and Mr. and Mrs. Oliva always (plays / play) bridge when they get a chance.

3. Words that come between the subject and verb may cause confusion. Phrases that begin with *in addition to, along with,* or *as well as* do not affect the number of the verb.

Phil, along with several friends, is attending Mardi Gras.

The apple pie, in addition to two dozen cookies, was eaten by the squirrels.

REMEMBER *A word in a prepositional phrase is never the subject of the verb. To help pinpoint the subject, you might cross out the prepositional phrases, as in these examples:*

The stamps ~~in the desk drawer~~ belong ~~to Harold~~.

Only one ~~of the books~~ is overdue.

Some of the common prepositions are *of, in, into, for, on, at, by, to, from, with, above, below, through, during, among, before,* and *after.* The noun or pronoun that comes after the preposition completes the prepositional phrase.

 **SPOTCHECK 7–2** Draw one line under the subject and two lines under the correct verb in parentheses. Cross out any prepositional phrases if that will help you locate the subject.

1. One of the Statue of Liberty's fingers (is / are) eight feet long.

2. The cause of the computer's problems (is / are) static electricity.

3. A banana, along with whole wheat bread and cereals, (adds / add) important nutritional values at breakfast.

4. Several workers in the front office (is / are) getting raises.

5. The waters of the Pacific Ocean (reaches / reach) a depth of six miles.

4. Sometimes the subject comes after the verb instead of in front of it. Remember that the word *there* is never the subject.

verb   subject

~~Inside the boxes~~ was a collection ~~of old magazines.~~

verb   subject

There are not many clues ~~in the case at this time.~~

 **SPOTCHECK 7–3** Draw one line under the subject and two lines under the correct verb in parentheses.

1. There (is / are) two lakes, Placid and Amore, in my home town.

2. The main attraction at the lakes (is / are) the swimming.

3. Only at Lake Placid (is / are) there swans.

4. Lake Amore (has / have) a Mother Goose Land for children.

5. Presenting the annual Fourth of July fireworks (is / are) the Park Department's responsibility.

5. Words called *indefinite pronouns* are usually considered singular, even though some of them seem to be plural. Here are some examples:

each   either   neither   everyone   everybody   someone

somebody   anybody   nobody   something   everything

When one of those words is the subject, the verb should be singular.

Everybody has [not *have*] to bring a hot dish or a salad to the party.

Everything the committee planned is [not *are*] taking place on schedule.

However, *both, few,* and *several* always take a plural verb.

Both of the vases are to be auctioned.

(compare) Neither of the vases is to be auctioned.

 **SPOTCHECK 7–4** Draw one line under the subject and two lines under the correct verb in parentheses. You may want to cross out prepositional phrases to make the subject more obvious.

1. Everything in the two trunks (was / were) at least one hundred years old.

2. Neither of the elephants (come / comes) from Africa.

3. Mattie hopes somebody at school (remember / remembers) her birthday.

4. Nobody among the mayor's aides (know / knows) where the police chief is.

5. Both of the referees (has / have) major league experience.

6. One of the Olsons (has / have) to be in court Monday.

7. Everyone in the group (live / lives) out of state.

8. Each of the chairs (copy / copies) a nineteenth century design.

6. When *who, which,* or *that* is used as the subject of a dependent clause, its verb may be singular or plural. It is singular if the word the pronoun stands for is singular; it is plural if the word it stands for is plural.

> Lake Tahoe is a resort area <u>that</u> <u>is</u> very popular. (The verb is singular because *that* stands for a word that is singular, *area*.)

> Lake Tahoe is one of those resort areas <u>that</u> <u>are</u> very popular. (The verb is plural because *that* stands for a word that is plural, *areas*.)

SPOTCHECK 7–5   **Underline the correct verb in parentheses.**

1. The vice president of the company is a woman who (has / have) a master's degree in business administration.

2. Houston has residents who (doesn't / don't) mind the summer heat.

3. Motorists who (drives / drive) Highway 5 know the meaning of boredom.

4. The leader of the expedition into the Himalaya Mountains is one of those people who (loves / love) adventure.

5. David's Camaro, which (costs / cost) him $90 a month just for insurance, will have to be sold.

7. Group nouns look plural but are usually singular. Here are some examples of group nouns:

family	team	class	committee	audience	band
flock	herd	group	department store	gas company	

They usually require singular verbs.

> The Dupree family <u>has</u> a cabin on Clear Lake. (The family is one unit or group.)

> This year's class <u>was</u> the largest in ten years. (The class is a single unit.)

But sometimes when we use group nouns we are thinking of individual members of the group acting separately. Then we need a plural verb. We are thinking "they" rather than "it."

> The Dupree family <u>have</u> interesting jobs. (Individual members have separate jobs.)

> This year's class <u>are</u> getting good job offers. (*Class* refers to individual members.)

8. Some nouns end in *-s* and look plural but take singular verbs. Examples: *politics, news, measles, mathematics, physics, economics.*

SPOTCHECK 7–6 Underline the correct verb in parentheses.

1. Economics (is / are) required for a business degree.

2. The Lions Club (meet / meets) once a month at the Elks Club Hall.

3. The Recreation Department (sponsor / sponsors) Little League baseball.

4. The crowd always (go / goes) wild when the band Toulouse 2 Lose plays.

5. The news from the Philippines (have / has) been encouraging lately.

DOUBLECHECK 7–1 Underline the correct verb in parentheses.

1. Everybody in the kayaks (has / have) to wear a life jacket.

2. Where (is / are) the photos of Jimmy's baptism?

3. The sandwiches on the counter (is / are) all vegetarian.

4. Ohio's Oberlin College, which (was / were) founded in 1833, was the first co-educational college in the United States and the first to admit students "without respect to color."

5. Neither Philadelphia nor Dallas (is / are) likely to win the Super Bowl this year.

6. The average American household (watches / watch) TV more than seven hours a day.

7. Among those at the concert (was / were) the Andrews sisters.

8. Taos, New Mexico, is one of those cities that (attracts / attract) visitors.

9. There (was / were) more than five hundred students at the rally.

10. Everyone in the English class (deserves / deserve) an "A."

EDITING CHECK 7

Some of the underlined verbs do not agree with their subjects. If the verb is wrong, write the correct form above the line. Underline the subject also. The first sentence is an example.

¹There <u>is</u> many <u>people</u> these days who are taking aerobic exercise classes or building muscles with weight training. ²Which one of the two kinds of exercise do you think <u>has</u> more health benefits? ³The answer to that question <u>lie</u> in understanding the terms *aerobic* and *anaerobic*. ⁴The first of the terms <u>mean</u> "with oxygen," while *anaerobic* means "without oxygen." ⁵One of the sports that <u>stimulates</u> beneficial activity of the heart and lungs is aerobic exercise. ⁶Activities like brisk walking, running, cycling, and swimming <u>are</u> healthfully aerobic. ⁷They make the body work hard and <u>increases</u> the demand for oxygen. ⁸Lifting weights, on the other hand, <u>is</u> anaerobic— building muscles but not strengthening the heart and lungs. ⁹Both walking and swimming <u>produce</u> good aerobic results without the risk of injury that is a drawback in running. ¹⁰Aerobic exercise, <u>says</u> medical experts, can increase endurance, lower blood pressure, and reduce stress.

QUICKCHECK ON SUBJECT-VERB AGREEMENT

Singular subjects take singular verbs; plural subjects take plural verbs.

Subjects joined by *and* are plural.

When two subjects are joined by *either . . . or* or *neither . . . nor,* the verb agrees with the nearer subject.

The object of a preposition is not the subject of a verb.

The subject usually comes before the verb, but sometimes it comes after.

There is never the subject of the sentence.

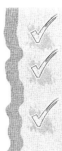

> Indefinite pronouns such as *each, either,* and *everybody* are singular.
>
> When used as subjects, *who, which,* and *that* agree with the words they stand for.
>
> Group nouns such as *committee, audience,* and *team* are usually singular.

CHECKPOINT 7

In the blanks at the left, write the subject and the correct verb form for each sentence.

(s) _____ 1. The crowd (was / were) well behaved at this summer's fair.

(v) _____

(s) _____ 2. There (is / are) several reasons why Mr. Ochoa votes as an independent.

(v) _____

(s) _____ 3. Neither the ambassadors nor the secretary of state (is / are) attending the conference.

(v) _____

(s) _____ 4. The restaurants in San Francisco (is / are) often praised.

(v) _____

(s) _____ 5. Neither of the chipmunks (was / were) interested in the bread.

(v) _____

(s) _____ 6. Either Mrs. Lozada or Mrs. Jones (is / are) singing the soprano part.

(v) _____

(s) _____ 7. Bouncing along the unpaved road (was / were) two old Jeeps.

(v) _____

(s) _____ 8. Toonerville has one of those bus lines that (is / are) always having problems.

(v) _____

(s) _____ 9. The E Street gang (has / have) turned over its guns to the police.

(v) _____

(s) _____ **10.** There (is / are) no trees in Iceland.

(v) _____

(s) _____ **11.** Of all his friends, Alex and Sam (is / are) Tim's best buddies.

(v) _____

(s) _____ **12.** The weather in St. Louis and Wichita (is / are) often cold in winter.

(v) _____

Wordcheck: Plurals

Using a dictionary when necessary, write the plural form of each word in the following list. The dictionary gives the plural form only for irregular plurals—those formed in some way other than by adding -s to the word. (The recommended spelling is usually given just after the pronunciation guide.)

woman	company
wolf	mother-in-law
potato	sheep
scissors	business

REVIEW CHECKUP This review quiz covers important terms used so far. Put the letter of the correct answer in the blank to the left of each definition.

_____ **1.** A part of a sentence mistakenly written as a complete sentence

    A. independent clause

    B. fragment

    C. run-together sentence

_____ **2.** The connectors that go with commas and independent clauses

    A. words like *although* and *since*

    B. words like *of, with, on, to,* and *by*

    C. words like *and, but, or, for, nor, yet,* and *so*

_____ **3.** The term for a word like *he, she, it,* and *they*

    A. pronoun

    B. preposition

    C. clause

_____ 4. A word that says what the subject does or is

    A. pronoun

    B. dependent word

    C. verb

_____ 5. A group of words containing a subject and a verb

    A. clause

    B. transitional words

    C. phrase

_____ 6. A group of words that could be a sentence

    A. fragment

    B. dependent clause

    C. independent clause

_____ 7. The name of a person, place, or thing

    A. noun

    B. verb

    C. preposition

_____ 8. The term for two sentences written as if they were one

    A. dependent clause

    B. run-together sentence

    C. fragment

_____ 9. A word like _although, since, because_

    A. dependent word

    B. fragment

    C. connecting word

_____ 10. The term that names who or what a sentence is about

    A. subject

    B. object

    C. verb

_____ 11. A word like _of, to, on, from,_ or _with_

    A. dependent word

    B. verb

    C. preposition

_____ 12. Transitional words that can be used after semicolons

    A. while, unless, although

    B. however, nonetheless, in fact

    C. through, among, between

GO ELECTRONIC!

For supplemental readings, exercises, and Internet activities, visit *Checkpoints Online* at
http://www.ablongman.com/page

Chapter 8

The Example Paragraph

READING PRECHECK

Two newspaper reporters give a chilling account of a gambling plague that is sweeping many parts of the country, destroying the lives not only of gambling addicts themselves but of their families as well. Notice how the writers use examples of actual people in telling this story.

> **JOURNAL TOPIC:** Write about your experiences with gambling or about other behavior that you feared might become a dangerous habit.

Addicted to Luck
Matea Gold and David Ferrell

Rex Coile's life is a narrow box, so dark and confining he wonders how he got **1** trapped inside and whether he'll ever get out. At 54, he never goes to the movies, never travels on vacation, never spends Christmas with his family.

compulsive uncontrollable
jackpots gambling winnings

Instead, Coile shares floor space in cheap motels with other compulsive **2** gamblers, comforting himself with dreams of jackpots that will magically wipe away three decades of wreckage. In the card clubs of Southern California, he lost his marriage, his home, his car, and not least of all, his pride.

And still, Coile is back at the card clubs. His pale eyes are expressionless, his **3** hair yellowish and brittle. It's hard to imagine he was once a prominent book editor.

At 11 p.m. one Tuesday, with a bankroll of $55—all he has—he is at a poker **4** table. The stack of $1 chips dwindles. Down $30, he says he'll stop at midnight. Midnight comes and goes. Coile starts winning. Chips pile up—$60, $70. "A

115

shame to go when the cards are falling my way," he says. "I'll go at two. Win, lose or draw."

The cards keep falling. At 2 a.m. Coile is up $97. He makes a new decision: "A few more hands." **5**

STEEP PRICE

Gambling is exploding across America, from the mega-resorts of Las Vegas to the gaming parlors of Indian reservations, from the riverboats along the Mississippi to the corner mini-marts selling lottery tickets. Now, with all but three states—Hawaii, Utah and Tennessee—sanctioning legalized gambling, evidence is mounting that society is paying a steep price. **6**

In 1997 bettors blew a whopping $50.9 billion—roughly five times the amount lost in 1980. That's more than the public spent on movies, theme parks, recorded music and sporting events combined. Of those losses an estimated 30 percent pours from problem gamblers **7**

Compulsive gambling has been linked to child abuse, domestic violence, bankruptcies, welfare fraud and other criminal ills. A survey of 228 members of Gamblers Anonymous found that almost half admitted to insurance fraud, embezzlement or arson. **8**

Today, 37 states run their own lotteries—generating almost $12 billion in net income—and spend millions on seductive advertisements. "When the cigarette industry did this with Joe Camel, the country was outraged," says Valerie Lorenz, executive director of the Compulsive Gambling Center in Baltimore. "Now our government is doing it." **9**

RUINED LIVES

Many gambling addicts share a common beginning: a hefty payday that they spend years trying to recapture. As they chase the elusive exhilaration of a big win, their families are often left to struggle for normality in a world of deceit and madness. Money starts vanishing: $200 here, $500 there. **10**

The husband of Jessica, a 42-year-old homemaker in Whittier, Calif., was making decent money as an industrial-plant manager. But, she says, "he fantasized about having this Monte Carlo existence." **11**

Lottery Keno became the rhythmic pulse of her husband's life. For five years he would leave the house at 5:30 a.m. every weekend and join other regulars at a local doughnut shop, watching the numbers flash on a monitor. He'd shuffle home hours later, refusing to divulge his losses. **12**

Like tens of thousands of spouses of compulsive gamblers, Jessica struggled to pay the bills. She hid money in cereal boxes, books, couch cushions. On paydays, when her husband's check was directly deposited into their account, they would race each other to the bank. Jessica would go to one branch and he'd head to another. She would sit at the drive-up window, jamming her withdrawal slip in the pneumatic tube the moment the bank opened. If she got the money, she could pay the utilities. If not, he'd be off to the races, the casinos, or the doughnut shop. . . . **13**

embezzlement theft in business

hefty big

NEW VICTIMS

Traditionally, compulsive gamblers have been middle-aged men. Today, though, **14** increasing numbers of women are getting hooked. And senior citizens are a lucrative new customer base. Lonely after the loss of a spouse or a career, some elderly see gambling as a harmless way to pass time.

A Florida resident, 62, started visiting the casinos in Biloxi, Miss., after her husband **15** died. "I withdrew from everything except gambling," she says. "It was a place to get away and no one was there who could remind me of Jim." The former school teacher lost almost $800,000 in 2 1/2 years and was arrested for writing bad checks . . . .

People like Gwen, a waitress and single mother, try to keep their heads **16** above water even as they are unable to comprehend their own obsession. Several years ago, on her son's tenth birthday, Gwen went to buy party supplies but ended up at the Commerce Casino. Hours passed as Gwen ran through the $2,000 in her bank account. Her family paged her, and her son begged her to come home. "Even if you don't have a present for me, it's okay," he said.

When she finally showed up the youngster was hunched in a corner, waiting. **17** "That's where he's been sitting all day," her sister said in disgust. Gwen approached him. "Mom," he asked, looking up, "why couldn't you come to my party?"

sears burns

The memory still sears. "I have hurt so many people with my gambling," says **18** Gwen, who now attend Gamblers Anonymous meetings. "A lot of people think gambling is harmless. They don't know it can make you steal and mistreat your loved ones. They don't know this is a deadly disease that can kill you."

Checking Meaning and Style

1. What career did Rex Coile once have? (Paragraph 3)
2. What new groups are getting hooked on gambling? (Paragraph 14)
3. Are Paragraphs 15 and 16 example or narrative paragraphs?
4. How did the one-year losses in gambling compare to money spent that year on movies, theme parks, recorded music, and sporting events? (Paragraph 7)
5. What social problems has gambling been associated with? (Paragraph 8)

Checking Ideas

1. Most states have legalized various types of gambling. Why do you think they have done this?
2. Do you favor states sponsoring and advertising lotteries? Explain.
3. In your opinion, are some types of gambling more addictive than others? If so, which?
4. There are many sources of addiction, such as cigarettes, alcohol, hard drugs, sex, and food. Are their causes at all related?

Analyzing Writing That Uses Examples

In "Addicted to Luck," the authors say America may pay too steep a price for legalizing gambling. They support this idea for most of the article with examples of specific people whose lives have been harmed by gambling. They also refer to gamblers in a general way: the "bettors" in Paragraph 7 and the gamblers in Paragraph 8 who are linked to child and spousal abuse, theft, and other criminal behavior.

Both approaches—using real-life examples and general or hypothetical examples—are illustrated in the model paragraphs that follow. In the first paragraph, a woman uses the real-life example of her parents to support the general idea in the topic sentence.

Model Paragraph 1

Even though it may sometimes be difficult, parents should give their teenage children considerable privacy. When my parents realized it was embarrassing for me to talk to boyfriends on the phone in the kitchen, they had a phone installed in my bedroom. If I was in my room with the door closed, they always knocked and asked if it was all right to come in. Of course I can't know for sure, but I'm confident they never searched my room for drugs or whatever else it is parents are often suspicious about. They respected my privacy, so I always tried to behave in a way that justified their trust.

The next paragraph, which takes a different view of privacy, uses hypothetical parents or "parents in general" as examples. Like Model #1, it starts with a topic sentence that states the main idea.

Model Paragraph 2

With more teenagers getting into serious drug trouble these days, parents need to keep a close watch on their children, even if it means "invading" their privacy now and then. Parents should listen in on their children's phone conversations and be sufficiently acquainted with slang to know that Johnny's remark about "snow" is not about a ski trip. When Mom puts clean clothes in the kids' dresser drawers, she should keep an eye out for suspicious bags or surprising wads of money. Dad might call the attendance office at school now and then just to be sure that's where Susie is spending her days. Parents may not like playing the role of narcotics agents, but that may save their children from the real narcs later on.

Writing Assignment: An Example Paragraph

Write an interesting, unified paragraph on one of the numbered subjects. Use either real-life or hypothetical examples to support the topic sentence.

1. Women (Men) can be hard to understand.
2. Some teachers bring out the best (worst) in a student.
3. Working mothers usually have busy lives.

4. AIDS can cause the victim and his or her family much suffering.
5. People who use drugs are inviting trouble.

 Writing Topic Bank

Making College Better

What are some ways that your college could be improved? Think about times you or your friends and classmates get frustrated in college. How could these aspects of college be improved? Write a paragraph that gives examples of helpful improvements.

Exploring Human Rights on the Internet

Go to the Amnesty International website library at www.amnesty.org/ailib/. Choose a country, region, or theme from the menu. Using one or more of the articles listed under your choice of country, region, or theme, write a paragraph giving examples of the human rights violations described in the article(s).

Writing About Media

A quick tour of your library's or your bookstore's magazine section will demonstrate the wide range of subject matter covered by the magazine industry. Choose a magazine that you consider unusual. Write a paragraph using examples of articles from the magazine to show how it is unusual.

WRITING CHECKLIST

 Start with a topic sentence that makes clear your central point. (One of the numbered topics above may be used as a topic sentence.)

 Develop the topic with a prewriting technique. Brainstorming, nonstop writing, or asking how and why would seem most useful.

 In revising your first draft, be sure the topic sentence leads to a unified, convincing paragraph. Correct any sentence fragments, run-together sentences, or faulty verb forms.

 Proofread the final copy, looking for small, overlooked mistakes.

Sentence Sense: Using the Right Pronoun

If we didn't have pronouns, our writing might read something like this:

> The man asked the woman what time it was. The woman told the man the time was ten o'clock. The man thanked the woman.

With pronouns, we can avoid the annoying repetition of nouns.

> The man asked the woman if *she* knew what time it was. *She* told *him* that it was ten o'clock. *He* thanked *her*.

The pronouns *she, her, he, him,* and *it* take the place of the nouns *woman, man* and *time* to make the writing smoother.

Pronoun Case

Pronouns change their form or case depending on whether they are used in a sentence as subjects or objects. In the previous example, we noticed that both *she* and *her* refer to *woman*.

Singular		Plural	
Subject	**Object**	**Subject**	**Object**
I	me	we	us
you	you	you	you
he	him	they	them
she	her	they	them
it	it	they	them

 **SPOTCHECK 8–1**   Enter the appropriate pronoun forms in the blanks.

Subject	Object		Subject	Object
1. he	_____	5.	I	_____
2. _____	them	6.	_____	us
3. it	_____	7.	you	_____
4. _____	her	8.	_____	him

Using Subject and Object Forms of Pronouns

Use the subject form when the pronoun is the subject of the sentence.

> I will deliver the message.

> They traveled in Nicaragua.

THE FAR SIDE® By GARY LARSON

"So, then ... would that be 'us the people' or
'we the people'?"

Notice that subject form pronouns usually come before the verb.

Use the <u>object form</u> in these situations:

1. When the pronoun is acted upon by the verb (is the direct object).

>   **verb object**
> The boss **praised *her***.

>   **verb   object**
> The biology test **confused *me***.

2. When the pronoun is the *indirect object* of the verb. To find an indirect object, ask *for whom* or *to whom* something is done.

> The doctor <u>gave</u> *us* blood tests.

To whom were the tests given? To *us. Us* is the indirect object of the verb *gave.* (*Tests* is the direct object.)

> Martin <u>has done</u> *me* many favors.

For whom were the favors done? For *me. Me* is the indirect object of the verb *has done.* (*Favors* is the direct object.)

Notice that direct object pronouns and indirect object pronouns usually come after the verb.

3. When the pronoun follows (is the object of) a preposition.

> The letter was addressed <u>to</u> *her.*

> The ball rolled <u>between</u> *us.*

SPOTCHECK 8-2   Indicate whether the underlined pronoun is the subject (S), the direct object (DO), indirect object (IO), or object of a preposition (OP). This will require some thinking!

_____ 1. The police found <u>him</u> under a bush.

_____ 2. The bus driver gave <u>us</u> a route schedule.

_____ 3. Henri's father warned <u>him</u> against using drugs.

_____ 4. Olivia saw <u>him</u> at the movie premier.

_____ 5. The guard stood between <u>us</u> and the president.

_____ 6. The officer decided not to give <u>them</u> a parking ticket.

_____ 7. At noontime, <u>they</u> walked around the lake.

_____ 8. The package was addressed to <u>her</u>.

SPOTCHECK 8-3   Substitute a pronoun for the underlined words. Indicate whether the pronoun is the subject, direct object, indirect object, or object of a preposition. Write your answers in the blanks.

    Example: The government sent <u>Mr. Nelson</u> a big income tax refund.

         <u> him </u>   <u>indirect object</u>

1. <u>The Nelsons</u> built a swimming pool in their backyard.

    _____   _____

2. Workers finished <u>the pool</u> in four weeks.

    _____   _____

3. The crew boss gave <u>Mr. Nelson</u> a pair of fins.

    _____   _____

4. Mr. Nelson gave the fins to <u>his son</u>.

    _____   _____

5. The son uses <u>the fins</u> almost every day.

    _____   _____

Pronouns in Compound Subjects and Objects

Usually we don't have much trouble using the correct pronoun form. For example, we're not likely to say or write, "*Me* saw *she* at the movies."

But there are a few times when pronoun errors are likely to appear. One of them is when there is more than one subject or object. Which pronoun is correct in these sentences?

Between you and (I / me), Yoshi should have got the job.

The object form *me* is needed as the object of the preposition *between.*

The family sent Mark and (he / him) thank-you letters.

Him is the indirect object of the verb *sent.*

The Pritams and (we / us) deserve credit for the job.

We is part of the subject, along with the *Pritams.*

The audience applauded the violinist and (she / her).

Her is the object of the verb *applauded,* along with *violinist.*

If you had trouble with any of those, here's a tip that should clear up your problem: When the pronoun is accompanied by another word in a compound subject or object, cross out the other word. Your ear then will probably tell you the correct form.

The audience applauded ~~the violinist and~~ (she / her).

"Sorry, but I'm going to have to issue you a summons for reckless grammar and driving without an apostrophe."

Of course, the audience applauded *her.* In the same way, your ear would tell you, in sentence 2, that the family sent *him* a letter.

> **NOTE** It is considered a courtesy to refer to the other person first in such uses as "Mildred and I went . . ." or ". . . sent to my husband and me."

 **SPOTCHECK 8–4**   Underline the correct pronoun after crossing out any accompanying words that might cause confusion.

Example: The package was addressed to ~~Bill and~~ (I / <u>me</u>).

1. The umpire and (he / him) got into an argument.

2. The store gave the other shoppers and (we / us) free passes.

3. The doctor handed the prescriptions to my husband and (I / me).

4. The fire siren frightened (we / us) pedestrians.

5. The station attendant told Marlys and (he / him) to return in an hour.

6. (We / Us) Texans should be proud of our state.

7. Lilith and (he / him) are looking for part-time jobs.

8. The race ended in a tie between the Spartan runner and (she / her). (Note that the crossout method doesn't work with the preposition *between.*)

Pronouns in Comparisons

Problems in choosing the right pronoun can also appear in comparisons. Which pronoun is right in this comparison?

Alfredo studies harder than (I / me).

At least in somewhat formal writing, *I* would be preferred. Why? Because I is the subject of the implied verb *study.* Look at these comparisons in which the verb is implied but not stated:

We go to the movies more often than *they* [*do or go*].

Calvin is not as interested in jazz as *I* [*am*].

(Always include the verb if you're worried about sounding "prim," like Mr. Fleagle in the reading "The Art of Eating Spaghetti.")

Who and *Whom*

Many people feel a little uncomfortable when they have to choose between the pronouns *who* and *whom*. Keep in mind that *who* is the subject form and *whom* is the object form.

> Mr. Lee saw the thief *who* had robbed his market the night before. (*Who* is the subject of the verb *had robbed*.)
>
> It was Irene *whom* the class elected. (*Whom* is the object of the verb *elected*.)
>
> To *whom* was the package addressed? (*Whom* is the object of the preposition *to*.)

Whom is not much used in conversation or informal writing. It seems too fancy or pretentious. For instance, many people would prefer to say "Who was the package addressed to?" and avoid the formally correct *whom*. You will have to decide when the formal approach is better. If in doubt, use *who*.

Watch out for sentences like this one:

> It was Meredith (who / whom) the judge thought had the best painting.

Who is the subject of the verb *had*. It is not the object of the verb *thought* in the parenthetical expression *the judge thought*.

Self Pronouns

Careful writers do not use *-self* pronouns like *myself* and *themselves* in place of regular pronouns (*me, them*, etc.)

> The President awarded medals to Sergeant Washington and *me*. (not *myself*)
>
> Nancy and *you* (not *yourself*) will arrange the centerpiece.

The *-self* words have two uses. One is to provide emphasis.

> The President *himself* presented the medals to us.

The other use is to reflect the action back to the performer of the action.

> Mrs. Nakano stuck *herself* with a pin while arranging the flowers.

> **NOTE** Avoid using *hisself* and *theirselves* for the standard *himself* and *themselves*.

 **SPOTCHECK 8-5** Underline the correct pronouns.

1. Monica studies harder than (I / me).

2. The actors applauded (theirselves / themselves) with enthusiasm.

3. The president never said (who / whom) he suspected of leaking the story.

4. Did you notice (who / whom) gave the teacher an apple?

5. Scott (himself / hisself) put out the fire.

DOUBLECHECK 8–1   **Underline the correct pronouns.**

1. The superintendent sent the accounting staff and (we / us) sales people to the second floor.

2. It looks as if you and (they / them) will have to do all the work.

3. Deliver the package to the person (who / whom) is at the front desk.

4. The discussion between the mayor and (he / him / himself) finally ended in agreement.

5. My husband and (I / me / myself) are both from Birmingham.

6. The boys will have to clean up the bedroom (theirselves / themselves).

7. That is the person (who / whom) I think got out of the taxi.

8. The tailor will finish Nona's suit (himself / hisself).

9. Was it Shakespeare (who / whom) said, "Always have a friend with a truck"?

10. Guillermo has more money than (I / me) since he got his raise.

11. Just between you and (I / me), the Knicks will win the championship.

12. (We / Us) farmers are the backbone of the nation.

13. Either the sophomores or (we / us) freshmen will lead the parade.

14. Senator Foghorn is the candidate (who / whom) experts say will win the election.

15. (I and the pediatrician / The pediatrician and I) live on the same block.

DOUBLECHECK 8–2   **Write sentences using the words in parentheses.**

1. (herself) _____

_____

2. (whom) _____

_____

3. (me) _____

_____

4. (themselves) _____

_____

5. (who) _____

_____

6. (Patrick and she) _____

_____

7. (the mayor and me) _____

_____

 **EDITING CHECK 8**   **Edit the following paragraph to correct any pronoun errors, as in the first sentence.**

¹"This is just between you and <s>I</s> me," Helen said to her friend Gloria. ²"I don't trust Bill for a minute. ³He said he would pick up Francine and myself at nine o'clock outside the library. ⁴Francine and me stood there until ten without any sign of Bill. ⁵Luckily, the last bus was still there for Francine and me. ⁶This morning Bill told us that we women are always taking advantage of he and the other guys. ⁷He said that he hisself has been stood up by women plenty of times. ⁸I don't doubt it, him being the way he is. ⁹Guys like Bill should straighten theirselves out before it's too late." ¹⁰"No one knows that better than me," Gloria responded.

✓ **CHECKPOINT 8**   Write the formally correct pronouns in the spaces at the left.

_____ 1. The palm reader said Harry and (I / me) would be famous before we're thirty.

_____ 2. Angela can sing much better than (I / me).

_____ 3. On Vicente's team, it's every man for (himself / hisself).

_____ 4. Shawna was pleased when Harmon gave (she / her) an engagement ring.

_____ 5. Was it Tom Cruise (who / whom) we saw in the movie Friday night?

_____ 6. The relationship is close between the Herzogs and (we / us).

_____ 7. José can play the saxophone better than (he / him).

_____ 8. The invitation was intended for both Pat and (you / yourself).

_____ 9. Everyone in the library heard the argument between Lester and (I / me).

_____ 10. Luciano Dante is the produce man (who / whom) it seems wins all the prizes.

_____ 11. Francisco never should have tried to lift the box (himself / hisself).

_____ 12. Anitra can dance better than (she / her).

_____ 13. About (who / whom) were Pam and Cindy arguing?

_____ 14. Rita and (she / her) always get along well.

_____ 15. Except for you and (I / me), no one seems to know what is going on.

Wordcheck: Synonyms

Synonyms are two words with the same or similar meanings—*car* and *automobile,* for instance. A dictionary lists synonyms after the definitions of some words. Notice that two synonyms do not usually mean *exactly* the same thing. (For a reference work specializing in synonyms, turn to a thesaurus.)

List at least two synonyms for each of these words:

1. mysterious   _____   _____

2. magic   _____   _____

3. poor   _____   _____

4. anger   _____   _____

5. deceive   _____   _____

GO ELECTRONIC!

For supplemental readings, exercises, and Internet activities, visit *Checkpoints Online* at
http://www.ablongman.com/page

The Comparison/ Comparison/ Contrast Paragraph

READING PRECHECK

Are guns like cars, and should they be licensed like cars? If so, David B. Kopel argues in this 1999 essay, then they should be treated similarly across the board. Kopel shows what changes this would require by offering numerous comparisons in the ways guns and cars are sold, regulated, and thought about.

> JOURNAL TOPIC: A bumper sticker that was popular for a while read "If guns are outlawed, only outlaws will have guns." Do you agree?

Taking It to the Streets
David B. Kopel

Should we treat guns like cars? Handgun Control Inc. has been saying so for years, and this summer Vice President Al Gore agreed. "We require a license to drive a car in this nation in order to keep unsafe drivers off the road," Gore said. "As president, I will fight for a national requirement that every state issue photo licenses [for handgun buyers]. We should require a license to own a handgun so people who shouldn't have them can't get them." Prospective licensees should have to "pass a background test and pass a gun safety test." Gore predicted that his plan would cause the gun lobby to "have a fit." 1

prospective   likely to become

Actually, if Gore follows through with his promise to treat guns like cars, he will oversee the most massive decontrol of firearms in America since 1868, when the 14th Amendment abolished the Southern states' Black Codes, which 2

130

lobbyist person who tries to influence public officials

prevented freedmen from owning guns. Although anti-gun lobbyists who use the car analogy are pushing for additional controls, laws that really did treat guns like cars would be much less restrictive, on the whole, than what we have now.

The first thing to go would be the 1986 federal ban on the manufacture of **3** machine guns for sale to ordinary citizens. We don't ban cars like Porsches just because they're high-powered and can drive much faster than the speed limit. Even though it's a lot easier to go 50 miles per hour over the highway speed limit in a Porsche than in a Hyundai, we let people own any car they want, no matter what its potential for abuse.

analog something that is similar to another thing

After getting rid of the machine gun ban, the next step toward treating cars **4** like guns would be repealing the 1994 federal "assault weapon" ban and its analogs in California, Massachusetts, New Jersey, and a few other jurisdictions. So-called assault weapons are actually ordinary guns that fire just one bullet each time the trigger is pressed, but they happen to look like machine guns. Just as we don't ban powerful Porsches (which actually can go very fast), we don't ban less-powerful vehicles that simply look like high-performance cars.

Likewise, we don't ban autos because they are underpowered, or because **5** they're made with low-quality metal. If you want a Yugo, you can buy one. So the state-level bans on inexpensive guns (a.k.a. "junk guns" or "Saturday night specials") will have to go, along with the federal rules against the import of cheap guns.

a.k.a. "also known as"

Also slated for elimination under the treat-cars-like-guns rule are thousands of **6** laws regulating the purchase of firearms and their possession on private property. The simple purchase of an automobile is subject to essentially no restrictions. When you show up at a dealer's showroom, he will not conduct a background check to find out if you have a conviction for vehicular homicide, or if you've been arrested for drunk driving, or even if you have a driver's license. All you need is money.

The only "waiting period" to buy a car runs from the time you pay for it (with **7** cash, a certified check, or a loan document) to the time the salesman hands you the keys. This waiting period tends to run from 30 seconds to five minutes. In contrast, firearms are the only product in this country for which FBI permission (via the national background check) is required for every single retail purchase. . . .

Now suppose that you want to use your car on public property, such as a **8** street or an old logging trail in a national forest. Then a licensing system comes into play—but only because the car will be used in public. For a license that allows you to drive a car anywhere in public, most states require that you (1) be at least 15 or 16 years old; (2) take a written safety test that requires an IQ of no more than 75 to pass; and (3) show an examiner that you know how to operate a car and how to obey basic safety rules and traffic signs.

Your license may be revoked or suspended if, while driving in public, you violate certain safety rules or cause an accident. Except in egregious cases (such as **9** killing someone while driving with extreme recklessness), first or second offenses do not usually result in license revocations. Once the driver's license is issued, it is good in every state of the union.

These driver's license requirements seem to be what Gore has in mind for **10** handguns, although he fails to recognize that the requirements apply only to cars used in public, not cars possessed in private. The vice president's mistake is understandable, given his lack of driving experience in the years since the taxpayers have been paying for his full-time chauffeur. (In July, Gore warned that the 2000 election is "no time to take a far-right U-turn." He apparently did not realize that on American roads, it is impossible to make a U-turn to the right.)

concealed hidden

The guns-like-cars licensing system touted by Gore is already in effect in 30 states, where adults with a clean record can obtain a permit to carry a concealed handgun for lawful protection. (Vermont requires no permit.) Making the concealed handgun licensing system exactly like the driver licensing system would involve a few tweaks, namely: (1) reducing the minimum age for a license (21 or 25 in most states); (2) reducing the fees (which can run over $100 in many states); (3) mandating a written exam in the minority of states that do not currently have one; (4) adding a practical demonstration test, which most states do not currently have (but which Texas does); and (5) making the licenses valid everywhere, instead of just in the issuing state. And of course, the 19 states that currently don't give handgun carry permits to every person with a clean record would have to change their laws. . . . **11**

mandating requiring

prohibitionist a person in favor of making something illegal

Faced with the prospect of really treating guns like cars, gun prohibitionists tend to change their minds. They begin arguing that there are important differences in dangerousness between guns and cars. This is true. Cars are much more dangerous. **12**

The Independence Institute's Robert Racansky points out that in 1994 (the last year for which data are available), there were 32 auto deaths for every 100,000 autos in the United States. The same year, there were 16 firearm deaths for every 100,000 firearms in the United States. Put another way, in any given year, the average car is twice as likely as the average gun to cause a death. **13**

And more than 95 percent of gun deaths are intentional (suicide or homicide), while most auto deaths are accidents. This shows how dangerous cars really are: They are twice as likely to kill as guns are, even though the killer behind the wheel does not intend to take a life. Plus, most people who die from guns are suicides who choose to die, but almost none of the people who die in car crashes choose to die. **14**

explicitly clearly expressed

Another argument against treating guns like cars, of course, is that gun ownership is explicitly protected by the U.S. Constitution and by 44 state constitutions, while car ownership has no such special status. On the other hand, if the groups that call for treating guns like cars followed their own advice, they would immediately disband. There are no major Washington lobby groups arguing that people should be able to buy a car only if they government decides they need one, or that people should use only public transportation, instead of private vehicles, during life-threatening emergencies. **15**

Yet Handgun Control Inc.'s Sarah Brady favors "needs-based licensing" for firearms. "To me," she told the *Tampa Tribune*, "the only reason for guns in civilian hands is for sporting purposes." In response to the question of whether there are legitimate reasons for owning a handgun, Brady's husband and fellow anti-gun activist, Jim Brady, told *Parade* magazine: "For target shooting, that's OK. Get a license and go to the range. For defense of the home, that's why we have police departments." **16**

A few days after the Columbine High School murders last April, Steve Abrams   17
deliberately drove his Cadillac onto a playground in Costa Mesa, California, killing a
3-year-old and a 4-year-old. No one showed up on television to claim that General
Motors, car owners in general, or anyone other than Steve Abrams was responsible
for this crime. Politicians did not try to use Abrams' murderous act to create a cam-
paign issue or stir up support for restrictions on law-abiding car owners. If gun
owners were treated like car owners, they would not be vilified by smug moral
imperialists with the energetic assistance of the president and most of the national
news media. Sad to say, that would be progress.

vilify make vicious statements
about

Checking Meaning and Style

1. Kopel says that if guns are treated like cars in one way, then they should be
   treated like cars in many other ways. What are five of these ways?
2. This essay uses groups of paragraphs to discuss different general points of
   comparison. For example, paragraphs 3–5 discuss the banning of certain
   types of guns. Which groups of paragraphs cover these general comparisons: laws regarding the purchase of guns, licensing requirements and laws,
   the danger of guns, reasons for owning guns?
3. What is Kopel's main point? In what paragraph does he state the main
   point?
4. What statistics and examples does Kopel give to support the point that cars
   are more dangerous than guns?
5. How are the licensing requirements for driving and owning a gun similar?
   How are they different?
6. The last paragraph is a narrative about a driver who killed two children.
   What point is this anecdote intended to make?

Checking Ideas

1. Thirty-one states allow adults to carry concealed weapons. Is that a good idea?
2. Is it a good idea for the FBI to conduct a background check of anyone who
   wants to buy a gun? Why or why not?
3. Do you think that the same laws should apply to car drivers and gun owners?
4. Kopel states that gun ownership is protected by the U.S. Constitution as
   well as 44 state constitutions. Why do you think are there so many laws protecting citizens' rights to bear arms?
5. Do you think guns should be freely available, somewhat restricted, or taken
   off the market completely?

Analyzing Comparison Writing

In everyday life, you continually make comparisons: between your car and your
friend's car, between high school and college, between Rosa's new hairdo and her
old one, between Brand X toothpaste and Brand Y, between becoming a beach
bum and a nuclear physicist.

In college, exams and term papers often ask that you compare and contrast two poems, two characters in a play, or two economic policies. *Comparison* emphasizes the way things are similar; *contrast* emphasizes differences. However, *comparison* can cover both similarities and differences. We'll use the term *comparison* in this broad sense.

There are two basic ways of organizing a comparison of two items. One is the point-by-point method. In this method, the writer goes back and forth between the two items, discussing one point of similarity or difference at a time. This is the approach used in "Taking It to the Streets," as we see in the following outline of four major points of the essay.

POINT-BY-POINT METHOD

Point 1: Banning of certain types (Paragraphs 3–5)

Ban of machine guns similar to a ban on high-powered cars

Ban of assault weapons similar to banning cars that look like high-performance cars

Ban of inexpensive guns similar to banning underpowered cars

Point 2: Purchase requirements (Paragraphs 6–7)

Background check to buy a gun versus only needing money to buy a car

Waiting period to buy a gun versus no waiting period to buy a car

Point 3: Licensing requirements (Paragraphs 8–11)

Minimum age differences between gun and car ownership

Written and practical exams required for driving but only in some states for guns

Cost of fees typically less for driver's license than for gun license

Point 4: Dangerousness (Paragraphs 12–14)

Average car is twice as likely as the average gun to cause death

More than 95 percent of gun deaths are intentional while most auto deaths are accidents

The following paragraph shows how a single paragraph could be written following the point-by-point method.

Model Comparison Paragraph 1

My wife and I have had to make many adjustments in our marriage because she is from the North (New Jersey) and I am from the South (Georgia). For example, we sometimes seem to speak different languages.

She refers to a soda such as Coke as "pop." She congratulated me on taking up a "foreign language" when I enrolled in a college English course. When it comes to music, I have no enthusiasm for her Top 40 favorites, and she fails to appreciate my country music idols. I like my vegetables cooked just this side of mushy; she thinks the far side of raw is just right. Yes, we have our cultural differences.

BLOCK METHOD

Here is an outline of the <u>block</u> method that might have been used with the same material.

Block A: Husband

    1. Use of language

    2. Preference in music

    3. Preference in food

Block B: Wife

    1. Use of language

    2. Preference in music

    3. Preference in food

This block outline could have resulted in a paragraph such as this:

Model Comparison Paragraph 2

My wife and I have had to make many adjustments in our marriage because she is from the North (New Jersey) and I am from the South (Georgia). For example, we sometimes have different names for things; I certainly don't refer to a Coke as "pop." My favorite musicians are country singers like Reba McEntire. I like my vegetables to know they've been cooked. My wife, on the other hand, congratulated me on taking up a "foreign language" when I enrolled in an English class. Her taste in music runs to Top 40 performers like Prince. Properly cooked vegetables, to her, have had only a brief acquaintance with a stove. Yes, we have our cultural differences.

The following model paragraph compares two sisters to illustrate the block method of comparison.

Model Comparison Paragraph 3

One would never guess by looking at us that Carla and I are sisters. Carla is tall and slender: five-feet-seven and 120 pounds. She has blonde hair, which she cuts and perms in the latest style. Carla has blue eyes and fair skin.

She likes to wear tailored suits during the day and slinky dresses when she goes out evenings. I, on the other hand, am five-feet-two and weigh 130 pounds. My hair is dark and straight and reaches to the middle of the back; if I want to be fancy, I make braids or add a ribbon. My eyes are brown, and my skin has a perpetual tan. To complete the differences, I'm content to wear jeans on most occasions, but I will put on my best sandals and a peasant skirt to attend a friend's wedding. Carla takes after our mother, while I am more like my dad—Carl.

In the next paragraph, the sisters are compared using the point-by-point method.

Model Comparison Paragraph 4

One would never guess by looking at us that Carla and I are sisters. Carla is tall and slender: five-feet-seven and 120 pounds. I am five-two and 130 pounds. Carla has blonde hair, which she cuts and perms in the latest style. My hair is dark and straight and reaches to the middle of the back; if I want to be fancy, I make braids or add a ribbon. Carla has blue eyes and fair skin, while my eyes are brown, and my skin has a perpetual tan. To complete the differences, Carla likes to wear tailored suits during the day and slinky dresses when she goes out evenings. I'm content to wear jeans on most occasions, but I will put on my best sandals and a peasant skirt to attend a friend's wedding. Carla takes after our mother, while I am more like our dad—Carl.

Four categories are used in the point-by-point comparison of Carla and her sister: height and weight, hair style, eyes and skin, and clothing.

Writing Assignment:
A Comparison Paragraph

Write a paragraph of comparison using either the point-by-point method or the block method. Write on one of these topics:

1. Two movie stars, television performers, or musicians

2. College classes and high school classes

3. Part-time students and full-time students

4. Two houses or neighborhoods you have lived in

5. Two cities, states, or countries you have lived in

WRITING CHECKLIST

 Develop your ideas through journal writing, nonstop writing, clustering, or one or more of the other prewriting methods discussed earlier.

 Start with a topic sentence that makes clear the point of your comparison. Examples:

> College courses are more challenging than high school courses in several ways.

> Life is more comfortable since my family moved from an apartment to a house.

Your topic sentence:

_____

_____

 Answer the following questions to outline your paragraph.

1. What two people, places, or things are you comparing?
2. List three different ways you will compare the two.

_____

_____

_____

3. Will you organize the paragraph with the point-by-point method or the block method?

 Look out for pronoun and verb errors and the kinds of problems marked on earlier papers.

 As always, proofread the final copy before turning it in.

📓 Writing Topic Bank

Exceptions to the Rule

Think of a law, rule, or common social expectation (for example: using cross-walks, meeting deadlines, or opening doors for others) that you don't always follow. Write a paragraph comparing times when you follow the rule with times when you don't follow the rule.

Exploring Politics on the Internet

Use any search engine you like (such as Excite.com, Yahoo.com, Google.com, Dogpile.com) to locate the websites of a political candidate and her/his opponent(s) whose election efforts are of interest to you. Write a paragraph describing the differences between the candidates.

Writing About Media

Many popular songs have been "covered" or re-recorded by artists other than the one whose version of the song first made it popular. Also, some recording artists interpret their music quite differently in live concert than they do in the studio, or even in different studio sessions. Using two versions of a song that you enjoy, write a paragraph explaining why you like one version more than the other.

Sentence Sense:
Pronoun Agreement and Clear Reference

The word a pronoun refers to is called its antecedent. In this sentence, *Marta* is the antecedent of the pronoun *she:*

> Marta was given a scholarship because she is a talented violinist.

A pronoun must *agree* in number with its antecedent; that is, both must be singular or both plural.

> The robin has left its nest.

> The robins have left their nest.

It's easy to see that the singular pronoun *its* agrees with the singular antecedent *robin* and the plural pronoun *their* agrees with the plural antecedent *robins.* But you probably won't be surprised to learn that things are not always that simple.

> Each of the men brought (his/their) own tools.

You may have been tempted to choose *their,* but *his* is right. The singular pronoun *his* agrees with the singular subject *each. Men* is the object of the preposition *of* and, therefore, not the sentence subject. These *indefinite pronouns* are usually singular:

one	someone	each
anyone	everybody	either
everyone	nobody	neither

The indefinite pronouns *both, several,* and *few* are always plural.

 **SPOTCHECK 9–1** Underline the correct pronouns. It may help to cross out prepositional phrases first.

1. Each of the television sets was missing (its / their) remote control.

2. Both of the orchestras have (its / their) good points.

3. Neither Chris nor Clint could find (his / their) textbook.

4. Someone left (her / their) purse on the counter.

5. A woman who goes into carpentry will find (her / their) situation challenging.

6. Everybody should pay (his / their) taxes by April 15.

Avoiding Sex Bias

You may not have liked the answer for sentence 6 above. You might have asked yourself why *everybody* should take the masculine pronoun *his* when the word could just as easily refer to women as to men. In the past, indefinite antecedents (neither masculine nor feminine) have worked that way. But many people today believe that method gives a sexist bias to the language. Unfortunately, there is no easy way around the problem.

The most common "solution" is to use the plural pronoun *their*, which is neither masculine nor feminine. Thus we would have: "Everybody should pay their taxes. . . ." But this combination of plural pronoun and singular antecedent is considered ungrammatical by many and, at least in writing, should be avoided.

A somewhat better possibility is to say *his or her* in such situations, but this solution can be awkward if the words must be repeated very often.

> **(awkward)** Each applicant should bring *his or her* résumé to the office and be prepared to discuss *his or her* work experience with *his or her* interviewer.

A better approach, when possible, is to make the antecedent plural. This permits use of the gender-free pronoun *they.*

> **(revised)** All applicants should bring *their* resumes to the office and be prepared to discuss *their* work experience with *their* interviewers.

Other ways of wording a sentence sometimes can be used.

> **(awkward)** Did everyone remember to bring his or her sweater?
>
> **(better)** Did everyone remember to bring a sweater?
>
> **(biased)** Everyone should pay his taxes by April 15.
>
> **(better)** Taxes should be paid by April 15.

 **SPOTCHECK 9–2**   Rewrite these sentences to avoid sex bias and lack of pronoun agreement.

1. Everybody in the office brought his own lunch.

   _____

2. Each of the drivers had to show their license.

   _____

3. If a person takes a shower instead of a bath, he uses only about half as much hot water.

   _____

4. A fan who brings his ticket stub from the rained-out game will get in free.

   _____

Group Noun Antecedents

Group nouns—such as *team, committee, flock*—refer to more than one person or thing but usually are regarded as referring to a single unit. They therefore take singular pronouns.

> The committee will hold its [not *their*] next meeting Tuesday.

> The gas company promised to lower its rates before winter.

 **SPOTCHECK 9–3**   Underline the correct pronoun in parentheses.

1. The Minneapolis Symphony is on (its / their) fourth tour of Japan.

2. The women's soccer team scored (its / their) fifth straight victory.

3. After arguing for three hours, the committee revealed (its / their) decision.

4. Both of the daughters brought (her / their) textbooks home over the holidays.

5. Not one of the theaters opened (its / their) doors before 9 p.m.

 **DOUBLECHECK 9–1**   Put a check mark in front of the better sentence in each of the following pairs.

_____ **1a.** One of the companies gave its employees turkeys at Christmas.

_____ **1b.** One of the companies gave their employees turkeys at Christmas.

_____ **2a.** Anyone who sings well should put his name on the list.

_____ **2b.** Those who sing well should put their names on the list.

_____ **3a.** Neither France nor Germany would change their policy.

_____ **3b.** Neither France nor Germany would change its policy.

_____ **4a.** Not everyone will admit it when he has made a mistake.

_____ **4b.** Some people won't admit it when they have made a mistake.

_____ **5a.** The American Legion will hold their annual convention in Pocatello.

_____ **5b.** The American Legion will hold its annual convention in Pocatello.

_____ **6a.** Both the carpenter and the electrician lost his job.

_____ **6b.** Both the carpenter and the electrician lost their jobs.

_____ **7a.** Everybody brought a "We're No. 1" banner to the football game.

_____ **7b.** Everybody brought his "We're No. 1" banner to the football game.

_____ **8a.** Macy's will hold their "White Flower Day" sale Monday.

_____ **8b.** Macy's will hold its "White Flower Day" sale Monday.

_____ **9a.** Drivers who don't wear seat belts should have their heads examined.

_____ **9b.** A driver who doesn't wear a seat belt should have his head examined.

_____ **10a.** One of those lipsticks cost more than they're worth.

_____ **10b.** One of those lipsticks costs more than it's worth.

Clear Pronoun Reference

Pronouns like *he* and *they* have no meaning in themselves. They get their identity from the words they refer to, their antecedents. This connection must always be clear. Consider this sentence:

Chris told his father he needed a haircut.

Who needs a haircut, Chris or his father? The pronoun *he* does not have a clear antecedent. Assuming it is the father who needs a haircut, the problem could be solved this way:

Chris told his father, "You need a haircut."

In the next example, is it Judy or Beth who is in college?

(unclear) Judy phoned Beth once a week when she was in college.

(clear) When Beth was in college, Judy phoned her once a week.

Here's a real-life example from the broadcast of an outfield play in a baseball game (find the lost pronoun):

. . . Winfield goes back to the wall. He hits his head on the wall, and it rolls off. It's rolling all the way back to second base!

 **SPOTCHECK 9–4** Rewrite these sentences to make the pronoun reference clear.

1. As the cat approached the raccoon, it hissed loudly.

_____

_____

2. After Lewis beat Ted in the conference 100-meter race, he never raced again.

_____

_____

3. I never buy CDs at flea markets because they might be counterfeit.

_____

_____

4. The truck hit the police car, but it wasn't damaged.

_____

_____

5. Frank told the instructor that he had a poor understanding of geometry.

_____

_____

Vague Pronoun Reference

A pronoun should refer clearly to a specific word or group of words. The pronouns *it, this, that,* and *which* sometimes appear without clear antecedents.

(weak) Mr. Armajani gave his wife a dozen roses. This pleased her. (*This* has no specific antecedent.)

(revised) Mr. Armajani gave his wife a dozen roses. The gift pleased her.

(weak) Sue had always wanted to go into law, so she was excited when she finally achieved it. (*It* has no antecedent.)

(revised) Sue had always wanted to go into law, so she was excited when she finally got her law degree.

Avoid the vague use of the pronouns *you, they,* and *it.*

(weak) When you take an English course, you should revise your papers carefully.

(revised) Students who take English courses should revise their papers carefully.

(weak) They say a storm is on the way.

(revised) The weather bureau says a storm is on the way.

(weak) In the newspaper, it says Tenth Avenue will be closed for repairs.

(revised) The newspaper says Tenth Avenue will be closed for repairs.

 **SPOTCHECK 9–5**   Revise these sentences to avoid weak pronoun reference.

1. Clint did weight-training for a year before it became noticeable.

_____

_____

2. Jeffrey wants to be a rodeo rider, but he has never attended one.

_____

_____

3. If you want to keep a job, you have to get to work on time.

_____

_____

4. They always listen to the one who complains the loudest.

_____

_____

5. I did not respond to her invitation, <u>which</u> was not very polite.

_____

_____

6. Mr. Quach goes to the community pool every day because <u>it</u> is good exercise.

_____

_____

✓ **DOUBLECHECK 9–2** Rewrite these sentences to correct weaknesses in pronoun agreement or reference.

1. Not everyone knows where his ancestors came from.

_____

2. Queen Elizabeth told her maid that she was looking for the wrong kind of man.

_____

3. Neither of the male applicants could find their resumé.

_____

4. The City Council gave final approval to their consultant's street lighting plan.

_____

5. Delores got to walk down a shady lane, which made her happy.

_____

6. Some clerks talk to their customers as if they were idiots.

_____

7. After a long run on a hot day, you should drink lots of water.

_____

8. In this history text, it says the Panama Canal is fifty-one miles long.

   _____

9. Sylvia said she would tell Myra the news when she got home.

   _____

10. When touring France, you should be careful when driving the traffic circles.

    _____

EDITING CHECK 9 Edit this paragraph to correct weaknesses in pronoun agreement and reference, as in the first example.

Movie goers
¹~~Everyone~~ would have a hard time recognizing the cowboy depicted in films if they had actually lived in the "Wild West" themselves. ²For one thing, they say cowboys were greatly outnumbered—by about a thousand to one—by his neighbors, the unglamorous farmers. ³Although a person wouldn't guess it from watching old-time westerns, at least a quarter of them were black or Mexican. ⁴Furthermore, even a resident of Dodge City, which had a reputation as one of the toughest towns in the West, would scratch their head in puzzlement at the sight of all those gunfights on the screen. ⁵The town had only thirty-four bodies in their famous Boothill Cemetery, and almost all died of natural causes. ⁶The shootout at the O.K. Corral and the killing of Wild Bill Hickok became talked about just because this was so uncommon. ⁷In studies of the period, they say that the romanticized version of the Old West was largely due to two Easterners, Owen Wister and Zane Grey. ⁸Wister wrote a novel about cowboys called *The Virginian*. ⁹Zane Grey, a New York dentist who had never been out West, produced dozens of novels with a western setting. ¹⁰It included such "classics" as *Riders of the Purple Sage* and *West of the Pecos*. ¹¹His books are still read today; it's often found at bookstores and in the paperback section at drug stores.

 **CHECKPOINT 9**

In the blanks, write *weak* for sentences with faulty pronoun agreement or reference, including sex bias. Write *OK* for sentences without such problems.

_____ 1. In New York's Greenwich Village, you will find work by local artists.

_____ 2. Anyone who plans to attend the office party should see their supervisor.

_____ 3. A horse often "spooks" when they see a snake.

_____ 4. The ushers will assist those concertgoers who request help.

_____ 5. Anyone planning to travel abroad should order his passport well in advance.

_____ 6. Philip wanted to be a botanist, but he changed his mind after getting a C- in it.

_____ 7. Neither of the brothers mows his own lawn.

_____ 8. Elyse refused the gift, which surprised Richard.

_____ 9. They say that the world's population growth is creating problems.

_____ 10. Each of the actresses owed her success to hard work and talent.

_____ 11. Anyone who forgets their book will have to go home and get it.

_____ 12. They say the polar ice cap is melting.

_____ 13. You may be shocked at how much movie tickets cost these days.

_____ 14. Anyone who missed the exam should see their instructor about making it up.

_____ 15. Rowena thinks Texans are boastful although she has never visited it.

Wordcheck: Usage Tips

For some words, a dictionary will give special *usage* suggestions. Look up the underlined words to see which construction is recommended.

farther—further

1a. The gas station was farther than we thought.

1b. The gas station was further than we thought.

enthused—enthusiastic

2a. Marilyn was enthused about her new job.

2b. Marilyn was enthusiastic about her new job.

infer—imply

3a. Are you inferring that I took your pen?

3b. Are you implying that I took your pen?

former—latter

4a. We saw Tom and Dick, the former being home from college.

4b. We saw Tom and Dick, the latter being home from college.

fewer—less

5a. There were less students in class today.

5b. There were fewer students in class today.

GO ELECTRONIC!

For supplemental readings, exercises, and Internet activities, visit
Checkpoints Online at
http://www.ablongman.com/page

Chapter 10

The Definition Paragraph

READING PRECHECK

A word does not always have the same meaning for everyone who uses it. The author of this essay defines the term *macho* in two ways: as used in Latin America and as used in the United States. The essay won its author a journalism award for advancing social justice. Guilbault has degrees in journalism and business administration.

> **JOURNAL TOPIC:** How would you describe a "macho man"?

Tough on Macho
Rose Del Castillo Guilbault

subtlety   exact meaning

What is *macho?* That depends on which side of the border you come from. 1

Although it's not unusual for words and expressions to lose their subtlety in 2 translation, the negative connotations of *macho* in this country are troublesome to Hispanics.

alleged   accused, but not convicted

Take the newspaper descriptions of alleged mass murderer Ramon Salcido. 3 That an insensitive, insanely jealous, hard-drinking, violent Latin male is referred to as *macho* makes Hispanics cringe.

"Es muy macho," the women in my family nod approvingly, describing a man 4 they respect. But in the United States, when women say, "He's so macho," it's with disdain.

disdain   scorn, ridicule

The Hispanic *macho* is manly, responsible, hardworking, a man in charge, a 5 patriarch. A man who expresses strength through silence. What the Yiddish language would call a *mensch.*

chauvinist sexist

The American *macho* is a chauvinist, a brute, uncouth, selfish, loud, abrasive, **6** capable of inflicting pain, and sexually promiscuous.

Quintessential *macho* models in this country are Sylvester Stallone, Arnold **7** Schwarzenegger, and Charles Bronson. In their movies, they exude toughness, independence, masculinity. But a closer look reveals their machismo is really violence masquerading as courage, sullenness disguised as silence, and irresponsibility camouflaged as independence.

If the Hispanic ideal of macho were translated to American screen roles, **8** they might be Jimmy Stewart, Sean Connery, and Laurence Olivier.

In Spanish, macho ennobles Latin males. In English, it devalues them. This **9** pattern seems consistent with the conflicts ethnic minority males experience in this country. Typically the cultural traits other societies value don't translate as desirable characteristics in America.

ambiguity unclear meaning

recalcitrant stubborn
stoically without complaint

I watched my own father struggle with these cultural ambiguities. He worked **10** on a farm for twenty years. He laid down miles of irrigation pipe, carefully plowed long, neat rows in fields, hacked away at recalcitrant weeds and drove tractors through whirlpools of dust. He stoically worked twenty-hour days during harvest season, accepting the long hours as part of agricultural work. When the boss complained or upbraided him for minor mistakes, he kept quiet, even when it was obvious the boss had erred.

He handled the most menial tasks with pride. At home he was a good **11** provider, helped out my mother's family in Mexico without complaint, and was indulgent with me. Arguments between my mother and him generally had to do with money, or with his stubborn reluctance to share his troubles. He tried to work them out in his own silence. He didn't want to trouble my mother—a course that backfired, because the imagined is always worse than the reality.

Americans regarded my father as decidedly un-macho. His character was inter- **12** preted as nonassertive, his loyalty nonambition, and his quietness ignorance. I once overheard the boss's son blame him for plowing crooked in a field. My father merely smiled at the lie, knowing the boy had done it, but didn't refute it, confident his good work was well known. But the boss instead ridiculed him for being "stupid" and letting a kid get away with a lie. Seeing my embarrassment, my father dismissed the incident, saying, "They're the dumb ones. Imagine, me fighting with a kid."

I tried not to look at him with American eyes because sometimes the reflec- **13** tion hurt.

Listening to my aunts' clucks of approval, my vision focused on the qualities **14** America overlooked. "He's such a hard worker. So serious, so responsible," my aunts would secretly compliment my mother. The unspoken comparison was that he was not like some of their husbands, who drank and womanized. My uncles represented the darker side of macho.

In a patriarchal society, few challenge their roles. If men drink, it's because it's **15** the manly thing to do. If they gamble, it's because it's how men relax. And if they fool around, well, it's because a man simply can't hold back so much man! My aunts didn't exactly meekly sit back, but they put up with these transgressions because Mexican society dictated this was their lot in life.

In the United States, I believe it was the feminist movement of the early sev- **16** enties that changed macho's meaning. Perhaps my generation of Latin women was in part responsible. I recall Chicanas complaining about the chauvinistic nature of Latin men and the notion they wanted their women barefoot, pregnant and in the kitchen. The generalization that Latin men embodied chauvinistic traits led to this interesting twist of semantics. Suddenly a word that represented something positive in one culture became a negative prototype in another.

The problem with the use of macho today is that it's become an accepted 17 stereotype of the Latin male. And like all stereotypes, it distorts truth.

The impact of language in our society is undeniable. And the misuse of 18 macho hints at a deeper cultural misunderstanding that extends beyond mere word definitions.

Checking Meaning and Style

1. What is the meaning of *macho* for Hispanics, according to the author?
2. What is the meaning of *macho* for non-Hispanics in the United States?
3. The author uses examples, such as that of the murderer in Paragraph 3, to make clear the two meanings of *macho*. In what other paragraphs does she use examples for the same purpose?
4. What is a "patriarchal" society [Paragraph 15]? What are the roles of men and women in such a society?

Checking Ideas

1. If you described a male relative or acquaintance as "macho," would it be a compliment?
2. What actors, or other public figures, are macho in the ways described in Paragraphs 7 and 8?
3. Is the United States a patriarchal society?
4. Does the author's description of the "darker side of macho" in Paragraphs 14 and 15 weaken her argument about its idealistic meaning in Latin America?
5. All stereotypes distort the truth, Guilbault says. Can you give examples from your own experience or observation?
6. What do you think the author means when she refers in Paragraph 18 to a "deeper cultural misunderstanding" that goes beyond "mere word definitions"?
7. What is your idea of a "manly man"? A "womanly woman"?

Analyzing Definition Writing: Denotation and Connotation

In "Tough on Macho," Rose Del Castillo Guilbault says the word *macho* has troublesome connotations for many Hispanics in the United States. To be skilled in our use of language, we must recognize the difference between a word's *denotation*—its standard dictionary meaning—and its *connotations*—the meanings, often emotional, that attach themselves to words. For example, the words *house* and *home* have similar dictionary meanings, but they will awaken different feelings in a reader or listener.

The following words all denote "public official." Do they have favorable or unfavorable connotations? Are some neutral—neither favorable nor unfavorable?

statesman   public servant   politician   bureaucrat

Good (or bad) examples of making use of connotations often appear in political language. For example, we call troops trying to overthrow a foreign government "freedom fighters" if we want them to win; otherwise, they are "rebels" or "terrorists." Advertising also provides many examples of language used to sway our emotions. Consider these brand names: Mustang and Ram (cars) or Virginia Slims and Kool (cigarettes). What are their connotations?

We need to be alert to the connotative value of words for two reasons. One is to make our own writing clear, precise, and, yes, persuasive. Another is to detect efforts by others to influence our opinions through emotional language or "loaded" words.

SPOTCHECK 10–1   In these comparisons, describe yourself by using words with favorable connotations and describe the other person with words that have similar denotations but negative connotations.

Example: I am hard-working. You are a <u>workaholic</u>.

1. I am slender. You are _____.

2. I am lively. You are _____.

3. I am athletic. You are a _____.

4. I am _____. You are old.

5. I am _____. You are childish.

6. My clothes are colorful. Yours are _____.

7. I am firm in my beliefs. You are _____.

SPOTCHECK 10–2   After each sentence are several words with similar denotations but with different connotations. Fill in the sentence blank with the word that is most appropriate.

1. Claudette says she will never forget the love of her _____.

   female parent   old lady   mother   mommy

2. The Patels have built a charming _____ at the lake.

   cottage   shanty   shack

3. Mr. Lugo criticizes his son-in-law as a mere _____.

doctor   physician   pill-pusher

4. The grandmother boasted that little Sammy got good grades because he was so _____.

bookish   studious   nerdish

5. The driver said in court that he had been only a little tipsy, but the police officer testified he had been _____.

pickled   boiled   stewed   intoxicated

Study the following two model paragraphs. The first defines "bad habit" and the second "ambition."

Model Definition Paragraph 1

Smoking was a bad habit that threatened my health, irritated others, cost too much, and weakened my marriage. Newspaper and magazine articles, television programs, my own doctor, my friends—even warning labels on the cigarette packs—all said smoking was damaging to my health. At work and in restaurants, people complained if I lit up, making me feel like a criminal. My wife, who doesn't smoke, pointed out that we could go out to dinner once in a while with the money saved if I didn't smoke. She also complained that my smelly clothes and breath didn't exactly excite her. Quitting wasn't easy after ten years at two packs a day, but I'm glad I finally did it.

In the preceding example, the topic sentence specifies the bad habit—smoking—and also outlines the four points that will show why the writer considers smoking a bad habit: because it is unhealthful, irritating to others, expensive, and bad for the writer's marriage.

Model Definition Paragraph 2

My friend Anthony, who wants to be a lawyer, practically defines the word "ambition." He takes a full course load at a community college, attending classes from 8 a.m. to noon five days a week. He works forty hours a week for a janitorial service, cleaning office buildings at night. On weekends, he catches up on his sleep and his school homework, when he isn't doing yard-work for others. Tony says he can become a lawyer in six or seven years and cash in with a high-paying job with a big law firm—if he lives that long.

The writer announces the term to be discussed—"ambition"—and then defines the word with the example of his hard-working friend.

Writing Assignment:
A Definition Paragraph

Write a paragraph in which you define one of the following terms. Don't try to imitate a dictionary definition. Instead, you may want to use examples to make the meaning clear, as in "Tough on Macho." Or you might tell a story (narrative) that illustrates the word's meaning. With those methods, you could use a topic sentence along the lines of "I learned the meaning of fear the night our house caught fire" or "My Aunt Brenda is a good example of a person with common sense."

1. common sense

2. forgiveness

3. ambition

4. macho

5. friendship

6. a good neighbor

7. a bad habit

8. cool

 Writing Topic Bank

Alcohol Problems

What is meant when someone is described as an alcoholic? Write a paragraph defining alcoholism. How much do they drink? How often? What happens to them? How are they different from social drinkers?

Exploring on the Internet

We often assume that the words we use have the same meaning for everyone. Choose one word from the following list. Using the word you chose, enter a key word search on any search engine you like (such as Lycos.com, Google.com, Yahoo.com, Excite.com) and explore the websites listed as a result of your search. Write a paragraph defining the word based upon how it is used on the websites you explored.

love	terrorism
truth	beauty
intelligence	democracy
security	manipulation
hunger	habitat
sin	honor
satisfaction	identity

Writing About Media

How well known does someone need to be to be famous? How long must they be remembered? Is fame about their name, their face, their accomplishments, their thoughts? Write a paragraph defining the word "famous."

WRITING CHECKLIST

✓ Develop the topic through prewriting techniques such as journal writing and nonstop writing. Be sure to make your definition interesting with examples, specific details, an anecdote, or other methods discussed so far.

✓ Start with a topic sentence that includes the term you plan to define. Then build on that idea with supporting details, or, if an anecdote is used, the steps in that story.

Topic sentence:_____

First supporting detail:_____

Second supporting detail:_____

Third supporting detail:_____

Fourth supporting detail:_____

Fifth supporting detail:_____

✓ In revising the paper, look especially for errors in pronoun use, as well as the kinds of problems indicated on recent papers.

✓ Proofread the paper before turning it in.

Sentence Sense: Using Commas Correctly

We might be forgiven for turning to our TV sets if we ran into much writing like this:

> Having forgotten to let out her dog the faithful Poochie Isabel had to turn around at Abilene Texas and drive back home a trip of two hours.

That sentence makes a good deal more sense with the addition of a few commas.

> Having forgotten to let out her dog, the faithful Poochie, Isabel had to turn around at Abilene, Texas, and drive back home, a trip of two hours.

Obviously, those commas helped. Unfortunately, commas are the punctuation marks most likely to cause despair among inexperienced writers.

Here are some occasions for using commas:

RULE 1. Use a comma before the connecting words *for, and, nor, but, or, yet, so* (FANBOYS) when they join two complete thoughts or independent clauses. You may want to return to the section on clauses in Chapter 4 (page 49) for a quick review.

> The job is boring, but the pay is good.
>
> Mike liked the movie, so he told Fran to see it.

Be sure you are joining two independent clauses. In the next example, no comma is needed.

> Mike liked the movie and told Fran to see it. (a single clause with one subject and two verbs)

 **SPOTCHECK 10–3** Use a comma and one of the connectors *for, and, nor, but, or, yet, so* between independent clauses.

> **Example:** The book is valuable, but you may borrow it.

1. The movie was entertaining _____ it was too long.

2. Mr. Sahota will find a better job here in Omaha _____ he will move to Kansas City.

3. Estella should get a raise _____ she is a hard worker.

4. Cyril gets good grades in college _____ he lets everyone know it.

5. I studied hard for this test _____ I should get a decent grade this time.

 **SPOTCHECK 10–4** Write three sentences, each using a comma and one of the connectors *and, but,* and *so* between independent clauses.

1. _____

_____

2. _____

_____

3. _____

_____

RULE 2. Use a comma after introductory expressions—words that lead up to the main part of the sentence (the independent clause).

> After a long and snowy winter, we were eager for spring to come. (introductory prepositional phrase)

> Because the dog was limping, Arnold took it to the vet. (introductory dependent clause)

The comma is often omitted if the introductory expression is short.

> On Friday [no comma] the entire office staff played a game of softball at Live Oak Park.

But commas are used after such opening words as *well, yes,* and *no.*

> Yes, I returned the book to the library on time.

> Gee, I thought you had forgotten.

RULE 3. Use a comma to separate items in a series. A series is a list of three or more items.

> The hairdresser took out his comb, brush, and scissors.

> The truck driver jumped into the cab, turned on the ignition, and pressed her boot against the accelerator.

> The instructor opened the book and started to read. (no comma—two items do not make a series)

 **SPOTCHECK 10–5** Put commas after introductory words and between items in a series.

1. Grown in California and Oregon nectarines resemble peaches without fuzz.

2. The Chinese eat kumquats fresh preserve them or make them into jams.

3. Most papayas in the United States come from Florida Texas Hawaii Mexico or Puerto Rico.

4. To drink the juice of a coconut puncture a hole in the shell.

5. Known as "the poor man's fruit" in the Mediterranean area figs contain calcium phosphorus and iron.

6. No breadfruit is not used to make bread, but in the South Seas the wood of the plant is used to make canoes.

SPOTCHECK 10–6 Write two sentences using commas to separate items in a series.

1. _____

_____

2. _____

_____

Write two sentences using commas to set off introductory expressions.

3. _____

_____

4. _____

_____

RULE 4. Use commas to set off words that interrupt the sentence if those words are not essential to the main idea. This rule will be clearer after you study these examples:

Marie, who completed all the work, will pass the course.

Any student who completed all the work will pass the course.

In the first example, the main idea, "Marie will pass the course," makes sense without the interrupting words "who completed all the work." Since the extra words add nonessential information, they are set off by commas. In the second example, the main clause, "Any student will pass the course," is likely to be untrue. The interrupting words are essential to complete its meaning. Therefore, the interrupter is not set off by commas.

Here are some more examples of essential and nonessential interrupters.

> **(nonessential)** William Leong, who has been elected four times, will run for mayor again this year.

The interrupter "who has been elected four times" adds interesting but nonessential information. It is set off by commas.

> **(essential)** A man who has been elected four times will run for mayor again this year.

The main clause (underlined) doesn't make much sense without help of the interrupter. The interrupter is <u>not</u> set off by commas.

> **(nonessential)** We read a poem, "I Died for Beauty," in English class.

> **(essential)** We read the poem "I Died for Beauty" in English class.

RULE 5. Use commas to set off expressions such as "on the other hand" and "it seems to me" that interrupt the sentence.

> Saundra will, I suppose, marry Calvin if he asks her.

> Calvin, of course, has no intention of asking her.

> Columbus, according to some historians, was not the first European to discover America.

SPOTCHECK 10–7   Add commas to set off nonessential elements and interrupting expressions.

1. Bill's Diner which looks like it survived a tornado is a favorite student hangout.

2. Katrina's history teacher Mr. Jefferson has written a book on the Constitution.

3. The mating call of the Mediterranean fruit fly according to experts has the same frequency as the musical note F-sharp.

4. A goat that seems to be eating a tin can is probably just enjoying the glue on the can's label.

5. Pound cake which is one of my favorite desserts got its name from the pound of butter used in making it.

6. That fact of course won't keep some people from enjoying pound cake—and putting on pounds.

7. A rolling stone according to an old saying gathers no moss.

8. Benjamin Harrison who served from 1889 to 1893 was the last president to wear a beard.

RULE 6. Use commas to separate geographical names and items in addresses and dates.

Margarita lived in San Juan, Puerto Rico, before coming to the United States.

Susan was born on Tuesday, September 15, 1966, in Georgia.

The letter was addressed to 12500 Campus Drive, Oakland, CA 94619.

NOTE *Use zip code abbreviations for states only in addresses.*

Write a sentence in which you give the month, date, and year of your birth and the city and state (or country) in which you were born. Be careful with the commas.

_____

_____

 **SPOTCHECK 10-8** Add commas where needed.

1. The highest temperature ever recorded in California was 134 degrees, recorded July 10 1913 at Greenland Ranch.

2. The average daily maximum temperature in January in Chicago Illinois is 25.4 degrees.

3. The package was mailed to Mr. Oswald Roberts 213 Pine Street Chicago IL 60603.

4. Meg's son was born in Little Rock Arkansas on January 4 1962.

RULE 7. The final rule is, don't use a comma unless you know why you're using it. If in doubt, leave it out.

 **DOUBLECHECK 10-1** Add commas where appropriate.

[1]Sarah Winchester built one of the biggest oddest and most expensive private houses in the United States. [2]The mansion in San Jose California was enlarged continuously from 1884 until her death in 1922 but it was never completed. [3]When she died it had 160 rooms. [4]In 1862 Sarah married William Wirt Winchester whose father

had manufactured the famous Winchester rifle. ⁵When her husband died of tuberculosis in 1881 she inherited a twenty-million-dollar fortune. ⁶She was rich but she was not happy. ⁷She was afraid that the spirits of all the people killed by Winchester rifles including the spirits of many Indians would haunt her. ⁸The new house would keep the spirits away she believed as long as it was under construction. ⁹For thirty-eight years even on Sundays and Christmases carpenters kept building and rebuilding the house. ¹⁰They installed 10,000 windows 5 complete kitchens 13 bathrooms 5 heating systems 3 elevators and 48 fireplaces. ¹¹Many of the 2,000 doors opened on solid walls and there was a maze of secret passageways. ¹²The Winchester Mystery House as it is called today offers guided tours to the public.

Unnecessary Commas

Take care not to use commas where they aren't needed. Here are some of the spots where commas are unnecessary.

- Do not use a comma before a connector (*for, and, nor, but, or, yet, so*) not joining two independent clauses.

    (wrong) Marianne could read French, but couldn't speak it. (one independent clause with two verbs)

    (correct) Marianne could read French but couldn't speak it.

    (correct) Marianne could read French, but she couldn't speak it. (two independent clauses joined by *but*)

- Do not use a comma between a subject and its verb, a temptation if the complete subject (italicized in the examples that follow) is long.

    (wrong) *Fools and their money,* are soon parted.

    (correct) *Fools and their money* are soon parted.

    (wrong) *A knife, some string, and some matches,* are useful on a camping trip.

    (correct) *A knife, some string, and some matches* are useful on a camping trip.

- Do not use a comma between a verb and its object.

    (wrong) The supervisor said, that she would be back at three.

    (correct) The supervisor said that she would be back at three.

    (compare) The supervisor said, "I will be back at three."

    (wrong) The snow plow has finished, clearing our driveway.

    (correct) The snow plow has finished clearing our driveway.

- Do not use a comma before the first or after the last item in a series.

> **(wrong)** We could get along without, pollution, poverty, and war.
>
> **(correct)** We could get along without pollution, poverty, and war.
>
> **(wrong)** She found a brush, comb, and mirror, on the dresser.
>
> **(correct)** She found a brush, comb, and mirror on the dresser.
>
> **(wrong)** The sunset was a beautiful, breathtaking, inspiring, sight.
>
> **(correct)** The sunset was a beautiful, breathtaking, inspiring sight.

 **SPOTCHECK 10–9**   Circle unnecessary commas.

1. The well-known song "Happy Birthday to You," was originally called "Good Morning to You" and was a classroom greeting.

2. Confronted with the evidence, Susan admitted, that she had broken the vase.

3. Fred's new car is, economical, dependable, and quite handsome.

4. Making the dean's honor list, was Terry's goal for the semester, but he knew he would have trouble with math.

5. Yuko, who hated baseball, decided to attend the Dodgers game with her in-laws.

6. Under the cushion, Debra found, two quarters, a dime, and three pennies.

7. The camp counselor, Jim Smith, rowed out to the island in a canoe, and built a fire on the beach.

8. Next semester I will have to take algebra, history, and, English.

EDITING CHECK 10   **Add or remove commas where appropriate in this paragraph.**

¹According to archeologists men shaved their faces as far back as twenty thousand years ago. ²Drawings on caves show both bearded and beardless men and graves have contained the flints and shells that were the first razors. ³As soon as humans learned to work with iron and bronze razors were hammered out of those materials. ⁴Ancient Egyptians who sought status, shaved their faces. ⁵Greek soldiers shaved regularly because a beard was a handicap in hand-to-hand fighting. ⁶In the New World Indian men used tweezers made from clams, to pull out their beards one hair at a time.

 **CHECKPOINT 10**   Some of the numbered sentences that follow have a comma error. Find the errors on this list and, in the blanks, write the letter of the solutions listed below.

A. Use a comma with *and, but, or, for, nor, yet, so* to separate two independent clauses (complete thoughts).

B. Use a comma after introductory elements that lead up to the main clause of the sentence.

C. Use a comma to separate items in a series.

D. Use commas to set off nonessential words that interrupt the sentence.

E. Use commas to separate geographical names and items in addresses and dates.

F. If a sentence contains no error, write *F* in the blank.

_____   1. Giovanni's Restaurant which serves great spaghetti is on Main Street.

_____   2. It will be closed next Sunday Monday and Tuesday.

_____   3. The office lunch gang will be unhappy but they will just have to find another restaurant.

_____   4. It wouldn't hurt them of course to fix a lunch and bring it to work.

_____   5. A person who won't eat a bag lunch is going to spend a lot of money on food.

_____   6. When I worked at Smith and Co. nearly everyone brought a bag lunch.

_____   7. We ate our sandwiches in the company cafeteria or we took them to the little park across from the office.

_____   8. I have been working for Darwin and Associates which is a big law firm for six months.

_____   9. I joined the company on Monday April 16.

_____   10. What I like about the company are the flexible work hours the medical benefits and the lunches at Giovanni's.

Wordcheck: Biographical Names

A dictionary may list the names of famous people in the main section or in a special biographical section at the end. Use a dictionary to identify and to learn the birth dates of these people:

Harriet Tubman
Michelangelo

Mary Wollstonecraft Shelley
Confucius
Montezuma

GO ELECTRONIC!

For supplemental readings, exercises, and Internet activities, visit
Checkpoints Online at
http://www.ablongman.com/page

Chapter 11

The Opinion Paragraph

The White House wants to reduce poverty by encouraging marriage. Journalist Ellen Goodman suggests spending the $300 million proposed for the "wedding plan" on programs that fight poverty more directly.

JOURNAL TOPIC: What traits will you (or did you) look for in a marriage partner?

Marriage as Poverty Cure
Ellen Goodman

1 Last June, at the very height of the wedding season, twentysomething singles were asked what they wanted in a marriage partner.

2 These young Americans couldn't agree on the same pizza or politics. But 94 percent of them concurred that "when you marry, you want your spouse to be your soul mate, first and foremost."

3 The "soul mate study" caused a good deal of eye-rolling among my long-married friends. What about those days when you look across the breakfast table and soul mate is not the first image that springs to mind? How do you tell the twentysomethings about the goose bumps that arise from such passionate declarations as: "I'll do the laundry"?

4 Young singles weren't looking for a financial partner or even a parenting partner. They were looking for a deep, intimate, loving, and permanent superrelationship. The National Marriage Project, which commissioned this survey, characterized their portrait of marriage as "emotionally deep and socially shallow."

Fast forward now to the $300 million wedding plan that the Bush administration is proposing as part of the welfare reform package. This is not a federal matchmaking service or "a national soul mate policy." It is money for programs to encourage getting and staying married. **5**

The White House math goes like this: The families of single mothers are five times more likely to be poor than the families of married couples. Ergo, if single mothers would get and stay married, poverty would virtually disappear. **6**

Now, let it be said right off the bat that I'm in favor of healthy, stable marriages. I don't think this is a right-wing plot to get women to stay in abusive relationships or to reassert the patriarchal family. I, too, think there's something to be said for adding realism into the romantic mix and bringing wider social supports to fragile superrelationships. **7**

But where I drop off the love and marriage horse and carriage is when wedding bells are rung *as* an antipoverty program. As family sociologist Frank Furstenberg puts it, the belief that marriage policy will cure poverty is "an extreme case of magical thinking." **8**

For openers, 38 percent of all poor children already live in two-parent homes. As for single moms and dads, it's not clear whether they are poor because they are unmarried or unmarried because they are poor. **9**

Despite all the romantic ideology, poor mothers are at a disadvantage in what sociologists unromantically call the marriage market. Two paychecks are better than one, but the men around them don't always have a paycheck. Indeed, some economists believe that the most effective marriage policy would be a jobs program for poor men. **10**

As for men with good jobs, Stephanie Coontz of the Council on Contemporary Families muses, "Men don't go around saying, 'Gee, what's my contribution to the world today? I think I'll marry a woman to get her out of poverty.'" Studies show that they are looking for, um, soul mates with some earnings. **11**

And while we are talking about antipoverty programs, you could argue that the BA is a better bet than the Mrs. Only 1 percent of all the single mothers with a college education and a year-round job live in poverty. **12**

Of course, the president has not put all his hopes for reducing the welfare rolls on marriage. He is also pushing for stricter and longer work requirements on different moral grounds: "so that more Americans know the independence and dignity of work." **13**

So on the one hand, the administration thinks dependence on welfare should be replaced with the interdependence of marriage. Or, on the other hand, with the independence of work. That's not exactly a contradiction but a tension between the values of autonomy and mutuality that every soul mate can relate to. **14**

This tension became obvious as marriage gradually lost much of its institutional power. Marriage doesn't have the same kinship or legal permanence. It's no longer the most essential economic relationship. It's no longer even the sole acceptable child-raising unit. As those supports were shaken, we replaced them with love—and disillusionment. **15**

The big question, says Barbara Dafoe Whitehead, a co-director of the National Marriage Project, is: "How do we get people to pick the right person and stay mar- **16** ried?" The answer is the same whether we're talking about welfare mothers or Elizabeth Taylor: "We don't know."

It's fine to experiment with premarital counseling or couples workshops that build trust or communication skills. But the only way the administration's proposal would reduce welfare rolls is if they hired poor women to lead the workshops. 17

It's absurd to take $300 million from programs that actually help fight poverty—like child care or jobs—and lay them before the altar. Welfare reform and marriage? This is one knot we need to *untie*. 18

Checking Meaning and Style

1. Goodman opens her essay with four paragraphs about the "soul mate study." Why does she include these survey results in the essay?
2. What images that relate to weddings are given throughout the essay?
3. What is Goodman's main point about poverty and marriage?
4. Goodman suggests that the marriage program is based on errors in logical thinking. What are they? (Paragraphs 6, 9, 10)
5. What are two of the other possible solutions for reducing poverty that Goodman offers? Are all the solutions she offers realistic?

Checking Ideas

1. What are the strong and weak points of Goodman's argument?
2. What measures do you think would help get people out of poverty?
3. Goodman doesn't talk about what the unintended consequences might be of a program designed to encourage getting and staying married. What effects might such a program create?
4. Is it the responsibility of the government to ensure that people don't live in poverty? Why or why not?

Analyzing Opinion Writing

In "Marriage as Poverty Cure," Ellen Goodman gives her opinion about a controversial government proposal. To encourage the reader to accept her view, she gives a variety of reasons why the proposal should not be acted on, facts, and the words of experts. She gives her opinion and then backs it up with different kinds of evidence.

The following two paragraphs show different opinions about living wage laws. Living wage laws allow local governments to set a minimum wage in their area that is higher than the federal minimum wage.

Model Opinion Paragraph 1

Living wage laws are a good way to level the playing field for low-income working families. The laws are also a way for businesses that have received tax breaks for years to give something back to the community. In communities where living wage laws have been passed, fewer working families live below the poverty level. With more money, working families can afford better housing, health care, and education for their children. Even workers in jobs not affected by the living wage laws benefit because their employers will need to raise their wages to attract employees. Businesses benefit as well because higher wages encourage workers to be more productive and less likely to leave.

Model Opinion Paragraph 2

Living wage laws are not a good way to level the playing field for low-income working families. When government takes the wage decision away from businesses, workers can lose their jobs. For example, to make a profit in spite of paying higher wages, businesses may be forced to cut jobs, or to move out of communities that pass these laws. Anyway, businesses just raise their prices for goods and services when wages go up. Living wage laws affect only a very small number of workers and yet everyone suffers from the higher prices that result from higher wages. If higher prices are included, even those few working families who rise above the poverty level will not benefit very much.

An opinion paragraph on a different topic follows.

Model Opinion Paragraph 3

Newspapers and television need to do more to help cut down the number of automobile deaths in this country. The media issued a flood of stories when 230 people died in the explosion of a TWA 747 flying out of New York. However, comparatively little is said about the fact that about the same number die in traffic accidents every two days or that riding in a car is ten times more dangerous, mile for mile, than riding in a commercial airplane. Here are four steps the media should support: First, take away the licenses of first-time drunk drivers, who cause 40 percent of fatal accidents. Second, don't allow teens to drive; they are responsible for 5,500 deaths a year. Third, be strict in licensing the elderly, especially those over 80; they are second only to teenagers in accident frequency. Fourth, lower the speed limit; a study shows that the chance of death or serious injury doubles for every 10 miles per hour over 50. If the news media bring the problems of driving safety to the public, perhaps the politicians will pass the laws needed to save lives.

The writer offers facts and statistics to support the opinion that the news media need to emphasize the problems of auto safety.

Opinions and Facts

Others are more likely to accept our opinions if we back them up with some facts. Opinions can be argued about endlessly, but facts are statements that can be checked to see if they are true. Consider the following examples:

(opinion) Duke Ellington was the greatest American composer of the twentieth century.

(fact) Duke Ellington's compositions include "Solitude," "Mood Indigo," and the long concert work *Black Brown and Beige*.

(opinion) Women have easier lives than men in the United States.

(fact) Women outlive men by seven years in the United States.

(opinion) The United States has the best healthcare system in the world.

(fact) According to the Census Bureau, the United States ranks behind at least a dozen other countries in preventing infant death.

SPOTCHECK 11–1   In the blanks, write *fact* or *opinion.*

_____ 1. Roger Bannister of England was the first man to run a mile race in under four minutes.

_____ 2. Texas women are better looking than California women.

_____ 3. On June 18, 1983, Sally Ride was the first American woman in space.

_____ 4. Bill's new car has a six-cylinder engine.

_____ 5. Italian car designers are the best in the business.

_____ 6. The earth is about ninety-three million miles from the sun.

Writing Assignment: An Opinion Paragraph

Write an opinion paragraph on one of these topics.

1. The most shocking music group today

2. The TV program with the best family entertainment

3. The political party that best serves the country's needs

4. Immigration—for or against

 # Writing Topic Bank

Responding to Another's Opinion

Choose one of the readings in this book that gives an opinion, for example "Taking It to the Streets" in Chapter 9 or "Marriage as Poverty Cure" in this chapter. Respond to one of the writer's points in a paragraph that gives your opinion.

WRITING CHECKLIST

 Develop your ideas through journal writing, nonstop writing, or one of the other prewriting methods discussed earlier.

 Start your paragraph with a topic sentence that makes clear the opinion you want to put across, and support your opinion with persuasive facts and examples.

Topic Sentence: _____

First Support: _____

Second Support: _____

Third Support: _____

Fourth Support: _____

 Use a style (see "Choosing the Right Word" below) appropriate to a college assignment.

 In revising the first draft, check carefully for comma errors and the kinds of mistakes marked on recent assignments.

 Proofread the final copy.

Exploring Opinion on the Internet

Choose a current controversial issue (for example: same-sex marriage, school choice, immunization, human cloning) and, using any search engine you like (such as Lycos.com, Dogpile.com, Excite.com, Yahoo.com), review websites offering opinions related to the issue. Find what you consider to be the most outrageous point of view on the issue. Write a paragraph explaining why you consider that point of view to be outrageous.

Writing About Media

Examine the Letters to the Editor section, usually found near the editorial page, of your local newspaper. Choose an issue addressed in one of the reprinted letters. Write a letter to the editor stating your opinion on that issue.

Diction: Choosing the Right Word

In "Marriage as Poverty Cure," Ellen Goodman writes in a direct, informal style. She uses informal expressions like *right off the bat, for openers,* and *twenty something singles.*

You might write that way in a letter to a friend, but there are other occasions when that style might not be right. You probably wouldn't write a job application in so breezy a manner, or an important report to your boss, or a college term paper on Picasso's contributions to modern art. You probably would handle those subjects in a somewhat more formal style.

Good writing, then, is *appropriate* to its readers (audience) and its subject. Here are some specific points to keep in mind:

- Slang words and expressions are acceptable only in the most informal writing. Words like *groovy, far out,* and *boss* quickly go out of fashion and mark their users as the opposite of "cool." They also are usually vague and unclear. The *New Yorker* magazine gave some examples of slang popular with the "hip-hop aristocracy": "push a fly ride" (drive a great car), "sport butter gear" (wear sharp clothes), and "politick in the hot spots" (hang out in the right places). Have any of these expressions gone out of style?

LUANN/Greg Evans

LUANN reprinted by permission of United Feature Syndicate, Inc.

- Cliches or trite expressions were originally colorful and full of life but are worn out from overuse. Avoid expressions that pop into your mind fully formed: *neat as a pin, sadder but wiser, last but not least.*

- Jargon is the specialized language of a particular group or profession, such as football players, convicts, computer programmers, or doctors. The following make-believe memo contains jargon (in italics) that a group of business consultants found objectionable:

  "Your new *agenda:* Be *proactive* and *interface* with customers. Start *networking. Finalize* sales. Rack up the *done deals* that will *impact* the *bottom line.* We've got *world-class, state-of-the-art, user-friendly* products. That's our *competitive edge.*"

- Big words are often hard to resist. We like to sound impressive. But the person who lives in a *residence* instead of a house, or prefers to *commence* something instead of start it, is on the wrong track. "Write to express, not to impress." Your first goal is to be clear.

- Wrong words must be corrected, of course, after checking a dictionary. "The instructor ~~inferred~~ implied that I had copied the paper."

SPOTCHECK 11–2   Correct slang, cliches, jargon, big words, and wrong words.

Example: Rudy is really ~~uptight~~ about tomorrow's game. *(nervous)*

1. Sally is the most <u>pulchritudinous</u> woman I know.

2. George wants to <u>interface</u> with me at lunch.

3. The City Council wasn't <u>crazy</u> about the mayor's idea.

4. Most critics said the movie was <u>gross</u>.

5. Please <u>inquire</u> of your boss if you can leave early.

6. Amy <u>hit the nail on the head</u> in her paper on gun control.

7. Someone stole Hakim's new <u>wheels</u> last night.

8. The Petersons have bought a new <u>domicile</u>.

9. <u>Irregardless</u> of Tom's feelings, the family will vacation again at Lake Wobegone.

10. The judge was <u>mad as a wet hen</u> at the lawyer's remarks.

Sentence Sense:
Using Other Punctuation Marks

Ending the Sentence

Show that a sentence is completed by using a period, a question mark, or an exclamation mark.

A period marks the end of a statement.

Do you always remember to put a question mark at the end of a question?

Good grief! I thought you knew that an exclamation mark shows strong emotion.

PEANUTS® by Charles M. Schulz

PEANUTS reprinted by permission of United Feature Syndicate, Inc.

Questions: Direct and Indirect

Be sure to note the difference between a *direct* question and an *indirect* question. An indirect question is actually a statement and ends with a period, not a question mark.

(direct) Lee asked me, "Are you going home?"

(indirect) Lee asked me if I was going home. (This statement tells what Lee asked.)

A sentence may contain both a question mark and a period.

"Are you going home?" Lee asked me.

SPOTCHECK 11–3   Supply the correct end punctuation.

1. Mr. Kopish wondered if the bus would arrive on time

2. "Where's Sylvia" Gabriela asked

3. Allison asked her friend if she was ready to leave

4. Stand back That bottle contains acid

5. Did the doctor give you a prescription for your cold

Using Quotation Marks

Use quotation marks [" "] around direct quotations: the exact words of a speaker or writer. Do not use quotation marks around indirect quotations: the idea of the speaker or writer put in your own words.

(direct) "Reading is to the mind what exercise is to the body," said Sir Richard Steele. (his exact words)

(indirect) Sir Richard Steele said that reading develops the mind in the way that exercise develops the body. (his idea, your words)

(You will often find the word *that* before an indirect quotation.)

Study the use of quotation marks and the explanation for each in the following examples. Note especially the relation of the marks to other punctuation and to capital letters.

• The words identifying the speaker (the flight attendant said) are separated from the quotation by a comma.

"The plane will be twenty minutes late," the flight attendant said.

- All periods and commas go <u>inside</u> the ending quotation marks. The quotation begins with a capital letter if it is a complete sentence.

  The captain said, "Prepare to abandon ship."

  "Prepare to abandon ship," the captain said.

- If the quotation is interrupted, the next part doesn't begin with a capital letter unless it is a complete sentence. Be sure to put quotation marks around the quoted words only, not around the words naming the speaker.

  "The time to relax," wrote Sydney J. Harris, "is when you don't have time for it."

- This quotation goes on for more than one sentence without interruption. Use quotation marks only at the beginning of the first sentence and at the end of the last.

  Angela protested, "That's not fair. You should have told me that I was expected to attend class. I don't want to flunk."

SPOTCHECK 11–4   Supply quotation marks and any other needed punctuation.

1. According to sports broadcaster Frank Gifford Pro football is like nuclear warfare. There are no winners, only survivors. (direct quotation)

2. All weddings are happy said one observer. It's the living together afterwards that causes all the trouble.

3. Writing is the hardest way of earning a living, with the exception of wrestling alligators, said Olin Miller.

4. Georges Clemenceau said that everything he knew he learned after he was thirty.

5. In the seventeenth century, John Comenius said We are all citizens of one world; we are all of one blood. To hate a man because he was born in another country, or because he speaks a different language, or because he takes a different view on this subject or that, is a great folly.

Using Quotation Marks and Italics with Titles

Use quotation marks around the titles of short works like essays, short stories, songs, book chapters, and magazine and newspaper articles.

Underline (or type in *italics*) the titles of longer works, such as books, magazines, plays, movies, and television shows.

Wanda read an article titled "Buying Your First Home" in the September issue of <u>Skyrocketing Real Estate</u>.

For Monday, the class is supposed to read the short story "Paul's Case" in the book <u>Best American Stories</u>.

Use single quotation marks for a quotation or title within a quotation.

"We read the poem 'Patterns' in class," Sanjay said.

SPOTCHECK 11–5 Supply quotation marks, underlining (italics), and commas. Remember that quotation marks go outside commas and periods.

1. What are you doing tonight? Mary asked.

2. Oh, I don't know Cathy answered. I'll probably just stay home and watch a rerun of Friends on TV.

3. Mary said that she thought television was a waste of time.

4. So what are you going to do, Miss Intellectual? Cathy wanted to know.

5. Mary said I'll probably do some reading. There's an article called Lipstick and You in the new Teen World that looks good.

Apostrophes in Contractions

An apostrophe is used to show where one or more letters have been left out in a contraction of two words into one. Some examples:

isn't = is not	can't = cannot	they've = they have
I'm = I am	here's = here is	won't = will not (!)

Don't confuse the following contractions with other sound-alike words.

it's = it is	we're = we are	they're = they are	you're = you are

(The sound-alikes *its*, *were*, *there*, and *your* have other meanings. See Chapter 1 for a review.)

SPOTCHECK 11–6 In the blanks, write the contractions of the words shown in parentheses. Be sure to put the apostrophe where one or more letters have been left out.

1. (we will) If the plane is on schedule, _____ be home by 10 o'clock.

2. (will not) The car _____ run if it's too hot.

3. (you have) Henry! _____ some lipstick on your cheek!

4. (could not) The driver _____ see the street signs in the fog.

5. (There is) _____ no use crying over spilled milk.

6. (you are) If _____ ready to go, so am I.

7. (they are) The doctors said _____ going to operate tomorrow.

8. (has not) Fidelia _____ forgotten her mother's birthday.

9. (cannot) Stay out of the boats if you _____ swim.

10. (I have) With final exams around the corner, _____ several notebooks to review.

Apostrophes to Show Possession

Apostrophes are also used to show possession or ownership.

Bill's book   children's games
two mothers' opinions   the book's cover

A common problem is not knowing whether the apostrophe comes before or after the -s. Why is it *Bill's book* (apostrophe before the -s) but *mothers' opinions* (apostrophe after the -s)?

You can solve the problem by asking yourself this question: Who (or what) does it belong to? If the answer doesn't end in -s, add 's to the word. If the answer does end in -s, add only an apostrophe.

Who does the book belong to? (Bill)

Since *Bill* doesn't end in -s, add 's, It is <u>Bill's</u> book.

Who do the games belong to? (the children)

Since *children* doesn't end in -s, add 's. They are the <u>children's</u> games.

Who do the opinions belong to? (the two mothers)

Since *mothers* ends in -s, add only an apostrophe. They are the <u>mothers'</u> opinions.

What does the cover belong to? (the book)

Since *book* doesn't end in -s, add 's. It is the *book's* cover.

Be sure to place the apostrophe clearly in front of or behind the -s. Don't cheat by putting it on top of the -s!

These possessive pronouns, although they end in *-s,* never take apostrophes:

his   hers   yours   ours   theirs   its

Almost all nouns form the plural by adding an *-s.* Be sure a word shows ownership before giving it an apostrophe.

Two <u>cats</u> sat on the fence. (no ownership, no apostrophe)

SPOTCHECK 11–7   **Put apostrophes in the possessive words.**

1. the womens wages

2. two files

3. a days pay

4. a winners smiles

5. the ovens temperature

6. several of the cakes frosting

7. both of the dogs tails

8. the countries borders

SPOTCHECK 11–8   **Add apostrophes where needed.**

1. Have you seen Charles new skis?

2. Yings parents watched from the front row.

3. These magazines belong to Rachel.

4. Both students coats were hanging in the hall.

5. Six porters carried the mens duffle bags into the locker room.

SPOTCHECK 11–9   **Write sentences using the words in parentheses.**

1. (men's) _____

_____

2. (farmers') _____

_____

3. (Jennifer's) _____

_____

4. (mail carriers') _____

_____

✔ **DOUBLECHECK 11-1** Add quotation marks, apostrophes, and underlining (italics) as needed.

1. Why are you calling me at three in the morning? he yelled into the phone.

2. The college drama class is putting on Shakespeares play The Taming of the Shrew.

3. Im sure I saw you last night at Joes party.

4. We had to memorize Kilmers poem Trees in the third grade.

5. Surely, Joyce said, you don't expect me to drink day-old coffee.

6. Is that bicycle yours, or is it ours?

7. That used to be Dolores TV set, but now it belongs to Karen.

8. The two cowboys horses were tied to the hitching post.

9. Look before you leap is an old saying.

10. Dwight says that he will never forget the touchdown he scored in Central Highs Homecoming game.

Using Semicolons

Ordinarily, we use a period to separate two sentences. But we could use a semicolon [;] instead. A semicolon would show a closer link between the two ideas than a period would.

The rain stopped; we decided to continue our walk.

The semicolon can also be used when the second clause contains a transition word like *however* or *consequently.*

The rain stopped; therefore, we decided to continue our walk.

Periods could have been used instead of the semicolons; in fact, a good test of the semicolon is to ask if a period might have been used instead.

Another use of the semicolon (in which the above test does not apply) is to separate series items that already contain commas.

The new club officers are Hilda Jones, president; Franklin Hill, vice-president; and Rick Okamura, secretary-treasurer.

Using Colons

Use a colon [:] *after a complete statement* to introduce one of these: a list, an explanation, or a long quotation.

(list) Everyone should bring these items to class: the text, a notebook, and a pen.

(explanation) There are two things I like about Gerry: his sense of humor and his loyalty to his friends.

(quotation) The commencement speaker quoted Mark Twain: "When I was a boy of fourteen, my father was so ignorant I could hardly stand to have the old man around. But when I got to be twenty-one, I was astonished at how much he had learned in seven years."

SPOTCHECK 11–10   Supply semicolons and colons as appropriate.

1. The sun came up the dew quickly dried.

2. Here's what you should bring to the picnic paper plates, paper cups, and plastic forks.

3. Jessica has a quality I really admire enthusiasm.

4. Before you leave home, be sure to turn off the lights, turn down the furnace, and put the cat out.

5. Phil was drafted by the Miami Dolphins however he never made the team.

6. Among the top all-time money-making movies were *E.T. The Extra-Terrestrial*, 1982 *Jurassic Park*, 1993 *Star Wars*, 1977 *Return of the Jedi*, 1983 and *The Phantom Menace*, 1999.

Using Dashes and Parentheses

Use a *dash* [—] or two hyphens [--] to show an abrupt change in thought or to provide emphasis.

(abrupt change) We were married in 1982—no, in 1981.

(emphasis) Our neighbor—the scoundrel—still hasn't returned our lawn mower.

Use *parentheses* to set off extra information that is not emphasized.

Jason said weight-training (which he took up in January) helped him win the batting title.

The battle is discussed in Chapter 6 (pages 123–134).

SPOTCHECK 11–11   Add dashes and parentheses as needed.

1. I'd like a girlfriend just like Marsha a winner!

2. World War I 1914–18 caused 116,516 deaths to American servicemen.

3. My wife Mildred I mean Agnes went to visit her mother.

4. My friend Willie who owes me money, by the way was just named a vice-president at the bank.

5. Tina's brother in fact her whole family is a little odd.

 **DOUBLECHECK 11–2**   Add semicolons, colons, dashes, and parentheses as needed.

1. Among the largest cities of the world are Tokyo, Japan Sao Paulo, Brazil New York City Mexico City, Mexico Bombay, India and Shanghai, China.

2. Uncle Alfred he's my mother's late brother once went over Niagara Falls in a barrel.

3. The curtain rose the performance began.

4. Be sure to bring these on the camping trip a knife, a first aid kit, and a can of bear repellent.

5. Ludwig van Beethoven 1770–1827 was probably the greatest European composer ever known.

6. Allison lost would you believe it? ten pounds in two weeks.

7. Jon lost ten pounds in two months however he gained them back in one.

8. Everything the Garcias owned furniture, clothing, family keepsakes was destroyed in the fire.

9. Kareem Abdul-Jabbar was named rookie of the year in 1970 in addition he scored 38,387 points in his basketball career, more than any other player.

10. Katharine Hepburn do you remember her? won the Academy Award for best actress in 1981.

EDITING CHECK 11   Edit this paragraph about the McDonald's hamburger chain to supply needed apostrophes, semicolons, colons, dashes, parentheses, quotation marks, and question marks. Notice that the name McDonald's has an apostrophe when it refers to the restaurants.

¹Ill bet you didnt know that back in 1950 Americans ate more pork than beef

however twenty years later Americans were eating twice as much beef as pork nearly a hundred pounds of it a year. ²Half of that was in the form of you guessed it hamburger. ³The hamburgers success really took off in the 1950s. ⁴Can you guess what name is most closely associated with that success ⁵Yes, of course, its McDonalds. ⁶The McDonalds were two brothers. ⁷Almost everything were likely to think of when we think of fast food can be traced to the McDonalds the drive-through service, the simple menu, the single dressing for the meat, and the specialized labor one task per person. ⁸The McDonald brothers even had the golden arches and a sign out front announcing Over One Million Sold. ⁹Though pioneers in the fast food business, the McDonalds arent the ones were likely to think of today when we think of the Golden Arches. ¹⁰Better known is Ray Kroc, a salesman who bought the McDonalds name in 1954 and by the end of the century had Golden Arches all over the world. ¹¹If youre one whos been to McDonalds lately, you have lots of company almost 96 percent of Americans visit at least once each year.

CHECKPOINT 11

One sentence in each of the following pairs contains a punctuation error. Place a check mark in front of that sentence. (This time, quotation marks aren't used for the overall conversation.)

_____ **1a.** Who is that at the front door?
_____ **1b.** Its probably just the newspaper boy.

_____ **2a.** I asked him if he would put the paper inside the screen door.
_____ **2b.** He said "he would."

_____ **3a.** I enjoy reading the Tribune every day, don't you?
_____ **3b.** Well, I'd rather watch The Morning Show on TV.

_____ **4a.** I like the hosts, Tom and Toni, they're really smart.
_____ **4b.** However, I do wish Toni would do something about her hair.

_____ **5a.** Do you know what Mildred said about Tonis hair?
_____ **5b.** She said, "It looks like she's been in a hurricane."

_____ **6a.** I said that Toni has other qualities that make up for her hair: her intelligence and kind manner.
_____ **6b.** "Youre full of hot air," Mildred told me.

_____ **7a.** One part of the newspaper that I do like is that column Around Town.

_____ **7b.** One of the columnists, Hank Zilch, is pretty clever.

_____ **8a.** Did you read his item about the cat that couldn't get down out of the tree?

_____ **8b.** A fireman climbed the tree to rescue the cat, then he couldn't get down.

_____ **9a.** The other firemen asked him what the trouble was?

_____ **9b.** "I'm afraid of heights," he said.

_____ **10a.** They finally put up a ladder and helped him down.

_____ **10b.** He said hes also allergic to cats.

Wordcheck: Word Choice

Just because a dictionary lists a word doesn't mean the word is suitable for all occasions. These are some of the terms dictionaries use to guide us:

obsolete or archaic—words no longer in use
dialectal or regional—used only in certain areas of the country
nonstandard or illiterate—not used by educated people
colloquial or informal—more suited to conversation than to formal writing
slang—popular words that usually soon go out of fashion; suitable for only the most informal writing

What labels does your dictionary give the italicized words in these sentences?

1. Marcia's boyfriend is a good-looking _dude._
2. Who _hath_ seen the wind?
3. Alonzo fixed the car _hisself._
4. Some words _ain't_ in my dictionary.
5. Billie Joe carried the groceries home in a _poke._

GO ELECTRONIC!

For supplemental readings, exercises, and Internet activities, visit
Checkpoints Online at
http://www.ablongman.com/page

Chapter 12

Writing the Essay

READING PRECHECK

Being the parent of small children isn't always a joy, says physician Winston F. Wong in this Father's Day essay. Still, he says, the pleasures outweigh the pains. Notice that the main idea of the essay is stated in the first paragraph and that each of the next three paragraphs begins with a topic sentence. Observe also the use of specific details to develop the paragraphs.

> **JOURNAL TOPIC:** What do you think are the pleasures and pains of parenthood?

Fatherhood — It Has Its Moments
Winston F. Wong

Sometimes the last thing I want to eat is a McDonald's french fry, and I've stopped counting how many times I've seen "Sesame Street" videos. I've stuck my hand in my coat pocket only to find a lint-covered Gummi Bear. I've gone to work unaware that my baby spat up on my clean shirt. Being a father of three small children hasn't been a constant string of pleasures, but I can't think of a more fulfilling and rewarding adventure, and it's allowed me to relive the joys of being a child.   1

contemporary modern
repertoire special abilities

Like a lot of contemporary dads, I've taken on chores and responsibilities my own late father never had in his repertoire. Part of my routine includes giving the kids a bath, changing diapers, and bringing them shopping. But like my dad, I have   2

doodle scribble aimless designs

fun with the kids. I really get a kick when I doodle with my 6-year-old daughter, play "dinosaurs" with my 3-year-old son and build a tent for my 18-month-old daughter.

I especially like to laugh with my kids. I guess I picked up a certain corniness **3** from my father, who always seemed to crack a joke and poke a gentle tease even though he had other responsibilities. In my work as a family physician, I've worked in Chinatown with young immigrant families that remind me of my own childhood and father. As my parents did, these families struggle to learn a new language and culture—and make ends meet. The fathers that seem to cope well seem to really enjoy their kids, despite these pressures. Humor has kept them going.

I'm both pleased and a bit embarrassed today when my children and I laugh **4** together at the same slapstick humor I enjoyed as a kid watching the Three Stooges. I know it's not educational TV, but the laughter we share is precious. Hopefully, my kids will learn to laugh like I did as a kid growing up in San Francisco. That's why when Alisa, Connor, and Maya try to tickle me, ask me to make that "funny face" or scream, "Daddy, you're so silly!" I can't think of anything more complimentary.

So, while being a dad is a lot of responsibility, it's equally a ball. After all, being **5** a dad is supposed to be FUN!

Checking Meaning and Style

1. What is the thesis or central idea of the essay? (Paragraph 1)
2. What are some of the "chores and responsibilities" that fathers have? (Paragraph 2)
3. What are some of the pleasures? (Paragraphs 2, 3, and 4)
4. What helps immigrant families "keep going"? (Paragraph 3)
5. What is the function of the final paragraph (Paragraph 5)?

Checking Ideas

1. If fatherhood is so rewarding, as Winston F. Wong says, why are so many families without fathers?
2. Do immigrant families have a greater need for a sense of humor than other families, as Doctor Wong suggests? If so, why?
3. How has the role of fathers changed in recent years for many men?

Analyzing an Essay

The essay on parenthood and the student composition that follows are models for the essay, the kind of writing you will do for the rest of the term. Notice how Doctor Wong's essay starts with an introductory paragraph that states the main idea or thesis of the essay—that being a father can be rewarding. Paragraphs 2, 3, and 4 start with topic sentences that give the main idea of those paragraphs. The concluding paragraph sums up the writer's ideas.

Writing an Essay

Until now we have concentrated on writing paragraphs. It is time to tackle the larger challenge of writing the essay. If you have been having success with paragraphs, you shouldn't have much trouble with the essay. A paragraph is a brief development of one idea. An essay is a longer development of one idea or subject. You have been urged to use a topic sentence to express the main idea of each paragraph. You now are urged to use a thesis sentence to express the main idea of the entire essay. (An essay is sometimes called a *thesis*.)

Let's look at how the paragraphs are put together in a typical essay.

Paragraph 1	The introduction, including a thesis sentence that states the main point of the essay.
Paragraph 2	First support paragraph to back up the thesis sentence. Start with a topic sentence.
Paragraph 3	Second support paragraph, with a topic sentence.
Paragraph 4	Third support paragraph, with a topic sentence. (Paragraphs 2, 3, and 4 make up the body of the essay.)
Paragraph 5	The concluding paragraph, which brings the essay to a satisfying end, perhaps with a summary or restating of the main points.

Here is the essay in diagram form:

introductory
paragraph

thesis sentence

first body
paragraph

topic sentence

support

second body
paragraph

topic sentence

support

third body
paragraph

topic sentence

support

concluding
paragraph

conclusion

Now let's apply the outline to the essay "A Double Standard," in which a young woman complains that even her own family discriminates against her because she is not a man.

Model Essay

A DOUBLE STANDARD

Introduction

The Women's Movement has helped improve the lives of women in the United States in many ways. We can work at jobs formerly closed to us. We are more likely to get pay comparable to that of men. We are less likely to hear men call us "baby" and more likely to have them treat us as adults. But the Women's Movement hasn't had much impact on my family, especially on the way my brother and I are treated. Just because he is male he has many privileges and advantages that are denied me just because I am female. **1**

First Support

Even though he is two years younger than I, he is much more free to stay out late and to come and go as he pleases. If I come home after midnight, my dad throws a fit. He wants to know where I've been, who I was with, and who drove me home. Even if I tell him I went to a church meeting and had a hamburger afterwards with several girlfriends, he tells me that if it happens again I won't be allowed out of the house after dark for a month. Meanwhile, my brother is coming home at one or two in the morning, and all my dad says the next day is, "Well, did you have a good time last night?" **2**

Second Support

It irritates me that my brother doesn't have to do nearly as much work around the house as I do. I'm expected to set the table for all meals, help Mom with the cooking, and wash the dishes by myself. On Saturdays, it's my job to mop and wax the kitchen floor and vacuum all the rugs. And what does Little Brother do? Once in a while he carries out the garbage. He's supposed to keep the lawn mowed, but somehow he always seems to have baseball practice or some other crucial activity just when the grass gets a bit long. So Dad does it, saying he needs the exercise anyway. **3**

Third Support

Then there's the matter of the car. You can guess who gets to use it and who doesn't. He drives to classes. I take the bus to my morning job and the bus to my afternoon classes. I told my friend Shauna that I thought I could get the car to take us to the new Spielberg movie on Saturday night. But Brother gets the car to drive his buddies to a rock concert at the auditorium. Mother said it was too dangerous to take the bus to that part of town. **4**

Conclusion

It isn't fair that my brother has more freedom than I, that he gets out of household chores, and that he monopolizes use of the car. Whoever said it's a man's world must have been peeking into our house. **5**

Luann

By Greg Evans

LUANN reprinted by permission of United Feature Syndicate, Inc.

Now let's examine more closely how the essay "A Double Standard" fits the earlier outline.

Thesis Sentence "Just because he is male, [my brother] has many privileges and advantages that are denied me just because I am female."

(The purpose of the next three paragraphs is to support or show the truth of the thesis sentence.)

1st Support topic sentence: ". . . He is much more free to stay out late and to come and go as he pleases." (This idea is *developed* by using specific examples and comparison. The next two paragraphs are developed in the same way.)

2nd Support topic sentence: ". . . My brother doesn't have to do nearly as much work around the house as I do."

3rd Support topic sentence (implied): He gets to use the car more than I do.

Conclusion: It's a man's world (implied).

Of course, not every essay is organized just this way. An essay might have as few as two paragraphs to support the thesis—or many paragraphs. Essays written by professionals often do not contain a written-out thesis sentence; the thesis is only implied. But all essays will have a thesis—a central point the writer wishes to make.

Why a thesis sentence? Using a thesis sentence forces a writer to decide ahead of time just what point is to be made. It helps the writer stay on track once the writing begins. On a smaller scale, the topic sentence offers the same kind of help in writing the paragraph.

Some writers (and instructors) like an essay to start with a thesis sentence that outlines the entire essay. Using that approach, the essay "A Double Standard" could have had this thesis sentence:

Just because he is male and I am female, my brother has more freedom, has fewer household chores, and has first call on the family car.

That clearly sets up an essay with three developing paragraphs: one on freedom, one on chores, and one on use of the car.

Whatever method you use, it is important that you know before you start writing just what it is you want to say. One or more of the prewriting techniques discussed earlier should be helpful.

A Closer Look

Let's examine the three parts of the essay and the title a little more closely.

The introduction (first paragraph) serves two purposes. One, as we have already seen, is to present the thesis or main idea of the essay. The other is to arouse the readers' interest so they will want to continue reading. Perhaps the thesis sentence alone will do that. But often a more complex introduction is effective. The introduction to "A Double Standard," for example, puts one young woman's problems in the framework of progress made by women in general in this country.

Any introduction can be used that sets the stage for the rest of the essay. It might be a brief anecdote or description that leads into the thesis sentence. It might be an interesting quotation or startling fact. A question can be an effective opener—but be sure it implies very clearly what point you intend to make in the essay and is not just a way of postponing that decision.

The body is the main part of the essay. It should be at least two or three paragraphs long. (Your instructor may require at least three.) It is in these paragraphs that you support the thesis sentence. You prove your point with specific details, illustrations, examples, comparisons, and the other methods of paragraph development already studied. Each paragraph will take up one particular aspect of the general subject announced in the thesis sentence. Remember to start each body paragraph with a topic sentence. Look at "A Double Standard" again for examples.

How long should a paragraph be? The logical answer: long enough to develop the idea of each paragraph in a way that satisfies or convinces the reader. In general, if a paragraph doesn't have at least four for five sentences, it probably needs more development.

The concluding paragraph should bring the essay to a satisfying close. Often it will summarize the main points made, as in "A Double Standard," although in a short essay this reminder of what has just been read may not be thought necessary. It might be appropriate to suggest actions based on what has been said or to predict future developments.

The title (for example, "A Double Standard") is usually a short and catchy phrase intended to arouse the reader's interest and perhaps to give a hint about the subject of the essay. Center the title at the top of the first page (on the top line of notebook paper). Capitalize the first word and other important words. Do not underline the title or put quotation marks around it (unless it is a quotation). The title really isn't part of the main essay; any information it contains must be repeated in the essay itself.

Writing Assignment: An Essay

Write an essay with at least two or three paragraphs of development on one of the following subjects:

1. What I like (dislike) about being a parent

2. Causes of family arguments

3. Why I would (not) want to be a police officer (or other occupation)

4. Why I chose to attend this college

5. Two or three things I would hate to do without

 # Writing Topic Bank

Decisions, Decisions, Decisions!

Consider a decision that you made that continues to influence your life. Write a paragraph about your decision. What choices did you have? What influenced the choice that you made? How does the decision affect you now? How will the decision affect your future?

Exploring Animals on the Internet

Choose an interesting animal and, using any search engine you like (such as Lycos.com, Google.com, Yahoo.com, Dogpile.com), gather information to write an essay with at least two or three paragraphs of development describing that animal. Use an informal or humorous tone.

Writing About Media

Choose a media spokesperson (news anchor, talk show host, sports commentator, editorial writer) whom you admire and whose opinion you trust. Write an essay with at least two or three paragraphs of development explaining why you trust and admire that person.

WRITING CHECKLIST

 To develop your thoughts on your chosen topic, ask how and why or use freewriting, clustering, or nonstop writing.

 Write a sentence outline of the essay.

1. Thesis sentence

   _____

   _____

2. First support—topic sentence

   _____

   _____

3. Second support—topic sentence

   _____

   _____

4. Third support—topic sentence

   _____

   _____

5. Conclusion

   _____

   _____

(continued)

WRITING CHECKLIST (continued)

 Develop each support paragraph with at least three to five sentences, using interesting and convincing details.

 Center a title on the top line of the first page.

 In revising the paper, look especially for punctuation errors and those problems marked on recent papers.

 Proofread the final copy for errors in such things as spelling and punctuation.

Sentence Sense: Being Consistent

You will probably notice right away that there is something wrong with each of the following sentences. (The underlined words will give you some clues.)

1. The waiter <u>puts</u> our hamburgers on the counter and then <u>returned</u> to the kitchen.
2. When <u>one</u> drives into Yosemite Valley, <u>you</u> are overwhelmed by the magnificent scenery.
3. The president walked slowly to the lectern, carefully adjusted his glasses, and gave a <u>nifty</u> address on the state of the nation.

Each of the sentences is inconsistent; each contains a confusing or annoying shift.

- Sentence 1 shifts from the present-time verb *puts* to the past-time verb *turned*.
- Sentence 2 shifts from the third-person pronoun *one* to the second-person pronoun *you*. (This use of person will be explained in a moment.)
- Sentence 3 shifts from a formal tone or style to the casual style of *nifty*.

Consistent Time (Tense)

Be consistent in your use of the time (tense) of verbs unless there is a good reason to shift. Sentence 1 could have been written in either of these two ways:

The waiter <u>puts</u> our hamburgers on the counter and then <u>returns</u> to the kitchen. (Both verbs are in present time.)

The waiter <u>put</u> our hamburgers on the counter and then <u>returned</u> to the kitchen. (Both verbs are in past time.)

Sometimes a shift in time is necessary:

Rosalia remembers [present time] that her parents owned [past time] a ranch in Texas when she was [past time] a little girl.

SPOTCHECK 12–1 **Make the second verb in each sentence consistent in time with the first.**

opened

Example: Jackie Robinson <u>was</u> an outstanding athlete who ~~opens~~ the door for other African-American athletes.

1. Jackie Robinson joined the Brooklyn Dodgers in 1947 and becomes the first black player in modern major league baseball.

2. Robinson went to high school in Pasadena, California, where he becomes a star in track, football, and baseball.

3. He attends the University of California at Los Angeles on a football scholarship and, in 1939, gained more yards than any other college player.

4. After service in World War II, Robinson joined the Kansas City Monarchs and plays for $400 a month in the Negro American League.

5. When Dodgers general manager Branch Rickey signs Robinson, he warned Robinson to expect acts of prejudice from other players and the fans.

6. During the ten years he plays for the Dodgers, Robinson batted .311 and helped the team win six National League championships and a World Series in 1955.

SPOTCHECK 12–2 **Rewrite the six sentences in Spotcheck 12–1, leaving out the numbers and writing all the verbs in <u>past</u> time.**

_____

_____

_____

_____

_____

_____

_____

_____

_____

SPOTCHECK 12–3 ········· Cross out any verbs that are inconsistent and write in the correct <u>past</u> <u>time</u> forms above.

[1]The first tinted glasses were not intended to protect eyes from the sun. [2]Darkened with smoke, the glasses are worn by judges in China in the fifteenth century. [3]The idea was to conceal the judge's eyes so that witnesses couldn't tell if the judge thinks they are lying. [4]The earliest dark glasses were not vision-corrected, but by around 1430 judges are taking advantage of that factor too. [5]Outside the courts, others start wearing tinted glasses to reduce glare from the sun. [6]In America, the military played a major role in the development of sunglasses. [7]In the 1930s, the Army Air Force commissions Bausch & Lomb to develop glasses to protect pilots from high-altitude glare. [8]The resulting dark-green glasses became available to the public as Ray-Ban aviator glasses.

Consistent "Person"

A pronoun is said to be in the first, second, or third *person.* It depends on whether the pronoun refers to the person speaking, the person spoken to, or the person spoken about.

	Singular	Plural
First person	I, me, my, mine	we, us, our, ours
Second person	you, your, yours	you, your, yours
Third person	he, him, his she, her, hers it, its	they, them, their, theirs

Third person also includes the names of persons, places, and things and indefinite pronouns like *one, everyone, anybody.*

Remember to avoid unnecessary pronoun shifts. Let's revise our earlier example.

(shift) When <u>one</u> drives into Yosemite Valley, <u>you</u> are overwhelmed by the magnificent scenery.

(consistent) When <u>one</u> drives into Yosemite Valley, <u>one</u> is overwhelmed by the magnificent scenery.

Watch out especially for the most common shift—from the first- or third-person pronoun to the second-person *you,* as in the last example.

SPOTCHECK 12-4   Get rid of shifts in person by crossing out incorrect pronouns and writing the correct words above. Also change verbs when necessary.

> **Example**: I used to think Lola was perfect, but as ~~one gets~~ ^{I get} to know her, ~~one sees~~ ^{I see} she has a few faults.

1. When students are late for class, you often interrupt the activities there.

2. If motorists drive defensively, you can avoid many problems.

3. Pierre writes his parents every week, which is a thoughtful thing for you to do.

4. When you do the homework, students should be able to pass this class.

5. When an employee gets a promotion, you feel proud.

Although newspaper and magazine writers often use the word *you* in addressing the reader directly, this informal approach is not always appropriate in college writing, unless you are speaking directly to the reader, as in this text:

(weak) You could easily understand the president's problem.

(better) A person could easily understand the president's problem.

(also better) The president's problem was easily understood.

SPOTCHECK 12–5   Rewrite each sentence to get rid of the inappropriate *you.* Make the sentences as short as you can without leaving out information.

1. You don't need a ticket to attend the Doodle Brothers concert.

   _____

   _____

2. After eating at Charlie's Restaurant, you feel you got your money's worth.

   _____

   _____

3. You can imagine how glad I was to see Ralph again.

_____

_____

4. Foreign travel helps you understand your own country.

_____

_____

5. If you drove 55 miles an hour, it would take you 193 years to travel the 93 million miles to reach the sun.

_____

_____

Consistent Tone

Your writing in college and in your career will usually have a fairly serious or formal tone. You will want to avoid slipping into overly casual and slangy language. Such shifts in tone are jarring to the reader, as is the case in our original example.

(shift) The president walked slowly to the lectern, carefully adjusted his glasses, and delivered a <u>nifty</u> address on the state of the nation.

(consistent) The president walked slowly to the lectern, carefully adjusted his glasses, and delivered a <u>stirring</u> address on the state of the nation.

Of course, if you are jotting a note to a friend, you can be as informal as you like.

 **SPOTCHECK 12–6** Change the italicized words to keep a fairly formal tone.

Example: The United States must maintain alliances in the Middle East if it wants to protect its interests there.
~~wants to stay in the ball game there.~~

1. Anyone who thinks American schools will ever operate all year round is *full of beans.*

2. This year's top student is not only intelligent, she is a *foxy chick.*

3. The orchestra gave a *neat* performance of a Beethoven symphony.

4. The members of the Downtown Elite Association *boogied* until midnight after installing new officers.

5. Mr. Alberts was pleased to receive a raise of fifty *bucks* a week.

 **EDITING CHECK 12** Edit this paragraph to correct *italicized* errors in time, person, and tone. The first sentence has been done as an example.

Anyone who
~~¹If someone~~ likes potato chips ~~you~~ should thank Thomas Jefferson and George Crum. ²Jefferson, the future president, introduced French-fried potatoes after he *learns* to like them while serving as ambassador to France. ³The salted, thin-sliced chips so popular today *got in gear* because of a dispute between a chef and a customer. ⁴It happened in 1853 while chef George Crum *is employed* at a fancy resort in Saratoga, New York, where he fried potatoes in the thick-cut French style. ⁵A diner sent his French fries back to the kitchen because they were too thick and *yucky*. ⁶If anyone has ever worked in a restaurant, *you* know how difficult some customers can be. ⁷Crum *keeps* cutting the potatoes thinner, and the diner *kept* sending them back. ⁸Finally the angry Crum *slices* the *spuds* so thin they are almost like strips of paper. ⁹The diner is delighted with the potatoes, other customers request them, and the restaurant *became* famous for its "Saratoga Chips." ¹⁰So when people sit down in front of the television set with a bag of chips in hand, *you* should say thanks to Thomas Jefferson and George Crum (and to Crum's fussy customer).

 **CHECKPOINT 12** Cross out the word causing a shift in time, person, or tone and write the correct or appropriate word in the blank at the left.

Example: <u>crashed</u> The car sped around the corner and ~~crashes~~ into an ambulance.

_____ 1. I work out in the gym three times a week; you feel much better as a result.

_____ 2. Whenever Karen has a conversation with Julie, she gets angry.

_____ 3. When you visited San Francisco, do you see Alcatraz Island?

_____ 4. People should say "excuse me" when you step in front of someone.

_____ **5.** Fred said the writings of Tolstoy are awesome.

_____ **6.** Ng got up two hours early but still arrives late for the interview because the bus got held up in traffic.

_____ **7.** Antoine wore his new threads to the dance.

_____ **8.** If people feel the issues are important, you will vote.

_____ **9.** As we arrived at the camp, you could see the sunset reflected in the lake.

_____ **10.** I never have trouble finishing my homework; the first thing you do is turn off the TV.

Wordcheck: Places and Things

Among the many helps a dictionary provides is information about sites throughout the world. Use a dictionary to answer the following questions.

1. How tall is the Eiffel Tower?

2. What is the capital of South Carolina?

3. What is the population of Zambia?

4. Where is the Blarney Stone? (What is it?)

5. What are the names of the Great Lakes?

GO ELECTRONIC!

For supplemental readings, exercises, and Internet activities, visit
Checkpoints Online at
http://www.ablongman.com/page

Chapter 13

The Classification Essay

READING PRECHECK

This article warns that clever advertising can persuade us to buy unneeded products or to accept dubious ideas. It suggests five questions we can ask about an ad to reduce the chances of being manipulated.

JOURNAL TOPIC: Have you ever bought something because of an appealing ad or commercial and later wished you hadn't?

Ad It Up, Break It Down
Phil Sudo

sucker someone taken advantage of

manipulation improper influence

No one likes to be a sucker. If you don't pay attention, though, ads can make you one. You can protect yourself by learning how to analyze ads. Once you understand the strategies and techniques advertisers use—the buttons they're trying to push—you can spot attempts at manipulation and make better, more critical decisions about what's being advertised. You can even heighten your appreciation of ads—which ones you think are good and which ones you think are bad. 1

So the next time you notice an ad, ask yourself some of these questions: 2

WHAT KIND OF AD IS IT? The majority of ads are called product ads— those intended to promote the millions of different goods and services for sale, from baking soda to banking. Other kinds of ads include: corporate ads, which promote a company's image or philosophy rather than a 3

197

product; political ads, which aim to generate votes for a candidate or against an opponent; and public-service ads, which offer help, promote a cause, or seek donations.

WHAT'S THE TARGET? One reason we ignore so many ads is that they're not aimed at us. Advertisers seek to maximize an ad's effectiveness by identifying a target market—the audience they most want to reach. To do so, they divide the market into categories: by age, sex, income level, education, geographic region, ethnic background, political leaning, life-style—the list goes on and on. A maker of hockey sticks, for example, is going to target young males who live in cold-weather areas and take part in sports. Thus, its hockey-stick ads would be tailored to appeal to the likes and desires of that market alone. 4

A company with a wide target audience, like McDonald's, will develop several different ads, each aimed at a specific segment of the market—one for teenagers, one in Spanish, one for black families. It may cost more than having a single ad designed for everybody, but it is a more calculated, direct method of selling. 5

WHERE IS THE AD FOUND? It makes no sense for the seller of arthritis medication to run an ad on MTV, or for a skateboard maker to advertise on Oprah. Advertisers seek to place their ads in media viewed by their target audience. A public-safety department, for example, might put a billboard about seat belts near a site where accidents are high. Similarly, a ritzy mail-order house might send its catalogues only to ZIP codes like 90210 and other high-income areas. 6

WHAT IS THE SALES PITCH? The foundation of an ad is the sales pitch. To make the pitch, ads play on our needs and desires—those basic, often instinctive forces that motivate us to do something. Says one corporate marketing director, "Fear, envy, vanity, health, utility, profit, pride, love, and entertainment. If you ever spend money, it will be for one of those reasons." Here is where your guard should go up. If you can identify the buttons an ad is trying to push, you can avoid manipulation. 7

WHAT IS THE SUBTEXT? All ads have a subtext—that is, a meaning beneath the surface. The subtext of an ad is often what causes the most controversy, usually for fostering sexism or racial and ethnic stereotypes. Ads for laundry detergent, for example, are sometimes criticized for portraying women only as housewives. 8

By looking at the deeper level of ads, you can critique not only the attitudes of the advertiser, but our culture at large—what we value, how we see ourselves. With that knowledge, you can buy into those values or not. At least you'll know you're not getting suckered. 9

---

maximize increase to the fullest extent

ritzy stylish, expensive

fostering encouraging

Checking Meaning and Style

1. What does it mean to "have one's buttons pushed"? (Paragraph 1)
2. What three kinds of ads are discussed in Paragraph 3?
3. How do catalog companies decide where to mail their catalogs? (Paragraph 6)
4. What "needs and desires" does advertising often appeal to? (Paragraph 7)
5. What is an ad's "subtext"? (Paragraph 8)

Checking Ideas

1. What kind of advertising "target" are you, judging from the unsolicited mail you receive? (Paragraph 4)
2. What kind of products are advertised in a publication you are familiar with?
3. Judging from the ads, what groups would you guess are the audience for the evening national network news programs? Would the audiences be different for MTV or sports channels?
4. Have you ever responded to an ad out of "fear, envy, vanity"? What have you bought or wanted to buy after seeing a television commercial?
5. Have you seen any ads that foster racial, ethnic, or gender stereotypes?
6. Can you think of any ads that especially reflect the attitudes and values of American culture? Are these values positive or negative, in your opinion?

Analyzing an Ad

Use the ad on page 200 to answer the following questions.

1. What kind of ad is it—corporate, product, political?
2. Who is the target buyer—age, sex, income, education, ethnic, life-style, geography?
3. In what magazine would the ad likely be found—*Popular Mechanics, Reader's Digest, Glamour, Better Homes and Gardens?*
4. What emotion is the sales pitch aimed at—fear, envy, vanity, utility, pride, or some other? Why would a person buy the product?
5. What is the subtext? What cultural values does the ad promote? What are the connotations of the product's name?

Analyzing Writing That Uses Classification

In "Ad It Up, Break It Down," the author has organized his material by separating it into five categories—five questions to ask when analyzing an ad. You

A Harley-Davidson® motorcycle stands for something. We know it. You know it. And everyone else knows it, too. Ninety-five years on the road have seen to that. So there's no need to explain it. Once you've got a Harley® of your own, all you need to do is enjoy it. For the dealer nearest you, call 1-800-443-2153 or visit us at www.harley-davidson.com. The Legend Rolls On.

The Harley-Davidson Motor Company

might use this approach in writing a paper on, say, four kinds of popular music (for example, rap, reggae, country-western, and jazz), or you might write a memo at work on three ways to increase company profits. The model essay that follows discusses three different perspectives on the college library.

Model Classification Essay

LIBRARY PRIVILEGES

Walk into the college library, and you will see—and perhaps hear—at least three types of "customers": the scholars, the socializers, and the snoozers.   1

The scholars can be identified in a variety of ways. They wear serious   2
expressions, as can be seen in those rare moments when they glance up from their work. As a rule, they have their noses in textbooks or are busy writing something, an essay for an English class, perhaps. Also in the scholar category are the students sitting at the library computers. Assuming that the solitaire games have been removed, they're probably looking for a book or magazine article that will offer help in writing a term paper in sociology on three types of football fans or the various categories of ethnic groups. If the

library has a video collection, scholars will be the ones checking out the foreign films. They also look at their watches frequently to be sure they won't be late for their next class.

The socializers have other reasons for visiting the library. They find it a good place to go if the cafeteria is too noisy for a conversation with friends. Textbooks may be open on the study table, but they receive little attention. More important is chatting about the good-looking tennis instructor or last night's Academy Awards program on TV. The socializers can also be identified as the targets of annoyed looks from nearby scholars.   **3**

It isn't hard to guess what distinguishes the third category—the snoozers. They're the ones in the most comfortable chairs, or the ones with their heads resting on a study table. Sometimes they have a book in front of (or under) their faces; at other times, they don't even pretend to know the usual function of a library. The snoozers sometimes overlap with the socializers, as when there is a need to discuss last night's party that lasted until three o'clock. A conspicuous sub-category of the snoozers is made up of the snorers.   **4**

So, which are you—a scholar, a socializer, or a snoozer?   **5**

Notice that the first paragraph identifies the three classifications to be discussed and that each of the three body paragraphs begins with a topic sentence. Notice also the use of examples to explain each type.

Writing Assignment: A Classification Essay

In an essay, discuss a topic by breaking it into at least three classifications, as in these suggested topics:

1. Types of popular music
2. Types of restaurants
3. Types of sports or attitudes toward sports
4. Types of children or parents
5. Types of television programs
6. Types of teachers

 # Writing Topic Bank

Take a Chance

Gambling takes many forms in our society. Some gambling activities are illegal while others are managed by churches or government. People take risks with their money, their health, even their lives. Write an essay describing various forms of gambling by breaking gambling into at least three classifications.

WRITING CHECKLIST

 Use prewriting techniques to come up with specific details, examples, and so on to develop the paragraphs. Clustering (Chapter 3) might work well here, with separate clusters for each type of music, sports, or gambling.

 Be sure the first paragraph has a thesis sentence and that each of the other paragraphs begins with a topic sentence that says how that paragraph will support the thesis.

1. Thesis sentence

_____

2. First classification

_____

3. Second classification

_____

4. Third classification

_____

5. Conclusion

_____

 When revising the first draft, watch out for inconsistent sentence structure (shifts) and the kinds of errors made in recent papers.

 Center a suitable title at the beginning of the essay.

 Carefully proofread the final copy.

Exploring Motor Vehicles on the Internet

Use any search engine you like (such as Lycos.com, Google.com, Yahoo.com, Dogpile.com) to locate the websites of motor vehicle manufacturers. Write an essay describing several types of vehicles offered and explain why a person might want each type.

Writing About Media

Write an essay classifying several television shows that focus on current events. You might consider news programs, talk shows, political forums, special events coverage, or real-time video of legislative or courtroom sessions.

Sentence Sense: Achieving Variety

Sentence Patterns

A speaker who always uses the same tone of voice becomes boring. A writer who uses the same sentence patterns over and over can also become boring. The ability to construct sentences in a variety of ways makes our writing more interesting and allows us to express our ideas more effectively.

Notice how the repetition of short sentences makes the following paragraph boring and even irritating.

> More than a million earthquakes may take place in any one year. Most of them take place under the oceans. They usually don't cause any damage. Some earthquakes occur on land. Earthquakes near large cities may cause extensive property damage. They may even cause deaths.

With a variety of sentence patterns, the paragraph becomes smoother, more concise, and more interesting:

> More than a million earthquakes may take place in any one year. Most of them take place under the oceans, so they usually don't cause any damage. When they occur near big cities, however, they may cause extensive property damage and even deaths.

We will look at three basic patterns: simple, compound, and complex sentences.

Using Simple Sentences

The simple sentence is made up of one independent clause, with no dependent clauses. A clause, you will remember, has a <u>subject</u> and a *verb*. The clause is independent if it expresses a complete thought.

> The <u>detective</u> *left*.

Describing words (modifiers) may be added to form the *complete subject*. Words added to the verb make up the *complete predicate*.

> The <u>uniformed detective</u> *left in a blue car*.

A simple sentence can have a compound subject (more than one) or a compound verb.

> The <u>detective</u> and the <u>burglar</u> *left.* (compound subject)

> The <u>detective</u> *left* but *returned.* (compound verb)

A simple sentence can combine all these elements.

> The uniformed <u>detective</u> and the <u>burglar</u> *left* in a squad car but *returned* within half an hour and *entered* the interrogation room.

That is a long sentence, but it is still, grammatically speaking, a simple sentence. Why? Because it has only one independent clause and no dependent clause.

 **SPOTCHECK 13–1**

Combine the short simple sentences into one longer simple sentence containing a single independent clause.

> **Example:** The computer program was irritating. It always printed ¢ instead of $.
>
> <u>The irritating computer program always printed ¢ instead of $.</u>

1. Juan won a debating award. Franco won a debating award.

   _____

2. Juan won a debating award. He won a speech award.

   _____

3. The welder was weary. The welder put down his torch. The welder thought about lunch.

   _____

Using Compound Sentences

A compound sentence is made up of two or more independent clauses.

> <u>The moon came up,</u> and <u>we set off through the woods.</u>

> <u>Anthony got a raise,</u> so <u>he decided to celebrate.</u>

As in these examples, the two clauses are usually joined by a comma and one of the connecting words *for, and, nor, but, or, yet,* and *so.* The two parts of a compound sentence are considered equal in importance.

 **SPOTCHECK 13–2**

Edit the following sentences to change the simple sentences into compound sentences by joining them with one of the connectors *and, but, or, for, nor,*

yet, or *so.* Don't forget to put a comma and a lowercase letter (not a capital letter) after the first clause.

1. Thirteen percent of American women consider themselves pretty. Twenty-eight percent of men consider themselves handsome.

   _____

2. A penguin may look clumsy. It can swim faster than many fish.

   _____

3. Surrounded by water and glaciers, Juneau, Alaska, can be reached by boat. It can be reached by air.

   _____

Using Complex Sentences

A complex sentence has an independent clause and one or more dependent clauses.

      (dependent clause)   **(independent clause)**
Because Mrs. Larson was sick, her husband fixed breakfast.

      (independent clause)   **(dependent clause)**
Marian netted the fish while Bill steadied the boat.

A dependent clause begins with a dependent word such as *because, although,* or *since.* It needs an independent clause to complete its meaning. (See page 57 for a longer list of dependent words.)

In a compound sentence, the ideas in both clauses are given equal emphasis. In a complex sentence, the idea in the dependent clause is emphasized less than the one in the independent clause.

 **SPOTCHECK 13–3**   Edit each pair of simple sentences to combine them by adding a dependent word. The resulting complex sentence will contain one independent clause and one dependent clause. Start some sentences with the independent clause and some with the dependent clause. Put a comma after the dependent clause if it starts the sentence.

1. The mail carrier refused to enter the yard. The dog was barking.

   _____

2. Eighty-four percent of Americans believe in heaven. Only 66 percent expect to be admitted.

   _____

3. Doctor Winslow is the surgeon. He will marry Dolores.

_____

Don't assume that long sentences are always better than short ones. A mixture of long, short, and medium-length sentences usually is most effective.

 **SPOTCHECK 13–4** Change these compound sentences into complex sentences, that is, sentences with one independent clause and one dependent clause.

> **Example:** Martin repaired his bicycle, and Claudette read a novel. (compound)
> While Martin repaired his bicycle, Claudette read a novel. (complex)

1. The sun came out, and Jack knew it would be a nice day.

_____

2. The novel had an interesting plot, but it was boring.

_____

3. Claudette drives to her home town every weekend, for she is homesick.

_____

QUICKCHECK ON SENTENCE PATTERNS

 A simple sentence has one independent clause and no dependent clause.

 A compound sentence has two or more independent clauses and no dependent clause.

A complex sentence has one independent clause and one or more dependent clauses.

 **SPOTCHECK 13–5** The following paragraph contains only simple sentences. Edit the paragraph to make all sentences either complex or compound. The sentences have been numbered as a guide to joining. Join the sentences with a dependent word, as in the example, or with a connecting word (*for, and, but, or, yet, so*).

¹Thomas Edison (1847–1931) was a famous inventor. ~~He~~ who played a major role in shaping today's society. ²For example, one of his most important contributions was the

electric light. He developed it in the 19th century. ³His electric light was of no use without something to plug it into. He developed power plants and wiring for lamps and switches. ⁴New York became the first city to have electric street lighting. Edison threw a switch in 1882 to turn on eight hundred bulbs all over lower Manhattan. ⁵Among the many inventions in which he played a part are the phonograph and the motion picture projector. ⁶He attended school for only three months. He became famous throughout the world.

Building Effective Sentences

Many times, two or more short sentences can be combined to form a single sentence that provides variety, saves words, and gives more exact emphasis. Prepositional phrases, participial phrases, and appositives can be used in sentence combining.

Using Prepositional Phrases

Phrases are groups of related words that do not contain a subject and a verb. A prepositional phrase begins with a preposition and ends with a noun or pronoun: *to the beach, with them, under the gnarled oak tree.* See page 29 for a review.

Notice how prepositional phrases (underlined) are used in these two examples:

The executive finally made a decision. It took him four days of study.
The executive finally made a decision <u>after four days of study</u>.

The lieutenant picked up the grenade. He didn't give it a second thought.
<u>Without a second thought</u>, the lieutenant picked up the grenade.

Remember to put a comma after a phrase that starts a sentence.

SPOTCHECK 13-6 Combine these sentences by making one of them a prepositional phrase.

> **Example:** The hunter built a campfire. He built it near a stream.
>
> Near a stream, the hunter built a campfire.
> **(or)** The hunter built a campfire near a stream.

1. You will find the book you need. It is on the kitchen table.

   _____

2. Mrs. Elizonda found the ring. It was under the sofa cushion. (Start with *under.*)

   _____

3. Crows were in the tree's highest branches. They were holding a meeting. (Start with *in.*)

Using Participial Phrases

A participle is a word made from a verb. A *present participle* adds *-ing* to the verb. A *past participle* usually adds *-d* or *-ed.*

Verb	Present Participle	Past Participle
move	moving	moved
jump	jumping	jumped

Past participles of *irregular* verbs, you may recall, do not end in *-d* or *-ed.* Some irregular past participles are *begun, fought, eaten, sent, taught,* and *written.* For a longer list, see pages 88–90.

A participial phrase consists of a participle and its modifiers. Here are examples:

moving into position

encouraged by his parents

having risen to the top

A phrase must be joined to an independent clause to make a sentence.

Having risen to the top, the new president ignored those who had helped him.

The first noun or pronoun after a participial phrase usually must name the person or thing referred to by the phrase. Otherwise the error called a *dangling modifier* results.

(wrong) Having risen to the top, those who had helped him were ignored by the new president.

(correct) Having risen to the top, the new president ignored those who had helped him.

 **SPOTCHECK 13–7** **Underline the participial phrases in these sentences.**

1. Played in India in the sixteenth century, the game we now call Parcheesi was originally not a board game at all.

2. The game, enjoyed by the emperor Akbar the Great, took place in the royal garden.

3. Moving from bush to bush in the garden, the "pawns" were the most beautiful young women in India.

4. Their progress, determined by the throw of shells, finally brought them "home" to the emperor's throne in the center of the garden.

5. The English, changing the Indian name *pacisi* to *Parcheesi,* moved the game indoors and replaced the beautiful maidens with ivory pawns to mark progress around the board.

Using Appositives

An appositive helps identify a noun or pronoun in front of it.

Dr. Eugene Wilson, <u>a dentist</u>, needs a technician. (identifies Dr. Wilson)

The Ashleys saw a statue of George Washington, <u>the first president of the United States.</u> (identifies George Washington)

Appositives are set off by commas if they are not essential to the meaning, as in the examples just given. However, commas are not used if the appositives contain information essential to the sentence.

(no commas) The store <u>Spoiled Rotten</u> sells expensive toys. (Which store?)

(no commas) The movie <u>*Casablanca*</u> stars Humphrey Bogart. (Which movie?)

 **SPOTCHECK 13–8** Underline the appositives.

1. Vlad the Impaler, a fifteenth-century Romanian prince, was the inspiration for the novel *Dracula.*

2. The seventh-century story "Bluebeard" was based partly on an actual Frenchman who killed several wives.

3. According to New England legend, the original Mother Goose of nursery rhyme fame was a Boston widow, Elizabeth Goose.

4. The first words of recorded human speech were those of the nursery rhyme "Mary Had a Little Lamb."

5. The words were spoken in 1877 by Thomas Edison, inventor of the phonograph.

 **SPOTCHECK 13–9** Use appositives to combine these sentences.

Example: Minneapolis is the largest city in Minnesota. It has 153 city-owned parks.
<u>Minneapolis, the largest city in Minnesota, has 153 city-owned parks.</u>

1. Elizabeth Kenny was an Australian nurse. She developed a method for treating polio.

_____

2. The quartet played bebop. Bebop is a style of jazz developed in the late 1940s.

_____

3. Elvis Presley was the "King" of rock 'n' roll. He died in 1977.

_____

4. Alice Walker wrote *The Color Purple.* It is a novel.

_____

✔ DOUBLECHECK 13–1 Identify the underlined words as a prepositional phrase (Prep), a participial phrase (Part), or an appositive (Ap).

_____ 1. <u>Under her bed</u>, Mary kept all her childhood dolls.

_____ 2. Doctor Peterson, <u>a sprinter in college</u>, now runs marathons.

_____ 3. Renata, <u>one of four sisters</u>, has three brothers.

_____ 4. <u>Having lived on a farm all his life</u>, Milton was eager to attend college in a city.

_____ 5. The Ricardos, <u>annoyed by the poor acting</u>, left the performance after the first act.

_____ 6. <u>Clinging to a teddy bear</u>, the child climbed into her mother's lap.

_____ 7. Michael got a souvenir from his brother, <u>a center fielder for the Cardinals</u>.

_____ 8. <u>Encouraged by the appearance of the sun</u>, the boys went to the beach.

✔ EDITING CHECK 13 Combine sentences in this paragraph by using prepositional and participial phrases and appositives. The sentences are numbered as a guide.

[1]People have been trying to hide or get rid of body odor. They have tried for a long time. [2]The ancient Egyptians were among the first to avoid "offending." They used scented oils under their arms. [3]People favored two spices. They were citrus and cinnamon. [4]The body uses perspiration to cool off. The body can secrete several gallons

a day in hot weather. **⁵**A product to fight underarm odor was introduced. It was introduced in 1888. **⁶**It was called Mum. It was soon followed by other deodorants.

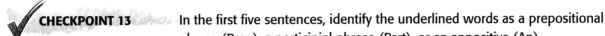 **CHECKPOINT 13** In the first five sentences, identify the underlined words as a prepositional phrase (Prep), a participial phrase (Part), or an appositive (Ap).

_____ 1. One of the earliest eye drops, <u>used in China 5000 years ago,</u> was made from the mahuang plant.

_____ 2. It contained ephedrine hydrochloride, <u>an ingredient still used today to treat eye irritations.</u>

_____ 3. <u>In Germany in the late nineteenth century,</u> Hermann von Helmholtz made an important contribution to eye care.

_____ 4. He invented the ophthalmoscope, <u>a device for examining the eye's interior.</u>

_____ 5. In 1890, Otis Hall, <u>a banker in Spokane, Washington,</u> accidentally helped bring about one of the best-known eye solutions.

Identify the next five sentences as simple (S), compound (C), or complex (X).

_____ 6. As he looked at a horse's broken shoe, Otis Hall was struck in the eye by a flick of the horse's tail.

_____ 7. His cornea was cut by the blow, and it became infected.

_____ 8. His injury was treated by two eye specialists, brothers James and George McFatrich.

_____ 9. Impressed by his quick recovery, Hall joined the brothers in a firm to market their eye drops, which contained muriate of berberine.

_____ 10. They combined the first and last syllables of the medicine for the market name Murine.

Wordcheck: Foreign Words

Words and expressions from other languages make their way into English. Look up the meanings of the italicized words in these sentences. Note what language they come from.

1. Cedric had a sense of *déjà vu* as he entered the English class.

2. Rebecca shouted, *"Shalom!"* as her friends drove away.

3. Mark said he would repay Al's loan *mañana.*

4. His rude attitude made William a *persona non grata* at the party.

5. Marcia's wedding was a *fait accompli* by the time John arrived at the church to propose.

GO ELECTRONIC!

For supplemental readings, exercises, and Internet activities, visit *Checkpoints Online* at
http://www.ablongman.com/page

Chapter 14

The Persuasion Essay

READING PRECHECK

The Drug Policy Foundation is a non-profit organization whose goal is to promote open debate and public education on possible approaches to the drug problem in the United States. The foundation ran this ad in national newspapers. Does it persuade you that policy changes are needed?

JOURNAL TOPIC: What are your views on current drug laws?

What Should Be Done About Drugs?
Drug Policy Foundation

Q: Will the next $150 billion make you safer?   1

A: Not if we spend it on the same old strategy.   2

Since 1981, well over 150 billion of our tax dollars have gone to fight the war   3
on illegal drugs. Annual spending has grown so fast that the next $150 billion will
be spent in three years. But if we do not change our basic drug strategy, it is
unlikely we will be any safer.

Current drug policies cannot deal with the excess crime, violence and disease   4
caused by drug prohibition.

FACT: According to FBI data, one out of three robberies and burglaries is com-   5
     mitted to obtain money for high-priced, black market drugs.

FACT: Up to 40 percent of the murders in major cities and 20 percent of the   6
     killings nationwide occur in the drug trade. Innocent children and police
     officers are often caught in the crossfire.

FACT: One out of three U.S. AIDS cases is traceable to the sharing of infected **7** needles by drug users. Criminalizing these users and prohibiting access to clean needles worsens the deadly AIDS epidemic.

These are just a few of the costs and consequences of maintaining strict drug **8** prohibition policies. This great nation can do better. With less waste. With more success dealing with hardcore users. And without fueling war in our cities.

What should new drug policies look like? We must study the legalization of **9** drugs. Support for this position comes from across the political spectrum.

Full legalization is not the only alternative. Different policies might make **10** sense for different drugs. Many options are available, including decriminalizing users only, permitting doctors to prescribe some drugs to addicts to undercut the black market, borrowing elements of the European public health model, or shifting the allocation of anti-drug resources to focus mainly on treatment and prevention rather than drug law enforcement.

No one can claim to know precisely what is best—not legalization advocates, **11** not prohibition's partisans. We all share concern over the problems caused by drug abuse in our society, but we must also concern ourselves with the harms caused by our policies. The question of pursuing alternatives must be fully and realistically investigated and debated.

What we cannot do is sit idly by while our nation continues to pursue mis- **12** guided drug policies. Much like alcohol prohibition did, our modern prohibition:

Enriches gangsters. At least $40 billion each year goes to the criminal under- **13** world as proceeds from drug sales.

Endangers and corrupts police. Police officers risk their lives enforcing prohi- **14** bition—but each drug dealer caught is immediately replaced. Drug profits have tempted too many public servants to become criminals themselves.

Fails to protect our children. Banned drugs are often easier for our kids to get **15** than regulated drugs like alcohol and tobacco. Pushers have a financial incentive to draw children into the drug trade and initiate them into drug use.

Insanity has been defined as doing the same thing over and over again and **16** expecting a different result. Despite some recent, commendable shifts in strategy, that is what our nation is doing now in drug policy.

It's time for a change. **17**

Checking Meaning and Style

1. What is the main idea of the selection?
2. What three "facts" support the idea that drug policy has failed? (Paragraphs 5–7)
3. What are some of the options besides legalizing drugs? (Paragraph 10)
4. In what ways does today's drug policy repeat the failures of the prohibition of alcohol—1920 to 1933? (Paragraphs 13–15)

Checking Ideas

1. Do you favor or oppose the legalization of hard drugs? Explain.
2. Which of the options listed in Paragraph 10 do you favor or oppose? Why?
3. The reading ends with the words "It's time for a change." Is it specific about what change it favors?

Analyzing Persuasion Writing

The ad "What Should Be Done About Drugs?" sets out to persuade the reader that recent drug policy has failed. It argues that the ban on hard drugs contributes to other kinds of criminal behavior and that the ban has been no more effective in preventing drug abuse than the Eighteenth Amendment (1920) was in prohibiting alcohol abuse. Its use of statistics and an unemotional tone encourage the reader at least to keep an open mind on the controversial subject.

You yourself might want to use persuasive writing techniques—to convince income tax officials that you really don't owe more taxes, for example, or to convince a sweetheart in a distant city that she or he should marry you. Many of the paragraphs you have already written for this class were meant to persuade, even though you might not have thought of them that way. If your topic sentence read, "English classes are a waste of time," your paragraph wasn't a success unless you argued that point convincingly. In other classes you may need to "prove" in a term paper or exam that John Lennon was a greater composer than Mozart, or that the United States should not send troops to settle disputes in the Middle East.

Let's say you want to write a paper showing that grades in college should be abolished. Here are some of the techniques of persuasion you might use:

1. Cite <u>facts or statistics</u> on student health problems or suicides blamed on grade worries.
2. Quote <u>expert authorities</u> who argue that grades inspire negative competition rather than positive cooperation.
3. Give <u>examples from history</u> showing that college students have not always been graded.
4. Offer <u>current examples</u> of colleges that don't assign grades.
5. Present a <u>narrative (anecdote)</u> about a rich and famous inventor who flunked out of college.
6. Give a <u>description</u> of a classroom full of students agonizing over an exam.
7. Describe a <u>personal experience</u>—the time you got a rash over a "D" in algebra.

Workers in most industrialized countries have shorter work weeks and more holidays than do American workers. The model essay that follows supports a shorter work week but admits that more leisure time can have drawbacks, too.

Model Persuasion Essay

WORKERS NEED A BREAK

Introduction, with thesis statement underlined

Some observers say Americans work too hard. They point out that many workers put in longer hours on the job these days, sometimes for less money; and increasing numbers of workers take second jobs to maintain their standard of living. To make matters worse, workers often find the drive to and from the job getting more and more time-consuming and frustrating. Is the solution a shorter work week with no reduction in pay, as some suggest? Such a change could have both benefits and drawbacks but is a good idea overall.

Body with first support, topic sentence underlined

A thirty-hour work week could have many advantages for workers and their families. For one thing, parents would have more time to spend with their children to strengthen the family ties that seem to be loosening these days. Not only would parents have the leisure to talk and play games with their children, they would also still have the energy to do so at the end of the work day. Increased leisure would permit workers to pursue hobbies and other interests that could enrich their own lives and refresh them for the return to work. There would also be more time for community activities. When the PTA at the children's school asks for help in the annual fundraiser, help is more likely to be offered.

Body with second support, topic sentence underlined

A pessimist, however, might see a downside to a thirty-hour work week and the increased leisure it would bring. Not everyone would use this time constructively. If more time off means more time in front of the TV set drinking beer and eating chips, no great gain (except in weight) will be made. Increased leisure could lead to an increase in what often seems to be Americans' favorite pastime, visiting the mall and buying items not needed with money better spent in other ways. Finally, increased time together could result in increased family tensions, arguments, and, in worst-case scenarios, family violence.

Body with third support, topic sentence underlined

Rudy, my neighbor, is an example of both the good and the bad sides of increased leisure. He is now a "telecommuter," working at home four days a week and going to the office only on Fridays. Assuming he actually does put in eight hours a day for his employer, he still saves four to six hours a week in driving time and another hour or so by not shaving so often. How does he use this new leisure? On the plus side, he plays tennis several times a week with his son when the high school sophomore gets home. The other day Rudy attended a conference with his daughter's sixth-grade teacher. And while Rudy and I were working in our yards last week (I'm glad to say he mows his lawn more often now), he told me how much fun the family was having evenings playing whist. However, his arguments with his wife seem to have increased. I heard her complain that since he was home so much, he should do more of the housework. She told my wife that Rudy spends far too much time and money surfing the net on his computer and buying the latest software. But I don't expect them to come to blows.

1

2

3

4

Conclusion Increased leisure is a mixed blessing, but on the whole it's a benefit that **5** more workers should receive.

Writing Assignment: A Persuasion Essay

Persuade the reader to accept your viewpoint on one of these topics: work, education, marriage, television, or popular music.

 # Writing Topic Bank

Selling Yourself

What career or profession would you like to pursue? Write an essay that convinces your readers to support your career choice.

Exploring Speed Limits on the Internet

Do speed limits save lives or do the fines paid by violators just provide another source of income for local and state governments? Use any search engine you like (such as Lycos.com, Google.com, Yahoo.com, Overture.com) to search for opinions on this issue. Using a combination of facts, statistics, quotes from experts, examples, and narrative or personal experience, write a persuasive essay defining your viewpoint.

Writing About Media

Is television a positive or negative influence on children? What are the risks? What are the benefits? Could the programming be improved? What about the violence, sit-coms, live coverage of news events, commercials? Write an essay taking one of the following positions:

1. Television watching should be required of everyone.
2. Television could be improved.
3. Television should be eliminated.

WRITING CHECKLIST

 Organize your essay with a thesis sentence and topic sentences. Start with a thesis sentence that makes clear the point you intend to make, as in these sentences:

Drug policy should put more emphasis on education and rehabilitation and less on enforcement and punishment.

A relaxed drug policy would just lead to more abuse by more people.

(continued)

The growing scarcity of leisure, the lack of time for families to be together, and the hours spent commuting show the need for a thirty-hour (four-day) work week.
My work and school schedule is too demanding.
Many workers do (not) make good use of their leisure time.

Use this outline to organize your ideas:

Thesis _____

_____

First support _____

_____

Second support _____

_____

Third support _____

_____

Conclusion _____

✓ Use prewriting techniques to make the preliminary outline and to develop the body of the essay. Asking how and why will be helpful in developing the essay.

✓ When revising the first draft, correct more than just grammar and punctuation; look also for ways to improve the content and organization.

✓ Center a title on the top line of the first page.

✓ Proofread the final copy carefully.

Sentence Sense: Solving Sentence Problems

We will now take up an assortment of problems that can weaken sentences: misplaced modifiers, dangling modifiers, nonparallel construction, other mixed constructions, and passive constructions. That's a lot, so go slowly!

Misplaced Modifiers

Notice what happens when we move around the word *only* in these sentences:

Stan *only* borrowed five dollars. (He didn't steal the money.)

Stan borrowed *only* five dollars. (He would have liked more.)

Only Stan borrowed five dollars. (The others had enough already.)

We see that it is important to be careful in placing words in a sentence, especially words that change the meaning of other words. Such words are called *modifiers*. A modifier usually should be placed near the words it modifies to avoid what is called a *misplaced modifier*. Sometimes the error is unintentionally amusing.

(misplaced) Tony was given a horse by the rancher that was old and sway-backed. (The *rancher* was old and swaybacked?)

(revised) The rancher gave Tony a horse that was old and swaybacked.

The lesson is clear: Put modifiers near the words they modify. Be especially careful with the modifiers *almost, only, just, even, hardly,* and *nearly.* They go in front of the words they modify.

Roderick ~~almost~~ ate almost the entire pizza by himself.

Nakia ~~nearly~~ saved nearly five dollars by buying the dress on sale.

✓ **SPOTCHECK 14–1**   Rewrite each sentence to correct misplaced modifiers.

1. Ladonna even likes to go shopping when it's snowing.

_____

2. The first members of Congress only were paid $6 a day.

_____

3. Felipe bought a pizza coming home from school.

_____

4. Wilhelm even likes his girlfriend when she is angry.

_____

5. The average marriage in the United States only lasts 9.4 years.

_____

Dangling Modifiers

A modifier is said to "dangle" if it lacks a clear connection to the words it is supposed to modify.

(dangling) Arriving home from work, her dog greeted Elena at the front door.

Of course it was Elena, not the dog, who arrived home. The modifier "arriving home from work" "dangles." A modifier that begins a sentence should be followed at once by the word it modifies.

(revised) Arriving home from work, <u>Elena</u> was greeted at the front door by her dog.

(option) When Elena arrived home from work, her dog greeted her at the door.

(option) The dog greeted Elena at the door when she arrived home from work.

SPOTCHECK 14–2   **Rewrite these sentences to correct dangling modifiers.**

1. Out of gas, Daniel parked the car at the side of the road

_____

2. Although twenty-one years old, my father expected me to be in by midnight.

_____

3. Able to bend a steel bar with ease, I watched Mighty Mo in awe.

_____

4. Jane watched as the stew boiled over in horror.

_____

5. Contentedly eating grass, Solomon took a photo of the cows.

Parallel Construction

Similar ideas are easier to read if they are in the same form—if, that is, they have *parallel construction*.

Not Parallel	Parallel
Seeing is to believe.	Seeing is believing.
Naomi is not only smart, she has a lot of luck.	Naomi is not only smart, she is lucky.
Kimberly likes to sail, to swim, and skiing.	Kimberly likes to sail, to swim, and to ski.
Aspiring models should be attractive, tall, and not be overweight.	Aspiring models should be attractive, tall, and slender.

The topic sentence of a paragraph or the thesis sentence of an essay may list several points. Be sure to put them in parallel form.

> **(not parallel)** Among the advantages of attending Centerville College are the low tuition, the small class size, and because it is close to my home.

> **(parallel)** Among the advantages of attending Centerville College are the low tuition, the small class size, and the convenient location.

The first example uses two nouns (*tuition* and *class size*) before switching to a dependent clause (*because it . . .*). The correction replaces the clause with a third noun, *location*.

SPOTCHECK 14–3 Revise the underlined words to achieve parallel construction by writing in the correct form above the line.

1. Whether right or when he is wrong, Dave likes to argue.

2. After playing soccer all afternoon, Matty was tired, thirsty, and he needed a bath.

3. Henry believes having a good family life is more important than to have a lot of money.

4. Working at Ajax Repair has taught me not only how to fix cars but also getting along with people.

5. Terrie was bright but being lazy.

6. Many industries are moving from the North to the South because wages are lower, the climate is often more pleasant, and <u>offers greater recreational opportunities.</u>

Mixed Constructions

Don't start a sentence off in one direction and then, without reason, go off in another.

(mixed) Because Simon was bored caused him to sleep in class.

(better) Because Simon was bored, he slept in class.

(mixed) When Rudy gets home early pleases his wife.

(better) When Rudy gets home early, his wife is pleased.

(mixed) The best part of a baseball game is where [or when] they hit home runs.

(better) Home runs are the best part of a baseball game.

(mixed) Ramon asked Cynthia did she ever eat at Dyspepsia restaurant.

(better) Ramon asked Cynthia if she had ever eaten at Dyspepsia restaurant.

Faulty Comparisons

Be sure comparisons are completed.

(incomplete) Puffy cigarettes have less nicotine. (Less than what?)

(better) Puffy cigarettes have less nicotine than Gaspers do.

(or) Puffy cigarettes have less nicotine than tar.

Be sure comparisons are clear.

(unclear) The days in July are longer than December. (Days is compared to the month December.)

(better) The days in July are longer than those [or the days] in December.

Watch out for incomplete comparisons that use the words *so, such,* and *too.* Careful writers will not stop short of the bracketed words in these sentences:

It was *so* hot yesterday [that I went swimming].

He is *such* an intelligent student [that he should do well in college].

The sunset was *too* beautiful [for me to describe].

(or) The sunset was beautiful.

 **SPOTCHECK 14-4**   Edit these sentences to get rid of mixed constructions and faulty comparisons.

1. Polly is a lot smarter.

2. A good sale is when Yolanda is happy.

3. The trees in the spring are greener than the fall.

4. Although sunshine is forecast, but Rocky has his umbrella.

5. A compact disk can hold more songs.

6. A sandwich from home costs far less than the cafeteria.

7. The dinner was so delicious.

8. I asked Tim did he expect to make the team.

Active vs. Passive Voice

Compare these two sentences:

Mrs. Donadio mailed a letter to her aunt in Italy.

A letter to her aunt in Italy was mailed by Mrs. Donadio.

In the first sentence, the subject (Mrs. Donadio) *acts;* in the second the subject (letter) *receives* the action of the verb *was mailed.* The first sentence is in the *active voice,* the second in the *passive voice.*

You should generally use the more vigorous active voice. However, you may prefer the passive voice if the receiver of the action is more important than the doer. For example, the first of these two sentences might be preferred.

(passive voice) Thirty-two home runs were hit by National League batters in games Sunday. (emphasizes the home runs)

(active voice) National League batters hit thirty-two home runs in games Sunday. (emphasizes the batters)

 **SPOTCHECK 14-5**   In the blanks, write *A* if the sentence is in active voice, *P* if it is in passive voice.

_____ 1. The country road was littered with bottles and paper.

_____ 2. Marietta read three novels during summer vacation.

_____ 3. The famous Halley's Comet was not discovered by the astronomer Edmund Halley.

_____ 4. The first hit rock and roll record, "Rock Around the Clock," was made by Bill Haley and the Comets.

_____ 5. Many of the most popular silent movies featured a dog, Rin Tin Tin.

SPOTCHECK 14–6 **Change the sentences from passive to active voice.**

1. "The Star-Spangled Banner" was not made the official anthem until 1931, 117 years after it was written.

_____

2. Many of his most famous works were composed by Beethoven after he became deaf.

_____

3. The songs "White Christmas" and "God Bless America" were written by Irving Berlin, who never learned to read music.

_____

4. The Braille reading system was invented by a fifteen-year-old blind boy.

_____

5. Only one of his more than 1,500 paintings was sold by Vincent Van Gogh.

_____

DOUBLECHECK 14–1 **Match the letter identifying these sentence problems with the sentences they describe. The first one has been done.**

A. Misplaced or dangling modifier

B. Nonparallel construction

C. Mixed construction

D. Faulty comparison

E. Passive voice

__D__ 1. The wings of hummingbirds travel much faster.

_____ 2. Although the sun had gone down, the lake still shining in the distance.

_____ 3. The guide showed us the waterfalls, the lake, and where the trails went into the caves.

_____ 4. The window was closed by Raymond.

_____ 5. While studying in the library, the lights went out.

_____ 6. Ernie is good at table tennis, chess, and playing backgammon.

_____ 7. The movie *Night of the Stranger* was a lot scarier.

_____ 8. The concert was attended by ten thousand fans.

 **EDITING CHECK 14** Edit this paragraph to correct any nonparallel or mixed constructions, dangling modifiers, passive voice sentences, and faulty comparisons.

[1]The Academy Awards organization gave no prize for best sound effects at the first awards ceremony in 1928. [2]That's because all the entries being silent films. [3]Although thought of as "golden," mostly tin was what the statuette called Oscar was actually made of. [4]The winning film that year, *Wings,* only had a small part for an actor named Gary Cooper, becoming better known when the "talkies" arrived. [5]Originally broadcast on radio, the first television show wasn't aired until 1952. [6]For creating Mickey Mouse, an award went to Walt Disney in 1932. [7]One of the films that movie fans watch on TV more often, *Casablanca,* was named best picture in 1943. [8]A non-actor got much of the attention at the 1973 awards, when an advertising man got back stage, stripped off his clothes, and streaking past the footlights.

 **CHECKPOINT 14** Match the letter identifying these sentence problems with the sentences that follow.

A. Misplaced or dangling modifier

B. Nonparallel or mixed construction

C. Faulty comparison

D. Passive voice

_____ 1. The essay was written by Stacy.

_____ 2. Because she had no car was the reason Ms. Flores took the subway to work.

_____ 3. Ned would rather play basketball than to play football.

_____ 4. The play was enjoyed by most of the parents.

_____ 5. Nine out of ten housewives say *Shiny* is better.

_____ 6. To save for the holidays is why I put money in the bank.

_____ 7. Thomas Jefferson was a scholar, an ambassador, and he served as the third president.

_____ 8. While away from the desk, the phone rang and rang.

_____ 9. Little Michael put the toys on a shelf that belonged to Richard.

_____ 10. The waitress is efficient and has a friendly manner.

_____ 11. While eating breakfast, the TV screen went blank.

_____ 12. Minh is a lot smarter.

Wordcheck: Abbreviations

The dictionary lists abbreviations just as it does words—that is, in alphabetical order. For example, the airport abbreviation *e.t.d.* ("estimated time of departure") appears right after the word *etching.* Look up the meanings of these abbreviations:

1. etc.

2. e.g.

3. D.D.S.

4. S.P.C.A

5. mm

GO ELECTRONIC!

For supplemental readings, exercises, and Internet activities, visit *Checkpoints Online* at
http://www.ablongman.com/page

Chapter 15

An Essay Using Mixed Modes

READING PRECHECK

A volunteer English teacher talks about his immigrant students' work and lives in the United States, using a variety of paragraph development methods.

JOURNAL TOPIC: How do you figure out what to do when you face a decision about whether to stay with the familiar or to venture out into the unknown?

Out of the Sweatshop and Into the World
David Masello

I was surprised last fall when my Chinese students didn't know the term "sweatshop." Lo, a woman in her mid-50s, told me during a class that she had spent 35 years working in a garment factory—not once getting a day off with pay. Sam, who is a few years younger, had stitched collars in Australia for 10 years before coming to New York and doing the same task for five more. He was an anesthesiologist in China but is content now to be working as an aide in an East Harlem nursing home where some of his medical training is put to use. Both he and Lo, co-workers at the Florence Nightingale Home, marveled at having two days off every week.

"Real luxury," Lo said, "no work two whole days."

Still not used to such luxury, Lo said she doesn't know how to use the time, so she often just sits in her favorite chair at home or goes to a second mass at church. And because Sam's workweek is now 40 hours, instead of the 70 he used to put in, he explained that he has time to attend to his Brooklyn garden—growing Chinese eggplant, "much better than American eggplant," he insisted.

For several years, I have taught English as a volunteer, to immigrants at a **4** Chinatown Manpower Project, a nonprofit organization that provides vocational training and tutoring for people of all ages. Sometimes, when I meet my students, I feel as if I've been handed the wrongly accused, people just released from a Devil's Island compound who never had the chance to learn the language of their adopted country or see neighborhoods beyond their own.

One evening a week, I stand before a blackboard in an old public-school **5** classroom, the occasional blur of a mouse disappearing behind radiators, writing down phrases and idioms. Typical conversation topics include happy memories (weddings, births of children), superstitions (it's proper to sprinkle food at grave site for relatives to enjoy), goals (living in a house with two bedrooms!) and first impressions of America (disappointment at bleak neighborhoods, awe at the variety of races).

When I used the word "sweatshop" and my students didn't understand, I sat **6** at a desk pretending to stitch at a sewing machine, pumping an imaginary pedal, mopping my brow with the drama of a silent-film star. "Sweating in a shop—or fac-tory—as you work, getting very tired," I explained.

"Sweatshop," Lo said, "make sense. Meaning is correct." **7**

I've often seen wisps of steam funneling from clouded windows in old build- **8** ings in Chinatown. Now I know that within those places some of my students are hunched over sewing machines, feeding garments under bobbing needles. The faster they work the more money they make, for payment is by the piece and not the hour.

One of the first topics I cover each semester is which sites my students have **9** visited. Lo, who has lived in New York 25 years, had been to Central Park once and never to the Metropolitan Museum of Art. I used to think some students were incu-rious. I've come to realize that after 70 hours a week at a sewing machine, with pay often below minimum wage, there is no time or energy to admire a Vermeer or see the whitecaps on the Central Park Reservoir some windy Sunday afternoon.

I take my students on occasional field trips and, during a tour of midtown last **10** September, as we were about to enter Saks Fifth Avenue, Lo bragged that she had made sample fabrics for a fashion show there. When we went inside, an aggres-sive perfume-company rep approached her and asked if she wanted a spritz of fragrance and the chance to purchase it and an accompanying silk scarf at a spe-cial price. But Lo didn't understand her and laughed out of self-consciousness, whereupon the perfume worker turned to a co-worker and said, "This one hasn't got a clue about fashion."

After class weeks later, Lo and I stopped at a bulletin board in a hallway that **11** displays adult-student projects. Among the items pinned to the board were shirt collars, plackets and zippers. I never knew there were four kinds of zippers—the kissing zipper, overlap, right fly and invisible. Lo ran the zipper up and down the gleaming track of one of the samples, an invisible.

"This is what I used to do. I was expert," she said with a wistfulness, certainly **12** remembering how hard the job was, but also how it allowed her to remain in the background of American life.

"Still scared at my job at nursing home," she admitted to me in class one day. **13** "Too many responsibilities and nobody understand my accent."

Over the semester, Lo remained uneasy in her nursing-home job, but never **14** said she missed the old work of zippers and plackets and collars.

Checking Meaning and Style

1. Paragraph 1 illustrates which method of paragraph development: cause and effect, example, or persuasion?
2. Paragraph 3 illustrates which method of paragraph development: example, specific details, or comparison?
3. Paragraphs 4 and 5 illustrate which method of paragraph development: narration, definition, or opinion?
4. Paragraphs 6 and 7 illustrate which method of paragraph development: example, definition, or comparison?
5. What are some of the effects of working very long hours? (Paragraphs 3, 9)
6. What methods of teaching English does the author use? (Paragraphs 5, 6, 10)
7. What does Lo feel about her former job in the sweatshop? (Paragraphs 11–14)

Checking Ideas

1. Should American citizens care about the existence of sweatshops?
2. What opinion does the author give about the limited life that many immigrants lead because of their long work hours?
3. There is an ongoing public debate about whether to allow more immigration or whether to limit immigration into the United States. What reasons can you think of to support each of these positions?
4. Is your city, county, or neighborhood home to many immigrants? What are the effects of having so many immigrants, or so few immigrants, on the character of the place?

Analyzing an Essay with Mixed Modes

Using this text, you have practiced a variety of methods for developing your ideas in paragraphs and essays—comparison, narration, description, and so forth. Much writing, of course, uses a combination of methods, as we see in "Out of the Sweatshop and Into the World." *Narration* tells the story of the author's classes with his students. *Examples* of different students' experiences show the long, unrelieved hours that immigrants are often forced to work. One *effect* of this constant work is that immigrants may not become familiar with the larger society. *Definition* of the word "sweatshop" is given by means of gestures to overcome the language barrier.

Model Mixed Mode Essay

Before going on to the final writing assignment, study the organization of this essay:

LOOKING AHEAD

Introduction, with thesis statement

Like everyone else, I have many goals in life. <u>Two of the most important are getting a solid education and leaving a healthy planet for those who come after me.</u>   1

1st support, with topic sentence and specific details

<u>I want an education that will prepare me not only to get a well-paying and worthwhile career but that will also help me live a satisfying life outside my work.</u> To prepare myself to get a good job, I am majoring in X-ray technology. Careers in radiology (as the field is also called) pay quite well. I would be able to support myself and my family comfortably; and some day, perhaps, I would be able to buy a house in a safe neighborhood with good schools. But I also want to get what is called a liberal education. For example, I want to take courses in literature and the arts to enrich my leisure time. I want to take courses in psychology and sociology to understand myself and my fellow citizens. I want courses in history to see where we humans have come from and where we are headed.   2

2nd support, with topic sentence and specific details

<u>Protecting the environment is also important to me.</u> Like everyone else, I have a duty to leave our Earth in at least as good a condition as I found it. I believe we should all be like those Native Americans whose beliefs required them to consider how their actions would affect the seventh generation of those who followed. One small contribution I can make is to limit the size of my family so as not to contribute to the exploding population growth that threatens the environment and the quality of life for everyone. I can also vote for those political candidates who can look further into the future than the next election.   3

Conclusion

No one wants to live in poverty, but it is not necessary for us to be rich to be happy, especially if our education has prepared us to lead a full life. At the same time, we cannot be happy if we think we are leaving an unhealthy planet to our grandchildren.   4

Again, we see an essay organized with thesis and topic sentences. The first body paragraph (Paragraph 2) gives specific reasons why the writer wants a good education. The next argues the need for a healthy planet.

Writing Assignment: An Essay on Life

Choose one of the following topics for your essay. The essay should have an introduction, two or three paragraphs of support, and a conclusion.

1. An essay discussing two or three goals you have that will make your life worthwhile.

2. An essay in which you discuss how your view of life differs from that of a friend or of one or both of your parents. Support paragraphs might compare their lives with your own life and goals.

3. An essay discussing two or three ways that population changes have made life better or worse, or both, where you live.

Writing Topic Bank

An Important Experience

Who has had the greatest influence in your life? What made her, him, or them influential? What are several ways that you were affected? What are some examples of these effects? What might have been different about your life without this influence? Write an essay using several methods of paragraph development to describe the greatest influence in your life.

Exploring Your Interests on the Internet

Use any search engine you like (such as Lycos.com, Ask.com, Yahoo.com, Dogpile.com) to locate websites related to a hobby, sport, or activity that interests you. Use the information available at those websites to write an essay encouraging others to become involved in your hobby, sport, or activity. Use several methods of paragraph development in your essay.

Writing About Media

The media is a great tool for learning. Instruction for developing skills ranging from agriculture to yodeling are available from books and audio/video sources. Classes, demonstrations, and tutoring are advertised through the media. What skill would you choose to explore through media sources? Look for sources of instruction in that skill in your local library, television schedule guide, community bulletin boards, newspapers, the Internet, and other media offerings. How many ways are there to learn the skill? How did you track down the information? Which source of instruction do you believe would be most effective for learning the skill? Write an essay describing your exploration. Use several methods of paragraph development in your essay.

WRITING CHECKLIST

 Use such prewriting techniques as asking how and why, freewriting, and journal writing.

 As was done in this chapter's reading, consider using different writing modes to develop your ideas. Use any of the methods discussed this term that will make your ideas interesting and convincing.

(continued)

WRITING CHECKLIST (continued)

 Be sure to include in the first paragraph a thesis sentence that states what point you want to make in the essay.

 Start each support paragraph with a topic sentence.

 Revise the essay as many times as needed, watching especially for mistakes made on recent papers.

 Center a title on the top line of the first page.

 Proofread the paper carefully before handing it in.

Sentence Sense: Adding Polish

By now you have learned most of the basics of effective writing. Finally, here are some tips that will help add polish to your writing.

Wordiness

Don't pad your writing with unnecessary words.

(wordy) Due to the fact that her essay had been written with a pencil, Melissa was asked to write it once more, this time with a pen.

(concise) Melissa was asked to rewrite her essay using a pen instead of a pencil.

Notice how one word can take the place of several.

due to the fact that (because)

LUANN/Greg Evans

LUANN reprinted by permission of United Feature Syndicate, Inc.

during the time period that (while)

at this point in time (now)

in the near future (soon)

Get rid of unneeded words.

After ~~the~~ class ~~ended~~, we went to the cafeteria.

The package was square ~~in shape~~.

Rich got home at 3 a.m. ~~in the morning~~.

Don't waste space with such expressions as "it seems to me" and "in my opinion."

~~In my humble opinion,~~ (T)he mayor should be thrown out of office.

Look carefully at sentences that begin with *there is* or *there are*. They are often both wordy and weak.

(wordy) There are several varieties of wheat grown in North Dakota.

(better) North Dakota grows several varieties of wheat.

SPOTCHECK 15–1   Rewrite these sentences to eliminate wordiness.

1. There are ten amendments in the Constitution's Bill of Rights.

   _____

2. Agnes' dress was bright blue in color.

   _____

3. Late in the month of June, heavy rain fell on the city and made everything wet.

   _____

4. Because of the fact that he is a pacifist, Eric opposes war.

   _____

5. As far as tomorrow night's game is concerned, it seems to me our team should win.

   _____

6. There are many occasions when we need good advice.

   _____

Adjectives and Adverbs

Adjectives and adverbs are words that describe (modify) other words.

Adjectives describe nouns or pronouns.

The campers watched the <u>beautiful</u> sunset. (*beautiful* describes the noun *sunset*)

She was <u>optimistic</u>. (*optimistic* describes the pronoun *she*)

With most adjectives, add *-er* when comparing two things; add *-est* when comparing three or more things.

Sheila is <u>taller</u> than Pat.

Sheila is the <u>tallest</u> member of the team.

Longer adjectives become awkward when *-er* or *-est* is added.

(awkward) The teacher is <u>intelligenter</u> than the banker.

With long adjectives, use *more* or *most* in front of the adjective instead of *-er* or *-est* at the end.

The teacher is <u>more intelligent</u> than the banker.

The plumber is the <u>most intelligent</u> person in town.

Never use *-er* and *more* together; never use *-est* and *most* together.

(wrong) My dog is <u>more smarter than</u> your dog. (omit *more*)

(wrong) That is the <u>most dumbest</u> thing I've ever seen. (omit *most*)

Some adjectives are irregular; that is, they are compared in a different way from the methods just discussed. Be sure to memorize the forms of these adjectives:

good	better	best
bad	worse	worst
many	more	most

Spelling tip: For adjectives ending in *y*, change the *y* to *i* before *-er* or *-est*.

happy	happier	happiest		easy	easier	easiest

 **SPOTCHECK 15–2** **In the blanks, write the correct form of the adjectives shown in parentheses.**

1. (faded) Robert's jeans are _____ than Pete's.

2. (bad) *American Beauty* was the _____ movie Natalie had ever seen.

3. (happy) Who is _____, Stacie or Carrie?

4. (many) The Coliseum holds _____ people than the Astrodome.

5. (intelligent) Of the three sisters, Chandra is the _____.

SPOTCHECK 15–3   **Write sentences using the adjectives in parentheses.**

1. (better) _____

2. (least) _____

3. (more athletic) _____

4. (bigger) _____

5. (best) _____

Adverbs

Adverbs describe verbs. They usually end in *-ly*.

The gas station attendant walked <u>slowly</u> to the pump. (*Slowly* is an adverb describing the verb *walked.*)

The student <u>gladly</u> gave his bus seat to the old man. (*Gladly* describes the verb *gave.*)

Don't make the mistake of using an adjective instead of an adverb following a verb.

Thomas spoke ~~angry~~ angrily to the dog's owner.

The child ran ~~quick~~ quickly to her mother.

In writing, don't leave off the *-ly* in *really* and *easily.*

The company president was ~~real~~ really angry when the vice-president contradicted him.

Terry can make an apple pie ~~easy~~ easily.

Mistakes are often made with the words *well* and *good*. Well is an adverb; it describes verbs. *Good* is an adjective; it describes nouns and pronouns.

Morgan is a <u>good</u> tennis player. (*Good* is an adjective modifying the noun *player.*)

Morgan played <u>well</u> in the tournament. (*Well* is an adverb modifying the verb *played.*)

SPOTCHECK 15-4   Underline the correct word in parentheses.

1. Calvin (quick / quickly) picked up the phone.

2. Annie won the 100-meter dash (easy / easily).

3. The child gazed (envious / enviously) at the neighbor's bicycle.

4. It is (good / well) that Yuko had the spare tire inspected.

5. The tetherball team did (good / well) in the conference finals.

6. Carmen knew Rodolfo (good / well) before he became famous.

SPOTCHECK 15-5   Write sentences using the adjectives and adverbs in parentheses.

1. (good) _____

2. (well) _____

3. (eagerly) _____

4. (careful) _____

5. (quietly) _____

Double Negatives

The error called a *double negative* occurs when the adverb *not* is used with another negative word. (*Not* often is disguised in such contractions as *can't, won't, hasn't,* and *couldn't.*)

(**wrong**) Susan <u>didn't</u> have <u>no</u> time to go dancing.

(**right**) Susan <u>didn't</u> have <u>any</u> time to go dancing.

(**right**) Susan had <u>no</u> time to go dancing.

The words *hardly* and *scarcely* are negatives and shouldn't be used with the word *not.*

(**wrong**) The millionaire <u>didn't</u> pay <u>hardly</u> any taxes.

(**right**) The millionaire paid <u>hardly any</u> taxes.

SPOTCHECK 15-6   Edit these sentences to get rid of double negatives.

Example: Bill doesn't like ~~no one~~ in the group.
          anyone

1. Amy didn't take none of Susan's advice.

2. The soccer team doesn't have scarcely enough money for uniforms.

3. Frank doesn't contribute nothing to charity.

4. The Gregorys don't know no one in San Antonio.

5. Since the accident, Mr. Quan can't hardly walk.

Faulty Logic

Your writing should be logical. If your reader's response is "That's ridiculous," you have lost your reader. Here are some common logical fallacies or errors in reasoning:

- Hasty Generalization—A sweeping statement that doesn't take into account likely exceptions.

    (**illogical**) Women workers are underpaid.

    (**illogical**) Never trust anyone over thirty.

Yes, *some, many,* a *few* women are underpaid. But the sentence implies that *all* are underpaid, and the reader knows that isn't true. As for those over thirty, surely a few of them are trustworthy.

  Watch out for sentences that use or imply the words *all, every, none, always,* or *never.* Instead use qualifiers like *some, most, the average,* or *sometimes.*

- Non Sequitur—These Latin words mean "it doesn't follow." Here's an argument in which the conclusion "doesn't follow" the evidence offered:

    (**illogical**) Maria had a frown on her face yesterday, so she must have flunked her history exam. (Her frown has many possible explanations.)

- Bandwagon—Because most people favor something is not necessarily a reason for everyone to "get on the bandwagon."

    (**illogical**) Senator Murphy is leading in the polls, so I guess I should vote for him.

- Either-or Fallacy—Saying there are only two choices or possibilities when there are actually more.

    (**illogical**) Either I get some new clothes, or I'll never get a girlfriend.

© Hilary B. Price. Reprinted with special permission of King Features Syndicate.

- Circular Reasoning—"Proving" a point by restating it (going around in a circle).

   (illogical) Professor Jones is a poor teacher because his classes are no good.

- Ad Hominem—"To the man." Attacking a person's ideas by attacking the person. Also, appealing to the emotions rather than to reason.

   (illogical) How can you agree with Joe Smith's politics? He never went to college.

   (illogical) Vote for Margaret Smathers; she lost both her children in a car accident.

- Post Hoc, Ergo Propter Hoc (*Post Hoc,* for short)—"After this, therefore because of this." Wrongly assuming that because one event follows another it is caused by the first event.

   (illogical) It's no use washing my car. The last two times I did, it rained.

- Glittering Generalities—Gaining favor with nice-sounding words that have little meaning by themselves.

   If elected, I will restore liberty, honor, and respect for the flag to this great nation.

SPOTCHECK 15–7   Identify the logical fallacies in these examples.

1. Everyone else cuts class, so why shouldn't I do it?

   Fallacy: _____

2. Either everybody stops using paper products, or we soon won't have any more trees.

   Fallacy: _____

3. The reason I like that band's music is that it sounds so good.

   Fallacy: _____

4. You just know that anyone who lifts weights is healthy.

   Fallacy: _____

5. Angela has a nice smile, so she will be good in sales.

   Fallacy: _____

6. Football players advertise beer, so drinking must improve athletic ability.

   Fallacy: _____

7. I'm in favor of home and family values; vote for me.

   Fallacy: _____

8. Since everyone else is getting a personal computer, I should too.

   Fallacy: _____

9. I went to a movie last night, and today I got an "A" in algebra. I'm going to go to a movie before all my tests.

   Fallacy: _____

10. You look like a smart person. You'll probably want to buy some life insurance.

    Fallacy: _____

DOUBLECHECK 15–1   Match the letters identifying these sentence errors with the appropriate sentences.

A. Wordiness

B. Adjective or adverb misused

C. Logic error

_____ 1. No other woman can match Gloria's sense of humor.

_____ 2. John can't hardly read without his glasses.

_____ 3. Many people believe that exercise helps them think clear.

_____ 4. Randolph tipped the scales at 190 pounds in weight.

_____ 5. Abdul had been married for five years at that point in time.

_____ 6. Both Mr. and Mrs. Jones play tennis, but she has the best serve.

_____ 7. My fight with Franklin is past history.

_____ 8. Joe Pugilist can't never remember his last boxing match.

_____ 9. Pete studied for a week for the English exam, and now he has an ulcer.

_____ 10. If you don't marry me, my life will be a disaster.

DOUBLECHECK 15–2   Rewrite or edit the sentences to correct problems with wordiness, misuse of adjectives and adverbs, and faulty logic.

1. The firefighters put out the blaze quick.

_____

2. All Swedes are blondes.

   _____

3. It seems to me that Jennifer should head the committee.

   _____

4. Alaska is more bigger than Texas.

   _____

5. Greg had the worse batting average on the team.

   _____

6. Due to the fact that Christmas will be here in the near future, I'm saving my money.

   _____

7. Rocky would make a good surgeon because he doesn't mind the sight of blood.

   _____

8. The company's sales figures are real good this year.

   _____

9. Although they are twins, Sonia is tallest by three inches.

   _____

10. Everett doesn't phone his parents hardly ever since he moved to South Carolina.

    _____

✓ EDITING CHECK 15 Edit the following paragraph to take care of problems with wordiness, logic, and adjectives and adverbs. Not all the sentences contain errors.

[1]In 1885, George Eastman gave up his bank clerk's comfortable salary of $15 a week to gain time to develop a small and simple camera that would be easy to use. [2]Up

until that time in the past, cameras were large and complicated. **³**Three years later he produced a camera that in size was only 3½ inches wide and 6½ inches long. **⁴**The small size was possible in part because the camera used rolled, paper-backed film, instead of the bulky glass plates generally used at that time. **⁵**Eastman called it the "Detective Camera" because it was more smaller than other cameras, and its small size might enable someone like the popular fictional detective Sherlock Holmes to use it without being noticed. **⁶**The camera had a button on the side and a key to advance the film forward. **⁷**The camera came loaded with enough film to satisfy anybody, enough to take one hundred pictures. **⁸**When all the pictures had been taken, the photographer returned the entire camera back to Rochester, New York. **⁹**Sometime later, one hundred circular pictures, 2½ inches in diameter, were returned. **¹⁰**Returned, too, was the camera, loaded with film for another hundred photos. **¹¹**"You press the button—we do the rest" was the company's slogan. **¹²**No one can think of a more better one. **¹³**In 1888, Eastman changed the camera's name to Kodak, a name that could be pronounced easy anywhere in the world. **¹⁴**The business itself soon before long became the Eastman Kodak Company. **¹⁵**It was the more successful camera company for many years.

CHECKPOINT 15   **Match the letter identifying these sentence errors with the appropriate sentences that follow.**

A. Wordiness

B. Adjectives or adverbs misused

C. Faulty logic

_____ 1. Either I play professional basketball or I'll end up on Skid Row.

_____ 2. The final payment on Jill's coat is due in the month of June.

_____ 3. Professor Daley is smiling, so she'll probably let us out early today.

_____ 4. That test on grammar was real easy.

_____ 5. Stinger is the most fastest racehorse I've ever seen.

_____ 6. In order to succeed in bird-watching, one will find that one needs patience.

_____ 7. It's always windy in Chicago.

_____ 8. In the opinion of this writer, smog control standards should be the same in all states.

_____ 9. Jennifer is more kinder than Constance.

_____ 10. The car moved slow through the parking lot.

Wordcheck: Miscellaneous Facts

Use a dictionary to answer these questions.

1. What was the nickname of George Herman Ruth?

2. In what year did President Abraham Lincoln die?

3. Whose faces are featured at Mount Rushmore National Memorial?

4. How many inches are in a meter?

5. What was Mark Twain's real name?

GO ELECTRONIC!

For supplemental readings, exercises, and Internet activities, visit *Checkpoints Online* at
http://www.ablongman.com/page

Writing Resources

Writing Resource A
Dictionary Overview

One of the most useful tools a writer or speaker can have is a good dictionary. Of course, dictionaries tell us the meanings of words and how to spell and pronounce them, but they also contain a surprising amount of other information.

Let's look at the dictionary entry for an everyday word, *bird*. First, here is the complete entry from the pocket edition of *The American Heritage Dictionary* (Dell Publishing Company). Small, paperback dictionaries of this kind can easily be carried to class in a book bag.

bird (bûrd)   n. A warm-blooded, egg-laying, feathered vertebrate with forelimbs modified to form wings. [<OE *brid*.]

Now let's look at the entry for the same word in the larger *American Heritage Dictionary of the English Language* (Houghton Mifflin). This is a hardback "college size" or desk edition. You can see at a glance that it contains much more information than the pocket edition. If you do not have one at home, you can use one in any library.

pronunciation

part of speech

spelling ——————— **bird** (bûrd) *n.* **1.** Any member of the class Aves, which
                   includes warm-blooded, egg-laying feathered
definitions ——————— vertebrates with forelimbs modified to form wings.
                   2. A bird hunted as game. **3.** *Aerospace Slang.* A — usage
                   rocket or guided missile. **4.** A target, a **clay pigeon**
                   (*see*). **5.** The feather-tipped object used in playing
                   badminton, a **shuttlecock** (*see*). **6.** *Slang.* One who is
                   odd or remarkable. **7.** *British Slang.* A young
                   woman. **8.** *Slang.* A derisive sound of disapproval or
                   derision. Used chiefly in the expression *give* — idiomatic
                   (*someone*) *the bird.* —**for the birds.** *Slang.* Ob- expression
                   jectionable or worthless. —*intr. v.* **birded, birding,** — inflected forms
part of speech ——————— **birds. 1.** To observe and identify birds in their
                   natural surroundings. **2.** To trap, shoot, or catch
                   birds. [Middle English *byrd, bryd,* young bird, Old
origins ——————— English *brid.*]

Pronunciation

Right after the first entry of the word is a special spelling of the word to show correct pronunciation. The special alphabet used for pronunciation is explained in the key at the bottom of the page (or, perhaps, in a section at the beginning of the dictionary). For example, you may be told that the *ûr* in *bûrd* is pronounced the same as the *ur* in the word *urge*. A heavy accent mark (') shows which syllable should get the most emphasis when spoken (not needed for a one-syllable word such as *bird*).

Parts of Speech

How a word may be used in a sentence is shown right after the pronunciation guide. You are told that *bird* can be used as a noun (abbreviated *n.*). Later you learn that *bird* can also be used as a verb *(v.)*. Some other parts of speech discussed in this text are pronouns *(pron.)*, prepositions *(prep.)*, adjectives *(adj.)*, and adverbs *(adv.)*.

Meanings

The definitions come next. Since more than one meaning is often given, you will have to figure out which one applies in your situation.

Usage

Not all words can be used on all occasions. Your dictionary will probably tell you which words are *slang* or *nonstandard,* for example. Here, you learn that the definitions numbered 3, 6, 7, and 8 are slang, to be used only in the most informal situations.

Inflected Forms

Some words change their endings to show how they are used in a sentence. Verbs, for instance, usually change for the past-time form and the past participle. Noun endings usually change to show the plural. The dictionary will indicate these changes only when they are "irregular"—not made in the usual way.

Origins

The words we use today often have their origins in words used many centuries ago in England or in such languages as Greek, Latin, German, and French. *Bird,* we are told, is derived from Old English (used in the eighth to twelfth centuries) and Middle English (used in the twelfth to fifteenth centuries).

Other Features

Your dictionary may also give you examples of words used in idiomatic expressions (*for the birds* is one). It may show differences among synonyms (words that mean almost the same thing) and may give usage tips (when to use *alternate* and *alternative*, for example).

SPOTCHECK A–1

Ten definitions are included in the definition just given for *bird*—eight as a noun (n.) and two as a verb (v.). In the blanks at the left, write N or V and the number of the definition that fits each sentence.

Example: <u>N-5</u> The badminton player tossed the bird to his partner and said, "It's your service."

_____ 1. Three birds splashed in the puddle.

_____ 2. Fred and Phoebe birded at the seashore.

_____ 3. The giant bird blasted off from the launching pad.

_____ 4. The Williams' neighbor is a strange bird.

_____ 5. The trapshooter waited for the release of the bird.

SPOTCHECK A–2

Use a dictionary to answer these questions.

1. Which syllable is emphasized in pronouncing *theater?*

2. Which spelling is correct, *athlete* or *athelete?*

3. What does *itinerant* mean?

4. Is *itinerant* an adjective, a noun, or both?

5. What is the plural form of *leaf?*

6. What language is *clone* derived from?

7. What usage label is given for *hoosegow?*

Reading in College

The ability to read well can bring rewards throughout our lives, but as you no doubt already have discovered for yourself, good reading skills are essential in college. It's hard to take part in class discussions, and impossible to do well on tests, if you don't understand the assigned readings. In addition, reading can make you a better writer. Reading will show you how experienced writers make use of words, sentences, and paragraphs. Reading will improve your vocabulary and spelling skills, often without your even being aware of the change. And it will give you new ideas, information, and insights to add strength to your own writing.

Whether you are zipping through a biker magazine or struggling with a chemistry text, these suggestions can help you understand and remember what you read.

- *Preview* the material. The more you know ahead of time about what you are going to read, the easier and more efficient your reading will be.
- Is there an *introductory note* with clues about the subject or about what the author's purpose is? This note often appears at the top of the piece, before the title, as in this text.
- Look at the *title.* Sometimes it reveals or hints at the subject or purpose.
- What do you know about the *author?* What is he or she an authority on? What ideas or prejudices have come through in earlier writings that you have seen?
- Are there *subheadings*—short titles within the work, usually set in contrasting type? These may (1.) signal points that the author wants to emphasize or (2.) show how the ideas are organized.
- Read the *first and last paragraphs.* Writers often present their main idea at the beginning and restate it at the end.
- Read the first sentence of each of the other paragraphs. This may be the *topic sentence,* giving a summary of the entire paragraph. (This approach is less useful with the very short paragraphs often found in articles in newspapers and magazines.)
- Read *actively.* Ideas and information are not going to leap off the page into your mind. You have to make an effort. It may be a good idea to turn off the TV and the radio and to take off your headset.
- Look for the *main idea.* Then keep asking how other details relate to that idea.
- Decide what the author's *purpose* is in writing. Is it to inform, to persuade, to describe, to entertain? Focus on those details that carry out the purpose.

- Mark up your book! *Underline key points.* When you review the material before a class discussion or a test, the most important details should be obvious. Underlining requires constant thought about what is and isn't important. Those who overdo it—who underline almost every sentence—are missing the point.

- *Read critically.* Just because something is in a book doesn't mean you have to accept it as true or worthwhile. Ask questions. Do the "facts" seem reliable? Are the opinions supported with sound evidence? Is the writer appealing mostly to your emotions or to your reason? Jot down your doubts and disagreements in the margin.

- Understand the *words.* If not knowing a word blocks your understanding of a passage, by all means look it up. But it isn't necessary to turn to the dictionary every time you come to a new word. Often you can guess what the word means from the way it is used, and you can skip over some unfamiliar words for the moment if they aren't essential to understanding. By the way, reading on a wide range of subjects is the best way to build up your vocabulary.

- When you've finished reading, *quiz yourself.* What was the thesis or main point of the material? What were the main supporting points? If necessary, read the material again to find the answers you missed. Rarely will reading the material just once provide the understanding expected in the classroom.

Writing Resource C

Words Often Misused

advice / advise   You get or give *advice,* a noun. *Advise* is a verb. "I advise you to study for the exam."

ain't   Avoid except in very informal or humorous usage.

a lot   Often misspelled as *alot.*

already / all ready   *Already* means "by a certain time": "When I arrived, Bill had already left." *All ready* means "completely prepared": "The class was all ready for the exam."

alright   Misspelling of *all right.*

among / between   In general, use *among* when discussing three or more items: "flew among the flowers." Use *between* when discussing two items: "between you and me."

and etc.   Omit the *and,* since *etc.* is an abbreviation of *et cetera,* meaning "and others." Spell it *etc.,* not *ect.* Generally avoid use of *etc.* in formal writing.

as (if) / like   *As* or *as if* introduces a dependent clause: "It looks as if [not *like*] it will rain." Use *like* as a preposition: "Frank looks like his father."

can / may   In formal writing, use *can* to show ability: "Susan can drive a car." Use *may* to show permission: "Susan may drive her parents' car."

conscious / conscience   *Conscious* means "aware": "conscious of his shortcomings." *Conscience* is the sense of right and wrong: "The thief's conscience bothered him."

 **SPOTCHECK C–1**   Underline the correct word in parentheses.

1. My (conscious / conscience) bothered me because of some unkind remarks I had made to Ernest.

2. So I went over to Pete's house for some (advice / advise).

3. Pete said everything would be (alright / all right) if I would always be (conscious / conscience) of Ernest's feelings in the future.

4. "You (can / may) tell Ernest that I said he should forgive you," Pete said.

250

5. It was (as / like) I knew it would be: Pete would have the answers.

More Words Often Misused--2

could of Write *"could have."*

dessert / desert *Dessert* is the after-dinner treat. Use *desert* for other meanings: "Will the soldiers desert their leader?" "The soldiers struggled across the hot desert."

except / accept *Except* shows exclusion: "everyone except Bill." *Accept* means to receive: "accept the compliment."

fewer / less *Fewer* is used with plural nouns: "fewer classes," "fewer bananas." *Less* is used with singular nouns: "less cake," "less money."

firstly, secondly, etc. Use *first, second* instead.

fun Avoid in formal writing as an adjective: "We had ~~a fun~~ an enjoyable time."

imply / infer *Imply* means "to hint at or suggest": "He implied I took the money." *Infer* means "to guess": "From my guilty look, he inferred I took the money."

input Computer jargon adapted to mean "opinion" or "advice." Avoid, as in "Sue wants my input on what car to buy."

irregardless Nonstandard. Use *regardless.*

is when, is where Avoid in definitions: "A good party is when . . . ," "a good friend is where . . . ."

✓ **SPOTCHECK C–2** **Underline the correct word in parentheses.**

1. We had a (fun / pleasant) time at Phoebe and Bob's house Saturday night.

2. All our friends were there (except / accept) the Greenes, who had (excepted / accepted) another invitation.

3. Actually, there were (fewer / less) guests than at the Oswalds' New Year's Eve party.

4. I don't mean to (imply / infer) that Phoebe and Bob are less popular than the Oswalds.

5. No friend will (dessert / desert) someone who makes (desserts / deserts) as good as Phoebe's.

6. A good party is (when / an occasion when) good friends get together.

More Words Often Misused—3

know / no   "We *know* that there is *no* free lunch."

literally   Do not use for emphasis—"I ~~literally~~ cried my eyes out"—unless that is exactly what happened (your eyes *fell out*).

lose / loose   *Lose* is a verb: "He will lose everything" *Loose* is an adjective meaning "not tight": "a loose sweater."

lot(s) of   In formal writing, use *a great deal of, much,* or *many.* "We saw ~~lots of~~ many wildflowers on our trip."

me and   Avoid in compound subjects: "~~Me and Bill~~ Bill and I are brothers."

morale / moral   *Morale* refers to spirit or attitude: "The team's morale was high." *Moral* refers to good character or conduct: "Sue had high moral standards."

most   Do not use instead of *almost:* "~~Most~~ Almost everyone liked the movie."

nice   Replace this vague word with a more exact one, such as *attractive, kind,* or *generous.*

ok, okay   Avoid in formal writing.

passed / past   *Passed* is a verb: "He passed the gravy" or "Our car passed theirs." If it isn't a verb, use *past:* "The car drove past" or "He lives in the past."

peace / piece   *Peace* is the absence of war. *Piece* means "a part of something": "a piece of pie."

SPOTCHECK C–3   Underline the correct word in parentheses.

1. Vic's (morale / moral) was low as he left Tony's house.

2. To (lose / loose) at chess was something he couldn't accept easily.

3. As he (passed / past) through the front door, he (most/almost) blew his top in disgust.

4. "(Me and Tony / Tony and I) have been playing chess for years," he muttered to himself.

5. "I (know / no) he won't beat me next time."

6. With that thought, Vic was once again at (peace / piece).

More Words Often Misused—4

quiet / quite   *Quiet* is the opposite of *noisy:* "The library was quiet." *Quite* gives mild emphasis: "The book was quite heavy."

reason is because   In formal writing, use *reason is that:* "The reason we are leaving is ~~because~~ that . . . ."

right / write   *Right* means "correct": "Sue had all the right answers." *Write:* "She had to write the paper before Monday."

sit / set   *Sit* is what you do in a chair. *Set* means "to place": "Sue set the vase on the table."

suppose to   Be sure to add the *-d:* "I am supposed to work this weekend."

theirself, theirselves   Use *themselves* instead.

threw / through   "He *threw* the baseball *through* the window."

try and   Write *try to:* "Try ~~and~~ to be home by six."

use to   Don't forget the *-d* on *used:* "We used to own a convertible."

weather / whether   "We didn't know *whether* [if] the *weather* would get better."

woman / women   *Woman* refers to one, *women* to more than one.

 **SPOTCHECK C–4**   Underline the correct words in parentheses.

1. Rebecca was (quiet / quite) sure she would see Martin again before long.

2. The reason (was because / was that) they had had spats before and gotten back together.

3. She (suppose / supposed) he would telephone or (write / right) her a note.

4. But she also wondered (weather / whether) it was all right for (woman / women) to call men.

5. She decided to (sit / set) down and (try and / try to) forget Martin for a while.

Spelling Tips and List

Adding Suffixes

A suffix is one or more letters added at the end of a word to form a different word. Some suffixes are *-ing, -ed, -ent, -ance*. Three rules will help you spell words with suffixes.

1. When a word ends in *-y,* change the *y* to *i* before adding a suffix—except the suffix *-ing.*

happy	happier
study	studies
easy	easily
but study	studying

2. Usually drop a final *-e* when adding a suffix that begins with a vowel.

drive	driving
sincere	sincerity
desire	desirable

3. Generally, if a word is accented on its final syllable, double the final consonant before adding a suffix.

permit	permitted
occur	occurring
regret	regrettable

The "*i* before *e*" Rule

The old rhyme usually works: "*i* before *e*, except after *c*, or when sounded like *a* as in *neighbor* and *weigh*."

Thus we have *field, grief niece, relief.* And we have *ceiling, deceive, conceit, freight.*

Some common exceptions to the rule: *science, efficient, leisure, either, neither, height.*

PEANUTS® by Charles M. Schulz

PEANUTS reprinted by permission of United Feature Syndicate, Inc.

✓ **SPOTCHECK D–1**

In the blanks, write the correct form of the word in parentheses.

1. (move) The Petersons are _____ to San Marino.

2. (control) Despite the blowout, Rick _____ the car.

3. (silly) Denise is the _____ member of the club.

4. (regret) The accident was very _____ .

5. (satisfy) We had a _____ meal.

6. (hope) We all were _____ Gloria would win.

7. (occur) Last night's accident _____ at an intersection.

8. (happy) Eugene seemed _____ in Idaho than in California.

✓ **SPOTCHECK D–2**

Underline the words spelled correctly.

1. The merchant (decieved / deceived) the tourists.

2. The butcher cut a (vien / vein) in his arm.

3. The farmer drove through the (field / feild).

4. We were (relieved / releived) when the drought ended.

5. The three teenagers met their (friends / freinds) at the mall.

6. Can you guess the (wieght / weight) of that pony?

7. Mark will never (believe / beleive) Fritz again.

8. William (recieved / received) an A in botany.

150 WORDS OFTEN MISSPELLED

1. absence	46. dependent	91. naive
2. acceptance	47. disappear	92. necessary
3. accidentally	48. disappoint	93. neighbor
4. accommodate	49. dissatisfied	94. neither
5. acquaintance	50. doesn't	95. ninth
6. acquire	51. easily	96. occasion
7. across	52. efficiency	97. occurred
8. address	53. eighth	98. paid
9. adolescence	54. eligible	99. particularly
10. against	55. embarrass	100. persuade
11. all right	56. environment	101. possess
12. almost	57. equipped	102. possible
13. always	58. especially	103. practically
14. answer	59. exaggerate	104. preferred
15. appearance	60. excellent	105. prejudiced
16. appreciate	61. except	106. privilege
17. argument	62. exercise	107. probably
18. asked	63. experience	108. proceed
19. athlete	64. February	109. professor
20. basically	65. finally	110. pronunciation
21. believe	66. foreign	111. psychology
22. benefit	67. fortunately	112. quantity
23. breathe	68. friend	113. questionnaire
24. business	69. grammar	114. receive
25. candidate	70. guarantee	115. recognize
26. careful	71. height	116. recommend
27. cellar	72. hoping	117. religious
28. cemetery	73. immediately	118. restaurant
29. certain	74. intelligence	119. rhythm
30. changing	75. jealous	120. ridiculous
31. choose	76. kindergarten	121. sacrifice
32. clothes	77. knowledge	122. schedule
33. coming	78. laboratory	123. scissors
34. committee	79. leisure	124. secretary
35. competition	80. library	125. seize
36. condemn	81. license	126. separate
37. confidential	82. literature	127. significance
38. conscience	83. loneliness	128. similar
39. conscious	84. marital	129. sincerely
40. counselor	85. marriage	130. sophomore
41. courteous	86. mathematics	131. statistics
42. criticize	87. medicine	132. strength
43. deceive	88. mileage	133. studying
44. decision	89. misspell	134. succeed
45. definite	90. muscle	135. surprise

136. sympathize	141. tragedy	146. Wednesday
137. therefore	142. truly	147. weird
138. thought	143. usually	148. whose
139. through	144. valuable	149. writing
140. till	145. vegetable	150. written

Add to the list words misspelled on your own papers:

Your Personal List of Spelling Troublemakers

A

_____

_____

_____

B

_____

_____

_____

C

_____

_____

_____

D

_____

_____

E

_____

_____

_____

_____

F

_____

_____

_____

G

_____

_____

_____

_____

Your Personal List of Spelling Troublemakers (continued)

H

_____

_____

_____

_____

_____

I

_____

_____

_____

_____

_____

J

_____

_____

_____

_____

K

_____

_____

_____

_____

L

_____

_____

_____

_____

_____

M

_____

_____

_____

_____

_____

N

_____

_____

_____

_____

O

_____

_____

_____

_____

_____

Your Personal List of Spelling Troublemakers (continued)

P

_____

_____

_____

_____

_____

Q

_____

_____

R

_____

_____

_____

_____

S

_____

_____

_____

T

_____

_____

_____

U

_____

_____

_____

_____

V

_____

_____

_____

W

_____

_____

_____

X

_____

Y

_____

_____

_____

_____

Z

_____

Capitals, Numbers, Abbreviations

Capital Letters

Capitalize the first word of a sentence and the first word of a direct quotation that is a complete sentence.

> The store manager said, "We close at midnight."

Capitalize names and nicknames of persons and the word *I*.

> Do you remember that I called you "Elephant Breath" Smith in high school?

Capitalize names of specific places, structures, and school subjects.

Asia	Kansas	the Midwest
Golden Gate Bridge	Hollywood	Tenth Street
Central High School	Ancient History 12	Alcatraz Island

Don't capitalize names that are general rather than specific.

> He went to high school near here.

> They lived on an island last summer.

> Ruth is majoring in history.

> The Finleys live east of town.

Capitalize names of races, nationalities, languages, and religions.

Caucasian	Russian	Swahili
Presbyterian	Buddhism	Jewish

Capitalize names of organizations.

Democratic Party	Congress	Bachelors Club
Red Cross	General Motors	Mafia

Capitalize days of the week, months, holidays, and historical events.

Tuesday	July	Independence Day
New Year's Eve	Homecoming Week	Vietnam War

Capitalize the first word and every important word in a title.

> *War and Peace*   *Sabrina the Teenage Witch*
> "Home on the Range" *The Tonight Show*

Capitalize a person's title only if it appears before a name.

> We saw <u>Professor</u> Smith in the cafeteria.

> Alfred Smith is a <u>professor</u> of economics.

SPOTCHECK E-1   **Supply capital letters as needed.**

1. college of the sequoias is in california.

2. her father is catholic, and her mother is baptist.

3. my language professor can speak six languages, including tagalog.

4. the olsons vacationed on an island in lake superior.

5. the kids in elementary school called sam "sparky."

6. the band named loud and funky performed the beatles' song "norwegian wood."

7. dave flunked math 1a, so i guess he won't major in accounting.

8. mr. and mrs. washington saw the grand canyon when they went to arizona in june.

9. the salvation army building is on the corner of tenth street and pine avenue.

10. vickie declared she would "never set foot in this town again."

Numbers and Figures

In general, spell out numbers from one to ten, and use figures for the others.

> ten cookies   11 cookies
> three miles   162 miles

But always use figures to show times, dates, addresses, decimals, percentages, fractions, and statistics.

> We have tickets for Flight 7, leaving at 3:15 a.m. on September 1.

> Megan lives at 4 East Spruce Street, Apartment 2.

Only 8 percent of the students know that in math *pi* equals 3.1416.

The Latin Club elected Liz president, 10–8.

Always spell out a number that begins a sentence. If the result is too long and awkward, rephrase the sentence.

(wrong)	123 bands marched in the parade.
(awkward)	One hundred and twenty-three bands marched in the parade.
(rephrased)	Members of 123 bands marched in the parade.

If two or more related numbers in a sentence call for different styles, use numbers for all.

The dictator's wife left behind 6 fur coats, 87 dresses, and 203 pairs of shoes.

SPOTCHECK E–2

Cross out any incorrect uses of numbers and write the correct forms.

Example: There were at least ~~8~~ *eight* chipmunks in the yard.

1. The mayor laid off three secretaries, 22 street cleaners, and 112 firefighters.

2. 12 percent of the police force was out sick.

3. Mimi wears shoe size six and a half.

4. Our candidate got only 9 percent of the vote.

5. The bus leaves at three p.m.

6. Ricky's birthday is on August third.

Abbreviations

Only a few abbreviations are acceptable in formal writing. Here are some of them:

A.M. and P.M. (or a.m. and p.m.)	B.C.		A.D.
Mr.	Mrs.	Ms.	Dr. (before a name)
Jr.	Sr.	III	M.D. (after a name)
A.A.	B.A.	M.A.	Ph.D. (academic degrees)
PST	MPH	35 mm	

If any of these abbreviations are unfamiliar, you can see the danger in using abbreviations: Your reader may not understand them.

It is generally safer to spell out a name once before switching to the abbreviation.

> We took poor Poochie to the Society for the Prevention of Cruelty to Animals. The workers at the SPCA said. . . .

Some names are perhaps better known in abbreviated form: *CIA, FBI, NBC, TV, VCR, IQ.* Use your judgment. Check a dictionary to see if periods are used with the abbreviations.

You may abbreviate titles like *Gen., Gov., Prof.,* and *Dr.* when they appear before a full name. Spell them out when they appear with the last name alone.

> Sen. Elmer Peabody will speak at the rally.

> Senator Peabody will seek a fourth term next year.

Spell out (do not abbreviate) the names of states, countries, months, days, and units of measurement (ounces, pounds, feet, yards).

SPOTCHECK E–3

Cross out abbreviations inappropriate in formal writing and substitute the full forms.

Example: Phoebe was born in ~~Minn~~. *Minnesota*

1. The police academy will hear a speaker from the FBI on Nov. 12.

2. The baby weighed seven lbs., three ounces, at birth.

3. I've heard that Prof. Parsnip trains attack dogs.

4. The college will offer a new poli sci course next semester.

5. Two-thirds of the land in downtown L.A. is used for driving, parking, or servicing cars.

6. Composer Scott Joplin was born in Texarkana, Tex., in 1868.

DOUBLECHECK E–1

Correct errors in capital letters, numbers, and abbreviations. Each sentence has one error.

1. 12 years ago I moved to Arizona.

2. Carrie is attending a University in the South.

3. Melissa has studied laotian for four years.

4. Nick still owes me thirty-six fifty for a sport coat.

5. Did world war II end in 1945 or 1946?

6. David lives at seventy-three Pine Street.

7. Rosanne earned a B.A. degree in Economics.

8. She attended High School in Tempe, Arizona.

9. That dog must weigh at least 50 lbs.

10. The bartender told the boys to return "When you're 21."

 **DOUBLECHECK E–2** **Correct errors in capital letters, numbers, and abbreviations. Each sentence has one error.**

1. The Earth's five billionth person was born in 1987, just 13 years after the four billionth person was born.

2. At that rate, there should have been 6 billion people by the year 2000; in fact, that number was reached on October 12, 1999.

3. The Census bureau said the United States population had passed 248 million in the 1990 census.

4. That was an increase of more than 34 million since the 1980 census.

5. The american family continued to change, according to the Census Bureau.

6. Only 28% of households were "traditional families" with a husband, wife, and children living together.

7. More than 1/2 of employed women who had babies were back on the job within six months.

8. According to the Nat'l Center for Health Statistics, divorced people wait about three years to get remarried.

9. Another Study indicated that a woman's standard of living dropped an average of 73 percent after a divorce, while a man's went up 43 percent.

10. Researchers said a typical working couple spends 4 minutes of "meaningful conversation" with each other each day.

EDITING CHECK E–1

Edit this paragraph, correcting any errors in capital letters, numbers, and abbreviations.

¹The Flea is a remarkable insect, says the magazine *national geographic.* ²If there were olympic games for insects, fleas would win most of the gold medals. ³Some fleas can jump one hundred and fifty times their own length. ⁴That's equivalent to a human jumping nearly a thousand ft. ⁵One flea was observed jumping thirty thousand times without stopping. ⁶Fleas are fast, too. ⁷A flea can accelerate 50 times faster than an Astronaut in a space shuttle after liftoff. ⁸Except for the creatures' athletic skills, Humans don't admire fleas. ⁹3 plague epidemics, spread by rats and their fleas, have ravaged the World, killing more than 200 million people. ¹⁰the last plague epidemic started in china in 1855 and was carried by steamships to all parts of the world. ¹¹In the U.S. in 1987 there were 12 cases of plague and 2 deaths.

**CHECKPOINT—
WRITING
RESOURCES E**

Each sentence has an error in the use of capital letters, abbreviations, or numbers. Underline the error and write the correct form in the blank.

_____ 1. Morehouse college is in Atlanta, Georgia.

_____ 2. Fred graduated from the University of Nebraska, but his brother never went to College.

_____ 3. The scenery is interesting along Hwy 66.

_____ 4. Cynthia jumped 17 ft, 6 inches, in the track meet Saturday.

_____ 5. Next fall, we hope to visit Yellowstone park.

_____ 6. Mary hopes Dr. Bell will be able to perform the operation.

_____ 7. I enjoyed the course "Theory of Capitalism," but I don't plan to take another course in Economics.

_____ 8. If I take a shower after P.E., I'm late for my English class.

_____ 9. Alejandro was born in Peru and still speaks fluent spanish.

_____ 10. Did you remember that Nov. 29 is Allison's birthday?

Writing Resource F

English as a Second Language

Non-native users of English sometimes have a problem choosing from the articles *a* and *an* and the adjective *some*.

Using A, An, and Some

The article *a* is used before words that do not begin with a vowel (*a, e, i, o, u*): a book, a scary movie.

An is used before words that do begin with a vowel: an alligator, an open door. (It often is helpful to say the two words together: It is easier to say "an apple" than "a apple." It is easier to say "a banana" than "an banana.")

A and *an* have no plural forms:

Singular: There is an apple in the refrigerator.

Plural: There are apples in the refrigerator. (no article)

The word *some* can be used before plural nouns: "There are some apples in the refrigerator."

A and *an* are not used before nouns that cannot be counted, such as gasoline, weather, music: "Be sure to buy flour at the store." Or, "It looks like we'll have good weather for the parade."

The word *some* can be used before both "countable" and "uncountable" words.

Countable: I need some new socks.

Uncountable: Some geometry should be required in high school.

 **SPOTCHECK F–1**   Write *a, an,* or *some* in the blanks.

1. She's buying _____ dress.

2. He's studying _____ English text book.

3. I'm looking for _____ blueberries.

4. She is eating _____ ice cream cone.

5. He is writing _____ letter.

6. Farmer Brown is selling _____ wheat.

Using *The* Instead of *A* or *An*

Use the article *the* before things already mentioned.

There is <u>a</u> clock on the cabinet. <u>The</u> clock is ten minutes slow.

Use *the* before specific things.

(nonspecific) We saw <u>a</u> movie at <u>a</u> downtown theater.

(specific) We saw <u>the</u> movie *Jaws* at <u>the</u> Paramount Theater.

SPOTCHECK F–2   Write *a, an, the,* or *some* in the blanks.

1. Rafael has _____ cap on backwards. _____ cap has "Astros" sewn on it.

2. There are _____ fishing reels in the box. _____ reels are new.

3. There is _____ bread dough in the bowl. _____ dough is ready for the oven.

4. Wilhelmina knows _____ author of children's books. _____ author will speak in the student lounge tomorrow.

5. _____ car is parked at the side of the road. _____ car has a flat tire.

DOUBLECHECK F–1   Write *a, an, the,* or *some* in the blanks.

Although he is 5 feet, 8 inches tall, Tony Figueroa weighs 180 pounds. _____[1]

doctor told him his weight was too high and that he should try to get _____[2]exercise.

Now Tony goes to _____[3]Downtown YMCA gym three times a week, where he does

_____[4]variety of exercises. _____[5]gym has _____[6]indoor running track, and

Tony starts out his exercise each day with twenty laps around _____[7]track. Then he

works out on _____[8]stair-climbing machine. _____[9]machine develops _____[10]leg

muscles and is good for his heart. Rather than "pump iron" like _____[11]more serious

exercisers, Tony uses _____[12]machines that develop upper body muscles, such as

_____[13]pectorals, _____[14]abdominals, and _____[15]biceps. On _____[16]

days, when he is feeling especially good, he ends up with _____[17]twenty-minute

swim in _____[18]gym's pool.

Verb-Preposition Combinations (Phrasal Verbs)

Non-native speakers of English may run into combinations of verbs and prepositions that seem odd. In the preceding sentence, *run into,* meaning "encounter," is an example. Here are similar expressions that are often used:

be or **get back by**—return: I'll <u>be back by</u> midnight.

be out of—not have any: The cafeteria <u>is out</u> of boiled spinach.

blow up—inflate: Maria's mother <u>blew up</u> twenty balloons for the party.

break down—stop working (machines): The motorcycle <u>broke down</u> near Tulsa.

break up—end a relationship: Is it true that Glenn and Gloria <u>have broken up?</u>

call back—return a phone call: I'm busy now. I'll <u>call</u> you <u>back</u> at noon.

carry on—continue an activity: When Juana comes back, just <u>carry on</u> as if nothing had happened.

carry on—act emotionally: Bill <u>carried on</u> like a 6-year-old when he didn't get the promotion.

clean up—put things in order: Who will be <u>cleaning up</u> after the banquet?

clear up—improve (weather): I hope it <u>clears up</u> before the game Saturday.

come on or **hurry up**—move faster: <u>Come on!</u> We don't want to be late for class again.

come across or **bump into**—meet unexpectedly: Guess who I <u>came across</u> in Florio's Cafe this morning.

cut down on—do or eat less: Boris lost ten pounds after he <u>cut down</u> on eating sticky buns.

cut in—interrupt: Antoine was talking to Becky when Felicity rudely <u>cut in.</u>

do with—related to: Ecology has something to <u>do with</u> protecting the environment.

do without—give up something: The pioneers had to <u>do without</u> sugar.

get back—return or have returned: I have to <u>get</u> that book <u>back</u> to the library by Monday.

give up—surrender or lose hope: I'm afraid that Ng will just <u>give up</u> if he doesn't get an "A" in the class.

give up—quit a behavior: Luana sings much better since she <u>gave up</u> smoking.

go ahead—do it (but you shouldn't): <u>Go ahead!</u> Spend your rent money on beer!

go against—(oppose) Our debating team <u>goes against</u> Springhaven in the tournament.

go away—leave: Are you staying in the dorm over spring break or <u>going away</u>?

go back—return: Rosa is <u>going back</u> to college in the fall.

go in for—enjoy: Jorge <u>goes in for</u> classical music.

go out—leave (to have a good time): No more TV viewing! I'm <u>going out</u> this weekend.

go up—increase: The price of gasoline has <u>gone up</u> again.

keep up with—match, equal: The Smiths can't <u>keep up with</u> the Joneses in buying expensive clothes.

leave behind—abandon: Tim had to <u>leave</u> his dog <u>behind</u> when he joined the navy.

let in or out—allow to enter or leave: Be sure to <u>let</u> the cat <u>out</u> before you leave for work.

look after—take care of: The neighbor <u>looks after</u> our children each Tuesday.

look out—be careful: <u>Look out!</u> That dog looks mean.

look up—do research: I'll have to <u>look up</u> *anthropomorphism* in the dictionary.

put in—deposit: Remember to <u>put</u> a quarter <u>in</u> the parking meter.

put on or turn on—<u>Put on</u> the light. It's too dark to read.

put up with—permit, tolerate: Cristina can't <u>put up with</u> her neighbor's loud music.

run out of—exhaust the supply: We'll stop at the next filling station. We're about to <u>run out of</u> gasoline.

send for—order (by mail, phone, etc.): My wife <u>sent for</u> a back scratcher that was demonstrated on the shopping channel.

set off—cause to sound: The burglar <u>set off</u> the car alarm.

stop at—go to a place: <u>Stop at</u> the supermarket on your way home and pick up a loaf of bread.

take after—resemble a relative: Little Jimmy <u>takes after</u> his dad; they both have freckles.

take off—leave the ground (aircraft): The plane <u>took off</u> two hours late.

take off—remove clothing: Spike's mother told him to <u>take</u> his cap <u>off</u> at the dinner table.

take out—display: The drug dealer <u>took</u> a hundred-dollar bill <u>out</u> of his wallet.

take out—remove: Don't forget to <u>take out</u> the garbage before going to work.

turn down or up—lower or increase the volume: <u>Turn down</u> the TV, please, so I can study.

turn on or off—cause or cease to function: <u>Turn on</u> the radio, and find out if the Giants won today.

be up to—be capable of : Are you <u>up to</u> the challenges of Marine Corps training?

 **SPOTCHECK F–3**   **Write the correct prepositions in the blanks.**

1. Who will clean _____ the mess after the party?

2. Frasier was worried when he realized that he was _____ money.

3. I hope this old car doesn't break _____ before we get home.

4. Melanie was surprised when she bumped _____ Alex in the night club.

5. Doesn't quantum theory have something to do _____ mathematics?

6. I hope Zu Shan doesn't go _____ before Sam comes home from college.

7. Lisa hopes the weather clears _____ for her wedding day.

8. When Anatol comes in, shout "Surprise!" and then turn _____ the light.

9. Claudette said the theater is already _____ tickets, so we can't attend.

10. How much money did you put _____ your savings account?

11. Lourdes got _____ the money Margarita had borrowed to buy books.

12. I could really go _____ a nice cool soda right now.

Writing Resource G
Revising and Editing a Paragraph

Revising and editing are two different steps in the process of writing. Revise a paragraph by making sure that your words communicate what you actually think and that readers will understand your points. Edit a paragraph to check for sentence sense. When you are finished with revising and editing, print a new copy of your paragraph and read it one last time to make sure everything is the way you want it to be.

Revising

Here are questions to ask as you revise a paragraph:

- Does it communicate your ideas clearly?
- Does it have a topic sentence that says what the paragraph is about?
- Is it unified? Do all the other sentences stick to the topic?
- Is it adequately developed with specific details to make it interesting and convincing?

Lynn Quesnel was using a college writing assignment to explore this question about her personal life: Should she work longer hours to be able to afford nicer things, or should she work fewer hours to have more time with her children? Lynn used clustering and then journal writing to develop a first, rough draft of a paragraph. Here it is.

Rough Draft

What is more important, having money or having time? If I work longer hours at my job, I can earn a lot of money. That money *should* buy me a lot of great things—like a nice house, new cars, and vacations! But how many hours of work a week would it take to get them—fifty? sixty? I already work 35 hours a week, and I'm nowhere near a new car or a vacation, although I do have a nice fat mortgage. And then if I worked longer hours, what about the kids—spending time with them, teaching them, just being with them? If I work less hours, I can stay home with the kids. Then, will I have any money to take them places, feed them, give them stuff they need, or will I just be

sitting around worrying about having enough money to pay the bills?

Lynn's Observations About the Rough Draft

Lynn read her draft after she wrote it. She decided to write down what she learned about her own ideas when she read the paragraph. Here is what she wrote.

—The paragraph seems to say that I think of time and money as opposites—are they really? Is there a real choice here, or am I painting the situation as too black and white?

—What are the possible solutions? The draft seems to be a long rant!

—There isn't really a topic sentence. Instead, I ask a question. The paragraph has some details.

Instead of starting with her rough draft and trying to "fix" it bit by bit, Lynn started a whole new paragraph. This time, she wrote more slowly and thought about her observations. She decided to start with what time and money have in common.

Second Draft

I love both time and money. I love time because it gives me chances to relax, to just "be" with my children, time to cook. Time to play, time to dance and run. But I also love money, and more importantly than money, I love my job. My job gives me space to myself away from my family, a chance to be creative, it gives me a lot of satisfaction because I do my job pretty well. I also like to have money to spend, to get my kids the toys they want (and that they learn from). If I had money but didn't have any time to spend it, or if I had time but didn't have any money to spend, I wouldn't be happy. When I really think about it, compared to a lot of folks, I have a lot of both time and money right now.

Lynn's Thoughts About the Second Draft

The second draft seemed better to Lynn. It seemed less like nonstop writing and more thoughtful. The act of writing this second draft also changed how Lynn was thinking about the topic. Lynn decided to start her next draft by writing a topic sentence. She also decided to make the paragraph sound less personal.

Realizing that a lot of working mothers probably share her dilemma, she started out with a new topic sentence.

Third Draft with Topic Sentence

For a working mother with children, time and money seem to be two opposing choices, but they are actually both important for different reasons. She needs time so she can be with her children, to teach them the values that she finds important, and simply playing with them. By not working too many hours, she can still have time to cook and do other household tasks. She can have time for herself—to dance, run, relax, whatever. But money is also important so Mom can have a share in the American dream. Live in a nice place, drive a decent car, and buy the things that her family wants, such as music CDs and books. Even more important, mothers need their work. I for one love my job. It gives me a chance to be creative. And a lot of satisfaction because I do my job pretty well.

Take out—off the topic

Even though it sometimes seems that a working mother needs to choose either time or money—staying home or going to work—the real question is how to find a balance between them, because neither one offers all the benefits that she needs.

Lynn was pleased with this draft. She thought it communicated her ideas well and that the details she had added explained her ideas better. The details also seemed to fit with the topic sentence for the most part. Lynn did make changes to the last few sentences, shown above in handwriting, because they seemed to go too far off the topic. She decided the draft was ready for editing.

Editing

Editing a paragraph means examining it for "sentence sense."

- Look at each sentence to make sure that is logical, grammatical, and error-free. For example, ask these questions about your sentences:

    —Are all the sentences complete, or are there some fragments that need to be revised?
    —Do the subjects and verbs agree?

—Is there some variety in the sentences?

- Does it communicate your ideas clearly?
- Check each word to be sure it is the best word for what you want to say.
- Check the punctuation, capitalization, and other small matters to make sure everything is correct.

Lynn read her paragraph and wrote notes to herself in the margin. (The notes are circled in the paragraph below.) Then she went back and edited each sentence in response to the notes.

Paragraph with Editing

All mothers have children!

verbs aren't parallel

what's the connection here?

kind of vague

sounds awkward

vague

fragment

For a working mother ~~with children,~~ time and money seem to be two opposing choices, but they ~~are~~ actually both ~~important for different reasons.~~ *provide important benefits* She needs time so she can be with her children, ~~to~~ teach them the values that she finds impor- tant, and simply ~~playing~~ *play* with them. ~~By not working~~ *A mother who doesn't work* too many hours, ~~she~~ can still *In addition to needing time to take care of others, she* have time to cook and do other household tasks. ~~She~~ can have time for herself— to dance, run, relax, ~~whatever.~~ *or* But money is also important so Mom can have a share in the American dream. ~~Live~~ *Money allows her to live* in a ~~nice~~ *she likes* place, drive a decent car, and buy the *and that her children can learn from* things that her family wants, such as music CDs and books. Even though it sometimes seems that a working mother needs to choose either time or money—staying home or going to work—the real question is how to find a bal- ance between them, because neither one offers all the benefits that she needs.

Lynn improved her paragraph with careful editing. Notice, however, that she did not begin editing until she thought she had a strong draft. By keeping revis- ing and editing separate, Lynn kept her focus, first on the big issues and later on the smaller ones.

Writing Resource H

Using a Computer and the Internet

If you have your own computer, you probably already know it can be a big help in your writing. If you don't have one, you perhaps can gain access to one in a computer lab on campus. A lab technician may be available to help you get started, and the "Help" option found on the top bar of many word processors can take you to on-screen instructions.

 Deleting and moving copy It is a simple matter to *remove* a sentence, a paragraph, or a larger unit. First "select" the material by running the cursor over it while the left mouse key is pressed. Or take the Edit and Select route at the top of the screen. The material you have now highlighted will be removed when you click Delete on the keyboard. To *move* material to a different spot, first select it, then use Edit/Cut. The selected material will disappear. Place the cursor at the desired insertion point and click Edit/Paste to restore and move the material. Since making changes is so easy, you have the advantage of trying several versions of a sentence—especially a thesis or topic sentence—without a lot of erasing or crossing out.

 Spelling Many word processing programs will check your spelling for you. Either select the material you wish to check or place the cursor at the point where you wish to begin checking. Click the spelling icon at a screen-top bar, or click Tools/Spelling. The program will identify any questionable spellings and present a list of alternatives. Remember, the computer doesn't know that your seemingly correct "their" should have been spelled "there."

 Vocabulary If you think a word you have written isn't quite the right one—or if you think you would like to use a more impressive word (let's hope not!)—some processors will show you a list of words that have a similar meaning. For example, if you're dissatisfied with "car," you might have access to a pull-down menu that will list these synonyms, among others: auto, limousine, convertible, sedan, jalopy, lemon. A dictionary may be needed to help you figure out which of the words best fits your needs. (If you are connected to the Internet, you can turn to on-line dictionaries, such as Merriam-Webster's at www.m-w.com.)

 Grammar Your computer may even be able to check your grammar—after a fashion. First, select the content you wish to check, or place the cursor at a starting point. Click the grammar icon. Then see if you agree with the computer on any of the "errors" found.

Prewriting   If the keyboard is faster for you than the pen, the computer can be an advantage in brainstorming, nonstop writing, list making, and other quick methods of coming up with topics, as well as details, for paragraphs and essays. Word processors can simplify outlining. The "columns" and "divide page" features are useful when, for example, you want to set up side-by-side lists for comparison prewriting.

 Editing and revising   Some writers prefer to print out a paper copy of the material for this stage of the process. Be sure to leave space in the margins and between the lines for your corrections and improvements.

 Internet   If your computer has an Internet connection that allows you to go online, you will find there an almost unlimited source of information and ideas. Even though the writing assignments in *Checkpoints* are based mostly on your personal experiences, thus not requiring outside research, you will still find it worthwhile to become acquainted with this remarkable aid. For example, if you think you might benefit from a little extra work in your grammar studies, you can turn to a website such as that of the Purdue University Online Writing Lab. The Internet address is http://owl.english.purdue.edu. One of several sites for English as a second language is that of Indiana State University, at http://indstate.edu.writing.esl.html. Be careful to credit material taken directly from the Internet—or any other source. Otherwise, you may be guilty of copying or *plagiarism,* a serious offense.

Using Outside Sources in Writing

Writing in college is like joining a conversation that people are already having about your topic, only the conversation is written on paper instead of being spoken. To show how your ideas fit into the discussion, you will need to refer to specific details of other people's written work. Be sure to handle these ideas and words carefully and honestly so that your readers will know whose ideas they are and where they were published. Follow these guidelines:

- Keep your ideas and words separate from those of your outside sources.
- Tell your readers exactly where you read the ideas you are responding to.
- Use a citation style (also called a documentation style) your teacher has approved.

Examples in this appendix are all in MLA style. MLA style is explained below.

Keep Your Ideas Separate from Your Sources' Ideas

You can refer to other people's ideas by quoting their exact words, paraphrasing their ideas in your own words, or summarizing their most important points. When you include a source's exact words in your paragraph or essay, you should indicate in three different ways that you are not the author of the material.

1. Introduce the material with a phrase that includes some information about the source, such as the person's name and their qualifications for writing about the subject at hand.
2. Enclose the exact words from the source inside a pair of quotation marks.
3. Give the page number of the source on which you read the words you are quoting.

Here is an example of direct quotation:

> William Damon, Director of the Center on Adolescence at Stanford University, defines the youth charter as "a coherent set of standards and expectations for youth behavior, shared by all the important people in a young person's life" (43).

Notice that you can tell easily why William Damon is being quoted as an expert on youth behavior. He holds an important position as the director of a center for studying teenagers. It is also easy to tell which words in the sentence are Damon's, not the student writer's. A pair of quotation marks shows where the quotation begins and ends. Finally, in parentheses at the end of the sentence, the page number from Damon's work is given. If you want to know more about what

Damon had to say, you can turn to page 43 in his work. In order to know what book the quotation comes from, you need to read the "Works Cited" page of the essay, where the publication information is given. We'll talk about that below.

It is important to keep your own ideas separate from the ideas of your sources. At the same time, however, you need to make your sentences sound polished, so the grammar of your sentence and the grammar of the quotation need to fit together and make sense. For example, this sentence is confusing:

> Ellen Goodman, a writer for the *Boston Globe*, disagrees with this view and "For openers, 38 percent of all poor children already live in two-parent homes" (A13).

The word "and" doesn't offer the reader enough information to understand the connection between the writer's words and Goodman's words. Removing "and" and adding the word "noting" suggests that the quotation offers one reason Goodman disagrees with the view:

> Ellen Goodman, a writer for the *Boston Globe*, disagrees with this view, noting that "38 percent of all poor children already live in two-parent homes" (A13).

Notice that in the revised sentence, the writer left out the first two words at the beginning of the quotation. If you omit words from the very beginning or the very ending of the passage you are quoting, you don't need to do anything special to indicate it. But if you omit words within the part you are quoting, you need to show where you have taken something out:

> Gene Logsdon states that one type of "biological degradation" on today's farm is human: "The quiet despair of farmers today is plainly due to the [. . .] strain of economic pressures" (41).

The three spaced dots that are inside brackets [. . .] show that you have omitted some words from the source. All words inside a pair of quotation marks are assumed to be from the source, so if you change something you need to show the reader what you did.

If you aren't using the exact words of the source, but just the ideas of the source stated in your own words (paraphrasing or summarizing), then you still need to give the author's name and the page number. You don't need the quotation marks since you aren't quoting the source word-for-word.

Here is an example of summary:

> Linguist Deborah Tannen has found that men and women have different habits of speech, and that this difference can lead to misunderstandings. For example, women may appear to be at fault even when they're not because they have a habit of apologizing (284). Men may appear to be harsh if they have a habit of giving direct criticism (285).

Notice that Tannen is identified as a linguist. Also notice that her exact words are not quoted, so no quotation marks are used. However, summaries of ideas that can be found on two different pages of her work are given, and a page number is provided for each one. The sentence about women is a summary of an idea stated on page 284, and the sentence about men is a summary of an idea stated on page 285. Using Tannen's name at the beginning of the source material and the page numbers at the end tell the reader when Tannen's ideas are stated.

Tell Readers Where You Got the Material

Readers need to know where your outside source material comes from:

- Who wrote the material?
- Where did it appear?
- What page did the words or ideas you are using come from?

The answers to the first two questions help readers know how much weight they want to give a particular opinion, or how carefully researched they believe a source to be. For example, a reader might find an article published in the *New York Times* or *U.S. News & World Report* more likely to be accurate than one published in the *National Enquirer*, which recently displayed this headline on the front page: "Dr. Phil Causes Guest to Have Leg Amputated." Or a reader might want to know whether the source of a political statement was a Republican, a Democrat, or a Green Party member to see what biases the writer might have. Finally, giving the page number allows readers to locate the material themselves in case they want to read further.

The examples of Damon, Goodman, Logsdon, and Tannen on pages 277–278 show one way of citing the author of an outside source: put the name of the author in your sentence. Another way is to add the author's last name into the same set of parentheses you use for the page number.

Here is an example of the citation with the author's last name and the page number inside the parentheses.

> One woodland worker provides an overview of woodland development in the British Isles from the Ice Age to the 21st century (Law 1–23).

A range of page numbers is given because the sentence summarizes what Law discusses for the first twenty-three pages of his book.

The reader now needs to know which work of Law's you are quoting from. On a separate sheet of paper at the end of your essay, you need to give the publication information:

> Law, Ben. *The Woodland Way: A Permaculture Approach to Sustainable Woodland Management*. Permanent: East Meon, Eng., 2001.

The author's name is given first, then the title of the book. Publisher's name, place of publication, and date of publication follow. This format is for a book. Other kinds of entries are given in the next section.

Notice that the parenthetical note and the beginning of the Works Cited entry both include the author's last name, Law. This is the connection that tells your reader which entry in the Works Cited list is the relevant one.

Use an Accepted Citation Style

Different citation styles are used by researchers in different fields. The citation style used in the humanities and the fine arts is usually the one recommended by the Modern Language Association (MLA). In the social sciences, the American Psychological Association (APA) style is typically used. In the natural and applied sciences, the Council of Science Editors (CSE) offers a choice of two styles. Here we will look at MLA style.

MLA style includes two main parts: an in-text citation, also called a parenthetical citation, and a corresponding Works Cited entry. In-text citations appear throughout your essay wherever you cite outside source material. All the Works Cited entries are listed on a separate page at the end of your essay, with the title "Works Cited" centered at the top.

In-text Citations

After you quote, paraphrase, or summarize a source, you must cite the last name of the author and the page number of the work, as shown below:

> A relatively small number of people immigrated to the United States in the fifty years following the American Revolution, but then a massive wave of immigration "came in the decades after 1840. More than two million new persons per decade entered the country" (Bischoff 22).

Notice that the quotation in this sentence is less than four lines in length. When a quotation is shorter than four lines, use a pair of quotation marks around the words of the source and add the parenthetical note before the final period of the sentence. If, however, the quotation is four or more lines in length, use a block format to show the quotation:

> Kingsolver introduces the relationship between the sisters in the first two sentences of the novel:
>
> > His two girls are curled together like animals whose habit is to sleep underground, in the smallest space possible. Cosima knows she's the older, even when she's unconscious: one of her arms lies over Halimeda's shoulder as if she intends to protect them both from their bad dreams. (Kingsolver 3)

In the block format, the quotation is indented ten spaces from the left margin, and no quotation marks are used. The other difference from a shorter quotation is that after the block quotation, the period or other final punctuation comes *before* the note in parentheses.

If there are two or three authors, give all the last names in the note:

> (Fowler and Aaron 125)
> (Waters, Weaver, and Brown 234)

If there are more than three authors, you can use the first author's last name followed by the phrase "et al." (meaning *and others*): (Abel et al. 14)

If you need to cite two or more works by the same author, add a title (if it's short) or a shortened version of the title to each citation so the reader can keep them straight. The short title has to include the first important words of the title so the reader can locate the work on the Works Cited page.

> (Kingsolver, Animal Dreams 25)
> (Kingsolver, High Tide 9)

Book titles are underlined. Article titles are enclosed in a pair of quotation marks.

You can find other rules for in-text citations in your handbook.

Works Cited Entries

Each in-text citation corresponds to an entry on the Works Cited list. The author's last name appears in the in-text citation, and it begins the Works Cited entry. The entries in the list are arranged alphabetically by author's last name. Sometimes, no author is named. In this case, alphabetize by the first word of the title, except for *A, An,* and *The.* For example, if the title were *The First Degree,* you would alphabetize by the word *First.*

If more than one work by the same author is cited, then after the first time you use the author's name, you don't have to repeat it. Instead, use three hyphens followed by a period.

> Kingsolver, Barbara. <u>Animal Dreams</u>. Harper: New York, 1990.
> ———. <u>High Tide in Tucson</u>. Harper: New York, 1996.

Here are the formats for some frequently used sources. Consult your handbook for others.

> A book:
> Riotee, Louise. <u>Carrots Love Tomatoes</u>. Storey: Pownal, VT, 1998.

Notice that if a city is not well known, you should give the postal abbreviation for the state as well. Also, the name of this publisher is "Storey Books," but in MLA style, you can omit all words such as "Books," "Publishers," and "Press." The exception is for university presses, for which you use "UP": for example, *Harvard UP.*

> An article or essay in an anthology:
> Berry, Wendell. "The Pleasures of Eating." <u>Our Sustainable Table</u>. Ed. Robert Clark. North Point: San Francisco, 1990. 125–131.

Note that Berry wrote the essay being cited. Clark is the editor of the whole anthology. The numbers at the end of the entry are all the page numbers of the essay.

> An article in a magazine:
> Langewiesche, William. "American Ground: Unbuilding the World Trade Center." <u>Atlantic Monthly</u>. July/Aug. 2002: 44–79.

Variations occur in the entries for scholarly journals and for weekly and biweekly magazines. Consult your handbook for periodicals other than monthly magazines.

> An article in a newspaper:
> Goodman, Ellen. "Marriage as Poverty Cure." <u>Boston Globe</u>. 7 Mar. 2002: A1.

Notice that the date is given in this order: day month year. The names of all months except May, June, and July are abbreviated. The section and page numbers end the entry. Sometimes there is an edition name also, such as "national edition." In this case, a comma is placed after the year and the abbreviation *natl ed.* is added.

A website:

Camping with the Sioux: The Fieldwork Diary of Alice Cunningham Fletcher.
2001. National Anthropological Archives, Smithsonian Institution. 9 July
2002 <http://www.nmnh.si.edu/naa/fletcher/fletcher.htm>.

No author or editor is listed for the site, so the website name itself is given first. Two dates are given. The first is the date the site was copyrighted (in this case), posted, revised, or updated. You can usually find this information on the first page of the site, or on an "About" or "Credits" page. The second date is the date you accessed the site. In between the two dates is the name of the institution that sponsors the site, if there is one. After the date of access, the complete URL is given between angle brackets. Be sure the URL is correct. The best practice is to cut and paste it from your navigation bar to your Works Cited page.

There are many variations of entries for different kinds of websites. In addition, the information available on the site will affect the entry.

Here is a sample Works Cited list with page format requirements shown.

(A) Jones 7

(B) Works Cited

Berry, Wendell. "The Pleasures of Eating." Our Sustainable Table. Ed. Robert
Clark. North Point: San Francisco, 1990. 125–131.

(C) Camping with the Sioux: The Fieldwork Diary of Alice Cunningham Fletcher.
2001. National Anthropological Archives, Smithsonian Institution. 9 July
2002 <http://www.nmnh.si.edu/naa/fletcher/fletcher.htm>.

Goodman, Ellen. "Marriage as Poverty Cure." Boston Globe. 7 Mar. 2002: A1.

(D) Kingsolver, Barbara. Animal Dreams. Harper: New York, 1990.

———. High Tide in Tucson. Harper: New York, 1996.

Langewiesche, William. "American Ground: Unbuilding the World Trade
Center." Atlantic Monthly. July/Aug. 2002: 44–79.

Riotee, Louise. Carrots Love Tomatoes. Storey: Pownal, VT, 1998.

(A) Your last name and page number are at top right of every page

(B) The title Works Cited is centered

(C) 1" margins are used all around

(D) Entries are alphabetical

A Note About Plagiarism

Plagiarism is the theft of someone else's words or way of expressing ideas. If you follow the rules above carefully—always separating your words and ideas from those of your sources, giving the complete publication information for each source, and using an accepted citation style—you will likely not plagiarize anyone else's work. There are two tricky situations to watch out for, however.

Internet Plagiarism

You can cut and paste almost any piece of information from the Internet, including photos and other kinds of files. But just because you *can* copy it doesn't mean you are *allowed* to copy it. Much of the material on the Web is someone's property, just like their cars and houses are property. The difference is that the Web material is intellectual property, not physical property. Treat the words and expressions of ideas on the Web just as you would words and ideas from print sources—that is, acknowledge the source.

Plagiarism by Paraphrasing Too Closely

Paraphrasing a source means putting it in your own words, being sure to convey the author's original meaning and emphasis. It does not mean changing a few key words in a sentence and leaving all the rest the same as the source. Here is an example.

Original source:

> The issue of undocumented or illegal immigrants in the United States is of recent vintage. It hardly entered public thinking during the first hundred years in the history of immigration in the United States, because no federal laws restricted immigration. (Source: Bischoff, Immigration Issues, p. 265.)

Plagiarized:

> The dispute of undocumented or illegal immigrants in the United States of America is of recent age. The public hardly thought about it during the first century of the history of immigration to America—no federal laws limited immigration (Bischoff 265).

All the underlined words in the plagiarized version are taken directly from the source. Most of the other words are simply synonyms (words with the same or similar meaning) for words from the original: *dispute* replaces the original *issue, age* replaces *vintage, century* replaces *hundred years*, and *limited* replaces *restricted*. The passage is plagiarized even though the in-text citation is given.

Acceptable paraphrase:

> Bischoff comments that public debate over illegal immigration is fairly new. There was no reason to discuss it previously because there were no federal laws governing immigration (265).

The writer could also have used a brief quotation if needed, but the words of the source would need to be enclosed in a pair of quotation marks:

> Bischoff comments that public debate over illegal immigration is fairly new: "The public hardly thought about it during the first century of the history of immigration to America" because no federal laws governed immigration (265).

Avoid plagiarism by using source material with care.

Writing Resource J

Grammar Terms: The Parts of Speech

Words are classified into eight *parts of speech* based on their use in a sentence.

Noun   A word such as *William, New York, sofa,* or *patriotism* that names a person, place, thing, or idea.

> **Proper nouns** name particular people, places, etc., and are capitalized: *Professor Smith, Lake Michigan, Pepsi, Buddhism.*

> **Common nouns** name people and things in general and are not capitalized: *doctor, river, soda pop, religion.*

> **Group (collective) nouns** refer to groups of people or things as if they were a single unit: *team, audience, flock.*

Verb

> **Action verbs** say what the subject does: "The boy *ran* home." **Linking verbs** connect the subject to a word that identifies or describes it: "The boy *was* tired."

> **Transitive verbs** have an object that receives the action of the verb: "The car *hit* the hydrant." **Intransitive verbs** do not take an object: "Birds *fly.*"

> A **verb phrase** is a verb made up of more than one word: *has run, could have run, will be running.*

> A verb in **active voice** shows the subject acting: "The singer also *played* a guitar." A verb in **passive voice** shows the subject being acted upon: "A guitar *was played* by the singer."

Adjective   A word that describes a noun ("*talented* actress") or pronoun ("she is *talented*"). An adjective tells which one, what kind, or how many.

Adverb   A word that describes a verb ("ran *slowly*"), an adjective ("*very* beautiful"), or another adverb ("moved *rather* quickly"). An adverb tells how, when, where, or to what extent.

Pronoun   A word that takes the place of a noun: "The students entered slowly. *They* dreaded Professor Higgins' exams."

> **Personal pronouns** refer to people or things: *I, we, she, he, it, they.* Besides those subject forms, pronouns also have object forms (*me, us, her, him, them*) and possessive forms (*my, mine, your, yours, his, hers, their, theirs, its*). Example: "We gave *them our* tickets."

> **Indefinite pronouns** (*each, neither, anyone, everybody,* etc.) do not refer to a specific person or thing: "*Nobody* knows the answer."

> **Interrogative pronouns** (*who, whom, whose, what, which*) begin questions: "*Whose* book is that?"

> **Relative pronouns** (the interrogative pronouns, plus *whoever, whomever, whichever, whatever*) begin dependent clauses: "The books were free to *whoever* needed them."

> **Intensive pronouns** (words ending with -*self* or -*selves*) give emphasis to a noun or other pronoun: "The doctor *himself* said it." "We *ourselves* will pay the bill."

> **Reflexive pronouns** (words ending with -*self* or -*selves*) show the subject acting upon itself: "The carpenter hit *himself* on the thumb."

> **Demonstrative pronouns** (*this, that, these, those*) point to a particular person or thing: "*These* are my favorite flowers."

Preposition   A word such as *to, for, of, in, with,* or *between* that connects a noun or pronoun (its object) to the rest of the sentence and forms a prepositional phrase: "They went swimming *in the river.*"

Conjunction   A word that joins other words.

> **Coordinating conjunctions** ("connectors") are *and, but, or, for, nor, yet,* and *so.* They join grammatically equal units, such as two independent clauses: "Sylvia attended the concert, *but* Glenn was out of town."

> **Subordinating conjunctions** ("dependent words") include words such as *although, because, since,* and *unless.* They join dependent (subordinate) clauses to independent clauses: "We went by train *because* Ernie doesn't like to fly."

> **Conjunctive adverbs** ("transitional words") join independent clauses: "Bernice got a pay raise; *however,* she remained unhappy." Other conjunctive adverbs include *moreover, nevertheless, finally,* and *meanwhile.*

Interjection   A word showing strong feeling, such as *wow, oh,* or *pshaw:* "*Oh!* I could hardly believe my eyes!"

Limited Answer Key

Chapter 1

SPOTCHECK 1–1
1. its
3. It's
5. It's

SPOTCHECK 1–2
1. their
3. Their, there
5. they're, their, there

SPOTCHECK 1–3
Answers will vary.

DOUBLECHECK 1–1
1. their
3. They're
5. there
7. its
9. its
11. their
13. it's
15. they're

SPOTCHECK 1–4
1. Are, our, or
3. hear
5. than
7. Where
9. You're
11. Then

DOUBLECHECK 1–2
Answers will vary.
1. June is taller than April.
3. Sam is in trouble, too.
5. Your lunch is ready.
7. I eat an apple every day.
9. Bill is too tired to play tennis.

DOUBLECHECK 1–3
1. too
3. our
5. there's
7. your, its
9. than
11. than, theirs
13. Your
15. You're, or

EDITING CHECK 1
1. our national anthem
3. then that Congress
5. However, a lot of people
7. he was there, he could hear
9. Key could have returned
11. and its words were

Chapter 2

SPOTCHECK 2–1
1. (Example) Mr. Wrigley was showing his age. Wrinkles covered his face like the lines on a road map. The few wisps of hair around his ears were white. His hands trembled as he lifted the coffee cup to his lips. When he stood to leave, it was with difficulty, and he needed a cane as he walked out the door.
3. *Answers will vary.*

SPOTCHECK 2–2
Sentences 3 and 9

SPOTCHECK 2–3
1. good
3. weak
5. weak

SPOTCHECK 2–4

Answers will vary.
1. textbooks, *Checkpoints*
3. office buildings, Empire State Building
5. governors, Governor Wilson

SPOTCHECK 2–5
1. weak
3. weak
5. weak

SPOTCHECK 2–6

Answers will vary.
1. My neighborhood has several attractive front yards.
3. My cousin is a fancy dresser.
5. My English class was boring Monday.

SPOTCHECK 2–7

Answers will vary.

SPOTCHECK 2–8
1. person
3. George Ferris
5. snow

SPOTCHECK 2–9
1. eat—action
3. look—linking
5. live—action

DOUBLECHECK 2–1
1. (s) soldiers; (v) fought
3. river; was
5. army; needed

SPOTCHECK 2–10

Answers will vary.
1. around midnight
3. in Chicago
5. with your help
7. through the telescope

SPOTCHECK 2–11
1. ~~In Germany, in 1910~~ service
3. ~~For American taxpayers, from paychecks, until 1943, during World War II~~, taxes

5. ~~After forty-one days, in New York's Museum of Modern Art, by Henry Matisse,~~ painting

SPOTCHECK 2–12
1. athletes
3. chance
5. You

SPOTCHECK 2–13
1. appeared, achieved
3. had resembled
5. would have
7. was taking

DOUBLECHECK 2–2
1. (s) Education; (v) is
3. rate; is
5. education; has been
7. values; are reinforced
9. half; attend
11. Four hours of sleep; is
13. Americans; have been

Chapter 3

SPOTCHECK 3–1

Answers will vary.
1. *Newsweek*
3. sports

SPOTCHECK 3–2

Answers will vary.

SPOTCHECK 3–3
A. 3, both
C. 2, v; 4, both
E. 3, s

SPOTCHECK 3–4
A. 2, both
C. 3, both
E. 2, both; 5, v

SPOTCHECK 3–5

Answers will vary.
1. Miriam received a gift from Uncle Alonzo.

3. During the final exam, a cat entered the classroom.

5. Mr. Loh swerved the car to avoid a large hole in the road.

SPOTCHECK 3–6

Example: Cheops, the largest

1. desert, it is

3. twenty years to build

5. being built, the pyramid

EDITING CHECK 3

Fragments: 2, 4, 5, 8, 9, 11, 13

Editing solutions may be different from this example:

[1]Helen Keller provides an inspiring example of a person who overcame great physical handicaps. [3]She was made deaf and blind by illness before the age of two. [5]With the help of a teacher, Anne Sullivan, Helen learned to communicate by spelling out words on a person's hand. [7]She learned to speak by the time she was sixteen as a result of her own hard work and Miss Sullivan's patience. [9]Graduating with honors from Radcliffe College in 1904, she began working to improve conditions for the blind, writing books, lecturing, and appearing before legislative bodies. [12]Two movies tell of her life, *The Helen Keller Story* and *The Miracle Worker*.

Chapter 4

SPOTCHECK 4–1

1. When

3. because

5. Whenever

SPOTCHECK 4–2

2, who

4, where

6, while

8, which

11, when

12, although

SPOTCHECK 4–3

Answers will vary.

1. Although the CD was expensive, I bought it anyway.

3. Whenever Macy's has a sale, Mrs. Fairhill is first in line.

5. Since the riot in the park, Stella doesn't walk there by herself.

SPOTCHECK 4–4

1. which is the day taxes are due

3. that hardly anybody knows

5. that was invented in the United States

SPOTCHECK 4–5

1. that

3. that

5. who

DOUBLECHECK 4–1

Answers will vary.

1. Nakia washed dishes while Bill took out the garbage.

3. I lose money whenever I gamble.

5. Franz skipped class, which was a mistake.

DOUBLECHECK 4–2

1. who love pizza

3. While the average American eats 22.5 pounds of pizza a year

5. that serves pizza

7. that 11 percent of restaurants feature pizza and 8.5 percent hamburgers

EDITING CHECK 4

(Sections showing editing are underlined.)

[1]The term *martial arts* covers a variety of fighting methods based on ancient Asian combat skills. [2]The martial arts are practiced today for a number of reasons, including self-defense, physical fitness, and sports competition.

[3]Styles, techniques, and teaching methods vary, even within a given branch of martial arts, such as karate, although adherence to ancient traditions is usually emphasized.

[5]Although the exact origins are uncertain, the Asian styles of the martial arts seem to have come to China from India and Tibet, where they were used by monks for exercise and protection against bandits. [8]The arts flourished in Japan, although Japan was among the last of the Asian nations to learn them. For a time, practice of martial arts was restricted to the Japanese warrior class, but the peasants practiced in secret.

[11]Martial arts can be divided into two categories, those that use weapons and those that don't. [13]In the weaponless methods, such as karate and kung fu, the contestant depends on kicks and hand and arm blows, as well as various holds, chokes, and twists, to subdue an opponent. [15]In one of the branches using weapons, kendo, based on ancient Japanese sword-fighting, contestants today use bamboo swords cased in leather.

T'ai chi is the most gentle of the martial arts. [18]It uses slow, graceful movements that bear little resemblance to the original blows and blocks on which the movements are based. [19]T'ai chi is used today for conditioning and flexibility. Some use it as a form of meditation.

Chapter 5

SPOTCHECK 5–1

1. believe, but today's
3. rugs, or they
5. mixer, for its

SPOTCHECK 5–2

Answers will vary.

1. One brother is a banker, and the other is a forest ranger.
3. Sara will move to Milwaukee, or she will stay in Topeka.

SPOTCHECK 5–3

Answers will vary.

1. Because the baseball game went into extra innings, the Ellisons had to leave before the game ended.
3. Because she was late for class, Deborah decided to skip dessert.
5. If Rex gets a raise, he will buy a new bicycle.

SPOTCHECK 5–4

Answers will vary.

1. Ng opened his umbrella when it started to rain.
3. Antoine will get a new car if he does well on *Jeopardy.*
5. Since he graduated from college last year, Enoch has had four different jobs.

SPOTCHECK 5–5

Answers will vary.

1. in education; in fact, they
3. in schools; however, we
5. "educational"; for example, television

SPOTCHECK 5–6

Answers will vary.

1. Felipe takes a full course load; in addition, he works thirty hours a week.
3. The baby was pouting; nevertheless, Ingrid took a few photos.

DOUBLECHECK 5–1

1. RTS—airships were called; name honored
3. C—airship exploded; thirty-six were killed
5. RTS—Fans can spot; it advertises

DOUBLECHECK 5–2
1. C—you are; you eat
3. C—Popcorn is; quart contains
5. RTS—popcorn has; it has

DOUBLECHECK 5–3
[1]Bathing suits did not make an appearance until the middle of the 1800s <u>because</u> recreational bathing was not popular before then; <u>however</u>, at that time doctors began to prescribe the "waters" for a variety of ailments. [2]Europeans flocked to the streams, lakes, and the ocean, <u>where</u> they sought relief from "nerves" or other disorders. [3]Standards of modesty were different in those days, <u>so</u> bathing suits covered more of the body than they do today. [4]Women wore knee-length skirts in the water; <u>in addition</u>, they wore bloomers and black stockings under the skirts. [5]<u>Since</u> a wet bathing suit could weigh as much as the bather, the accent was on *bathing*, not swimming. [6]<u>If</u> she wanted greater privacy, a woman could use a "bathing machine" at the ocean. [7]Attendants would wheel her and the portable dressing room into shallow waters. [8]<u>After</u> she had changed into a head-to-toe loose gown, she would step down a ramp into the surf <u>while</u> attendants shooed away any interested males. [9]A Danish immigrant to the United States named Carl Jantzen revolutionized swim wear in 1915 <u>when</u> he invented a knitting machine that yielded a stretch fabric. [10]The fabric resulted in a body-clinging fit; <u>however</u>, swimsuits still had sleeves and reached to the knees. [11]Swimsuits became more revealing in the 1930s <u>when</u> narrow straps and backless models paved the way for the two-piece suit.

[12]It wasn't until 1946 that the bikini made its appearance. [13]World War II had recently ended, <u>and</u> the United States was testing an atom bomb in the Pacific. [14]A French designer was about to introduce a skimpy swimsuit model, <u>but</u> he didn't have a catchy name. [15]<u>Thus</u>, the atomic blast at Bikini Atoll on July 1, 1946, gave him the name for the "explosive" suit he displayed to the world four days later.

DOUBLECHECK 5–4
A1. are worn out, so he
A2. Because Lowell's sneakers are worn out
A3. worn out; therefore, he will
B1. a computer, but he
B2. Although Fritz has a computer, he
B3. has a computer; however, he

EDITING CHECK 5
Answers will vary.
1. remarkable, for it
4. goes, went, gone

Chapter 6
SPOTCHECK 6–1
1. fly, flew, flown
4. goes, went, gone

SPOTCHECK 6–2
1. bought
3. threw
5. brought
7. ridden
9. gone

SPOTCHECK 6–3
1. taught
3. flew

5. drunk
7. saw
9. spent

SPOTCHECK 6–4
Answers will vary.
1. Chandra had never seen a porpoise before.
3. The phone rang three times.
5. The owner had driven the car 150,000 miles.

SPOTCHECK 6–5
1. excited
3. grown
5. prejudiced

SPOTCHECK 6–6
1. has
3. did
5. has
7. does
9. have

SPOTCHECK 6–7
1. commutes
3. supposed
5. knows

DOUBLECHECK 6–1
1. Example
3. he flies
5. he completes
7. he builds
9. he is

EDITING CHECK 6
1. was
3. started
5. had
7. did
9. did
11. are
13. is taken
15. poses
17. is inspired
19. sends

Chapter 7

SPOTCHECK 7–1
1. are
3. expects
5. play

SPOTCHECK 7–2
1. (s) one; (v) is
3. banana; adds
5. waters; reach

SPOTCHECK 7–3
1. (s) lakes; (v) are
3. swans; are
5. Presenting; is

SPOTCHECK 7–4
1. (s) Everything; (v) was
3. somebody; remembers
5. Both; have
7. Everyone; lives

SPOTCHECK 7–5
1. has
3. drive
5. costs

SPOTCHECK 7–6
1. is
3. sponsors
5. has

DOUBLECHECK 7–1
1. has
3. are
5. is
7. were
9. were

EDITING CHECK 7
1. (s) people; (v) are
3. answer; lies
5. sports; that stimulate
7. They; increase
9. walking and swimming; produce (C)

Chapter 8

SPOTCHECK 8–1

1. him
3. it
5. me
7. you

SPOTCHECK 8–2

1. DO
3. DO
5. OP
7. S

SPOTCHECK 8–3

1. They—subject
3. him—indirect object
5. them—direct object

SPOTCHECK 8–4

1. ~~The umpire and~~ he
3. ~~my husband and~~ me
5. ~~Marlys and~~ him
7. ~~Lilith and~~ he

SPOTCHECK 8–5

1. I
3. whom
5. himself

DOUBLECHECK 8–1

1. us
3. who
5. I
7. who
9. who
11. me
13. we
15. The pediatrician and I

DOUBLECHECK 8–2

Answers will vary.

1. Cordelia painted the picture herself.
3. The bee stung me on the finger.
5. It was Fred who won the race.
7. The honors were shared by the mayor and me.

EDITING CHECK 8

1. ~~I~~ me
3. ~~myself~~ me
5. correct
7. ~~hisself~~ himself
9. ~~theirselves~~ themselves

Chapter 9

SPOTCHECK 9–1

1. its
3. his
5. her

SPOTCHECK 9–2

1. All the office workers brought their own lunches.
3. A person who showers uses only about half as much hot water as a person who bathes.

SPOTCHECK 9–3

1. its
3. its
5. its

DOUBLECHECK 9–1

1. a
3. b
5. b
7. a
9. a

SPOTCHECK 9–4

Answers will vary.

1. The raccoon hissed loudly as the cat approached.
3. I never buy CDs at flea markets because the disks might be counterfeit.
5. Frank told the instructor, "I have a poor understanding of geometry."

SPOTCHECK 9–5

Answers will vary.

1. Cliff did weight-training for a year before the change in his body became noticeable.

3. Employees should get to work on time if they want to keep their jobs.
5. Not responding to her invitation was impolite of me.

DOUBLECHECK 9–2

Answers will vary.

1. Not everyone knows where his or her ancestors came from.
3. Neither of the male applicants could find his resumé.
5. The opportunity to walk down a shady lane made Delores happy.
7. On a hot day, long-distance runners should drink lots of water.
9. As soon as Myra gets home, Sylvia said she would tell her the news.

EDITING CHECK 9

1. Moviegoers would have . . . if they had actually lived
3. at least a quarter of the cowboys
5. town had . . . bodies in its
7. Studies of the period say
9. Correct
11. it's they're often found

Chapter 10

SPOTCHECK 10–1

Answers will vary.

1. thin, skinny
3. jock
5. youthful
7. stubborn, pig-headed

SPOTCHECK 10–2

1. mother
3. pill-pusher
5. intoxicated

SPOTCHECK 10–3

1. entertaining, but
3. raise, for
5. test, so

SPOTCHECK 10–4

Answers will vary.

1. Mary has a cold, and Bill has a headache.

3. Jan's shoes were too small, so she gave them to Sonia.

SPOTCHECK 10–5

1. Grown in California and Oregon,
3. Florida, Texas, Hawaii, Mexico, or Puerto Rico
5. in the Mediterranean area,

SPOTCHECK 10–6

Answers will vary.

SPOTCHECK 10–7

1. Bill's Diner, which looks like it survived a tornado, is a
3. the fruit fly, according to experts, has
5. Pound cake, which is one of my favorite desserts, got its name
7. stone, according to an old saying, gathers

SPOTCHECK 10–8

1. July 10, 1913, at
3. Roberts, 213 Pine Street, Chicago, IL 60603

DOUBLECHECK 10–1

1. biggest, oddest, and most expensive
3. When she died, it
5. in 1881, she
7. rifles, including the spirits of many Indians, would
9. years, even on Sundays and Christmases,
11. walls, and

SPOTCHECK 10–9

1. You," was
3. is, economical
5. Correct
7. canoe, and

EDITING CHECK 10

1. According to archeologists,
3. bronze, razors
5. Correct

Chapter 11

SPOTCHECK 11–1
1. fact
3. fact
5. opinion

SPOTCHECK 11–2
1. beautiful
3. enthusiastic
5. ask
7. car
9. Regardless

SPOTCHECK 11–3
1. on time.
3. to leave.
5. your cold?

SPOTCHECK 11–4
1. Gifford, "Pro football . . . only survivors."
3. "Writing . . . alligators," said Olin Miller.
5. Comenius said, "We are all . . . great folly."

SPOTCHECK 11–5
1. "What . . . tonight?" Mary asked.
3. Correct
5. Mary said, "I'll probably do some reading. . . . called 'Lipstick and You' in the new *Teen World* that looks good."

SPOTCHECK 11–6
1. we'll
3. You've
5. There's
7. they're
9. can't

SPOTCHECK 11–7
1. women's
3. day's
5. oven's
7. dogs'

SPOTCHECK 11–8
1. Charles'
3. Correct
5. men's

SPOTCHECK 11–9
Answers will vary.
1. The men's faces were brightened by smiles.
3. Jennifer's dance class meets on Tuesdays.

DOUBLECHECK 11–1
1. "Why . . . morning?"
3. I'm; Joe's
5. "Surely," Joyce said, "you don't expect me to drink day-old coffee."
7. Dolores'
9. "Look . . . leap" is

SPOTCHECK 11–10
1. The sun came up; the dew quickly dried.
3. admire:
5. Miami Dolphins; however, he

SPOTCHECK 11–11
Answers will vary.
1. Marsha—a winner!
3. Mildred—I mean Agnes—went
5. Tina's brother—in fact, her whole family—is a little odd.

DOUBLECHECK 11–2
1. are Tokyo, Japan; Sao Paulo, Brazil; New York City; Mexico City, Mexico; Bombay, India; and Shanghai, China.
3. The curtain rose; the performance began.
5. Beethoven (1770–1827)
7. two months; however, he
9. in 1970; in addition,

EDITING CHECK 11
1. I'll . . . didn't . . . beef; however, . . . pork—nearly
3. hamburger's
5. it's McDonald's
7. we're . . . McDonalds—[or colon] the drive-through. . . . labor (one task . . . person)
9. aren't . . . we're

11. you're . . . who's . . . McDonald's
. . . company—[or semicolon]
almost 96

Chapter 12

SPOTCHECK 12–1

1. (joined) became
3. (attends) gains
5. (signs) warns

SPOTCHECK 12–2

(**past time**) Jackie Robinson was an outstanding athlete who opened the door to professional sports for other black athletes. Robinson joined the Brooklyn Dodgers in 1947 and became the first black player in modern major league baseball. Robinson went to high school in Pasadena, California, where he was a star in track, football, and baseball. He attended the University of California at Los Angeles on a football scholarship and, in 1939, gained more yards than any other college player. After service in World War II, Robinson joined the Kansas City Monarchs and played for $400 a month in the Negro American League. When Dodgers general manager Branch Rickey signed Robinson, he warned Robinson to expect acts of prejudice from other players and the fans. During the ten years he played for the Dodgers, Robinson batted .311 and helped the team win six National League championships and a World Series in 1955.

SPOTCHECK 12–3

1. Correct
3. thought they were lying
5. started
7. commissioned

SPOTCHECK 12–4

1. ~~you~~ they
3. ~~you~~ him
5. ~~you~~ he or she feels

SPOTCHECK 12–5

1. No ticket is needed to attend the Doodle Brothers concert.
3. I was glad to see Ralph again.
5. A person driving 55 miles per hour would take 193 years to travel the 93 million miles to reach the sun.

SPOTCHECK 12–6

Answers will vary.
1. mistaken
3. exciting
5. dollars

EDITING CHECK 12

1. Example
3. originated
5. unappealing
7. keeps
9. becomes

Chapter 13

SPOTCHECK 13–1

1. Juan and Franco won debating awards.
3. The weary welder put down his torch and thought about lunch.

SPOTCHECK 13–2

1. pretty, and twenty-eight percent
3. by boat, or it can be

SPOTCHECK 13–3

Answers may vary.
1. The mail carrier refused to enter the yard because
3. Doctor Winslow is the surgeon who will marry Dolores.

SPOTCHECK 13–4

Answers will vary.
1. When the sun came out, Jack knew

3. every weekend because she is homesick.

SPOTCHECK 13–5
1. Example
3. plug it into, so he developed
5. Correct

SPOTCHECK 13–6
1. you need on the kitchen table.
3. In the tree's highest branches, the crows were

SPOTCHECK 13–7
1. Played in India
3. Moving from bush to bush
5. changing the Indian name *pacisi* to *Parcheesi*

SPOTCHECK 13–8
1. a fifteenth-century Romanian prince
3. Elizabeth Goose
5. inventor of the phonograph

SPOTCHECK 13–9
1. Elizabeth Kenny, an Australian nurse, developed
3. Elvis Presley, the "King" of rock 'n' roll, died in 1977.

DOUBLECHECK 13–1
1. Prep
3. Ap
5. Part
7. Ap

EDITING CHECK 13
1. body odor for a long time. (prepositional phrase)
3. two spices, citrus and cinnamon (appositive)
5. was introduced in 1888 (prepositional phrase)

Chapter 14

SPOTCHECK 14–1
1. Ladonna likes go shopping <u>even</u> when it's snowing.

3. While <u>coming</u> home from school, Felipe bought a pizza.
5. The average marriage in the United States lasts <u>only</u> 9.4 years.

SPOTCHECK 14–2
1. When the car ran out of gas, Daniel parked
3. Able to bend steel bars with ease, Mighty Mo filled me with awe.
5. Solomon took a photo of the cows contentedly eating grass.

SPOTCHECK 14–3
1. wrong
3. having a lot of money
5. lazy

SPOTCHECK 14–4
Answers will vary.
1. Polly is a lot smarter than Victoria.
3. The trees are greener in the spring than in the fall.
5. A compact disk holds more songs than an LP or tape.
7. The dinner was so delicious I could hardly stop eating.

SPOTCHECK 14–5
1. P
3. P
5. A

SPOTCHECK 14–6
1. The "Star–Spangled Banner" did not become
3. Irving Berlin, who wrote the songs. . . , never learned to read music.
5. Vincent Van Gogh sold only one

DOUBLECHECK 14–1
1. D
3. B
5. A
7. D

EDITING CHECK 14

1. Correct

3. . . . "golden," the statuette called Oscar was actually made of tin.

5. First broadcast on radio, the pro-gram wasn't aired on television until 1952.

7. . . . watched on TV most often . . .

Chapter 15

SPOTCHECK 15–1

Answers will vary.

1. The Constitution's Bill of Rights has ten amendments.

3. Late in June, heavy rain drenched the city.

5. Our team should win tomorrow night's game.

SPOTCHECK 15–2

1. more faded

3. happier

5. most intelligent

SPOTCHECK 15–3

Answers will vary.

SPOTCHECK 15–4

1. quickly

3. enviously

5. well

SPOTCHECK 15–5

Answers will vary.

1. Francisco is good at dominoes.

3. The child eagerly opened the present.

5. Walk quietly because Grandma is asleep.

SPOTCHECK 15–6

1. didn't take any, took none

3. doesn't contribute anything, con-tributes nothing

5. Mr. Quan can hardly walk

SPOTCHECK 15–7

1. bandwagon

3. circular reasoning

5. non sequitur

7. glittering generality

9. post hoc

DOUBLECHECK 15–1

1. C

3. B

5. A

7. A

9. C

DOUBLECHECK 15–2

1. The firefighters put out the blaze quickly.

3. Jennifer should head the committee.

5. Greg had the worst batting aver-age on the team.

7. Rocky might make a good sur-geon. . . .

9. Although they are twins, Sonia is taller. . . .

EDITING CHECK 15

1. Correct

3. ~~in size~~

5. ~~more~~ smaller

7. satisfy almost anybody

9. Correct

11. Correct

13. ~~easy~~ easily

15. most successful

Writing Resources

SPOTCHECK A–1

1. N–1

3. N–3

5. N–4

SPOTCHECK A–2

1. the first syllable: the'ater

3. traveling from place to place: an itinerant worker or preacher

5. leaves

7. slang (an unpleasant or disap-pointing experience)

SPOTCHECK C–1

1. conscience

3. all right, conscious

5. as

SPOTCHECK C–2

1. pleasant
3. fewer
5. desert, desserts

SPOTCHECK C–3

1. morale
3. passed, almost
5. know

SPOTCHECK C–4

1. quite
3. supposed, write
5. sit, try to

SPOTCHECK D–1

1. moving
3. silliest
5. satisfying
7. occurred

SPOTCHECK D–2

1. deceived
3. field
5. friends
7. believe

SPOTCHECK E–1

1. College, Sequoias, California
3. My, Tagalog
5. The, Sam, "Sparky"
7. Dave, Math, I
9. The Salvation Army Building, Tenth Street, Pine Avenue

SPOTCHECK E–2

1. 3
3. 6½
5. 3 p.m.

SPOTCHECK E–3

1. November
3. Professor
5. Los Angeles

DOUBLECHECK E–1

1. Twelve
3. Laotian

5. World War II
7. economics
9. pounds

DOUBLECHECK E–2

1. thirteen years
3. Bureau
5. American
7. half
9. study

EDITING CHECK E

1. flea, *National Geographic*
3. 150 times
5. correct
7. fifty, astronaut
9. Three, world
11. correct

SPOTCHECK F–1

1. a
3. some
5. a

SPOTCHECK F–2

1. a, the
3. some, the
5. a, the

DOUBLECHECK F–1

1. A
3. the
5. The
7. the
9. The
11. the
13. the
15. the
17. a

SPOTCHECK F–3

1. up
3. down
5. with
7. up
9. out of
11. back

Credits

"The Art of Eating Spaghetti" from *Growing Up* by Russell Baker. Copyright © 1982 by Russell Baker. Used by permission of Congdon & Weed, Inc.

"Lessons Learned During Ramadan" by Ameena El Jandali. Reprinted by permission of Ameena El Jandali. El Jandali is a board member of Islamic Artworks Group in Sartoga, CA (in 1996).

"My Mother" and "Nonnie's Day" from *Mary* by Mary Mebane. Copyright © 1981 by Mary Elizabeth Mebane. Used by permission of Viking Penguin, a division of Penguin Putnam.

San Francisco Chronicle, November 2, 1995 "Selling Off Pieces of Their Bodies" by Joan Ryan. Copyright © 1995 by *San Francisco Chronicle*. Reproduced with permission of *San Francisco Chronicle* in the format of a textbook via Copyright Clearance Center.

"The Write Stuff—A Different Drummer" by Jonathan Bailey from the September/October 1995 issue of *Stanford Magazine,* published by Stanford Alumni Association, Stanford University.

"The Jeaning of America" by Carin C. Quinn from *The American Heritage Magazine,* 1978. Reprinted by permission of American Heritage, Inc.

"Road Warriors of the Freeway" by Lonn Johnston from *The Los Angeles Times,* 1996. Reprinted by permission of The Los Angeles Times Syndicate International.

"Addicted to Luck" by Matea Gold and David Ferrell from *The Los Angeles Times,* July 21, 1987. Reprinted by permission of The Los Angeles Times Syndicate International.

"Taking It to the Streets" by David B. Kopel, reprinted, with permission, from the November 1999 issue of *Reason Magazine*. Copyright © 2002 by Reason Foundation, 3415 S. Sepulveda Blvd., Suite 400, Los Angeles, CA 90034. *www.reason.com*

"Americanization Is Tough on Macho" by Rose Del Castillo Guilbault. Copyright © by Rose Del Castillo Guilbault. Reprinted by permission of the author.

"Marriage as Poverty Cure" by Ellen Goodman from *The Boston Globe,* March 7, 2002, page A-13. Copyright © 2002, The Washington Post Writers Group. Reprinted with permission.

"Fatherhood—It Has Its Moments" by Winston F. Wong, M.D., in *The San Francisco Examiner,* June 18, 1995. Reprinted by permission.

"How to Analyze an Ad, Ad It Up, Break It Down" by Phil Sudo from *Scholastic Update,* 1993. Copyright © 1993 by Scholastic, Inc. Reprinted by permission of Scholastic, Inc.

"What Should Be Done About Drugs?" by the Drug Policy Foundation. Copyright © Drug Policy Foundation, *www.dpf.org*. Reprinted with permission.

"Out of the Sweatshop and into the World" by David Masello from *Newsweek,* June 24, 2002, page 18. All rights reserved. Reprinted by permission.

Index